THE *LIBER DE ORDINE CREATURARUM*

BREPOLS LIBRARY OF CHRISTIAN SOURCES

VOLUME 5

Editorial Board
Professor Thomas O'Loughlin
Dr Andreas Andreopoulos
Professor Lewis Ayres
Dr Lavinia Cerioni
Professor Hugh Houghton
Professor Doug Lee
Professor Joseph Lössl
Dr Elena Narinskaya
Dr Sara Parks

The *Liber de ordine creaturarum*

Translated, with an Introduction, by
MARINA SMYTH

BREPOLS

Latin text reprinted from Manuel C. Díaz y Díaz, *Liber de Ordine Creaturarum. Un anónimo irlandés del siglo VII* © Universidade de Santiago de Compostela, 1972. All rights reserved.

The English translation originally appeared in *The Journal of Medieval Latin* 21 (2011), 137-222, under the title: 'The Seventh-Century Hiberno-Latin Treatise *Liber de ordine creaturarum*: A Translation.' A revised version is published here with kind permission from the editor.

© 2023, Brepols Publishers n.v., Turnhout, Belgium.

All rights reserved. No part of this publication may be reproduced, stored in a retrieval system, or transmitted, in any form or by any means, electronic, mechanical, photocopying, recording, or otherwise without the prior permission of the publisher.

D/2023/0095/89
ISBN 978-2-503-59678-5
eISBN 978-2-503-59679-2
DOI 10.1484/M.BLCS-EB.5.126050

Printed in the EU on acid-free paper.

Table of Contents

Introduction   7
  Summary Review of the Evidence for the Origin and Dating of DOC   9
  Reception   25
  Division into Chapters and Chapter Headings   29

Text and Translation   33

Appendix   123

Notes   137

Bibliography   165

Indices   179
  Index of Biblical References   179
  Index of Patristic & Medieval Works and Councils   183
  Index of Modern Authors   186
  Index of Topics   188

Introduction

When speaking of *dispositio universitatis* in his treatise *De ordine*, St Augustine was referring to the divine disposition of the created world.[1] In contrast, when the author of the seventh-century *Liber de ordine creaturarum* (= DOC)[2] began his treatise with that same phrase, he was talking about the totality of all that exists, both the all-powerful God of Christianity and the universe he created, with the temporal dimension of the history of salvation thrown in for good measure. Such is the scope of the treatise translated here.

Long attributed to Isidore of Seville (d. 636) and later assumed to be influenced by formulations drawn up at the Eleventh Council of Toledo (675), *De ordine creaturarum* was first associated with Ireland at the beginning of the twentieth century, on account of its close ties with the treatise *De mirabilibus sacrae scripturae* [*On the Marvels of Holy Scripture*] written in Ireland and dated internally to 654.[3] In 1953, Manuel Díaz y Díaz demonstrated that DOC could not have been written by Isidore and argued for an Irish origin.[4] He believed that a sentence from the Epilogue of DOC was copied by Defensor of Ligugé in his *Liber scintillarum* composed around 700.[5] Allowing a few years for the Toledo decrees to reach Ireland, he therefore proposed the dating 680–700 in his 1972 edition of DOC.[6] My study of the accumulating evidence confirms the Irish origin of DOC. Moreover, having shown that the connection with the Spanish council of 675 no longer holds, my proposed dating is earlier than that of Díaz y Díaz: DOC was written in Ireland between 654 and c. 675, before new ideas on the fate

---

1 Augustine, *De ordine* 1.7.18 (CCSL 29, 98, line 31).
2 CLH 575; CPL 1189; CPPM iiA 1084; BCLL 342.
3 CLH 574; CPL 1123; CCPM iiA 1850–51; BCLL 291. Immo Warntjes correctly argues that common practice in the early Middle Ages and consular information which the author of *De mirabilibus* drew from a manuscript of Victorius of Aquitaine's *Cursus Paschalis*, both lead to a date of AD 654 (not AD 655, as was previously believed) for the composition of Chapter 4 in Book 2 of that treatise; see Warntjes (2010), LXXVIII–LXXIX, n. 209.
4 Díaz y Díaz (1953), 147–66.
5 See below, at n. 21.
6 Díaz y Díaz (1972), 27. I am grateful to Michael Lapidge and to the late Manuel Díaz y Díaz himself for their confidence in entrusting me with the translation of DOC for the *Scriptores Latini Hiberniae* series, where it was to appear facing a reprint of the generally unavailable 1972 edition. That plan did not come to fruition. Michael Herren encouraged me to submit the translation to *The Journal of Medieval Latin*, where it appeared in 2011. I am delighted that Thomas O'Loughlin has now made it possible to realize the original concept. I thank David Ganz, Thomas Hall, Michael Herren, Hildegund Müller, Daniel Sheerin and my husband Brian, for their help and support along the way.

of the soul after death reached Ireland after being introduced to the British Isles by Theodore of Tarsus.[7]

The author of DOC had been commissioned by an important church dignitary to clarify the orthodox view of reality. A number of significant sources were available to him, and he felt the need to enunciate a guiding principle for dealing with contradictory opinions: 'In such difficult and ambiguous cases, one should first examine which opinion is most strongly supported by the authority of the Holy Scriptures. If this fails, one should prefer the views which most catholic believers have reconciled with their faith. As for differing opinions put forward by catholic believers and which either do not contradict the words of both the holy canons of Scripture or are equally congenial with them, these should remain uncertain in the judgement of readers.'[8] One of the unresolved issues is surprising in a treatise purporting to describe the universe: the shape of the physical universe and that of the earth itself remain unclear — are they spherical or flat?[9]

While many ideas expressed in DOC are borrowed from earlier Christian authors, they are synthesized and integrated into a consistent overall view of the universe — both spiritual and material. Bookended between an account of the Trinity and the angels and a discussion of the final destiny of mankind, the central chapters of the treatise correspond to the sequence of descending layers in a universe blending traditional secular ideas with exclusively Christian concepts: the supercelestial waters, the firmament, the sun and the moon, the higher space of air (and the celestial Paradise where the souls of the truly good await the final resurrection), the lower space of air immediately above the earth (the domain of the fallen angels), the layer of water, the earth (where man once dwelt in the garden of Paradise), and finally Hell (where the souls of the truly evil are punished immediately after death).

Various doctrinal points are considered along the way: the Trinity, Creation, the Fall (both of the angels and of man) and its consequences, evil, sin, redemption, grace, free will, baptism, the importance of charity, and the threat of damnation. Several surprisingly explicit semi-Pelagian statements, particularly in DOC 12, add to the evidence gathered by Michael Herren and Shirley Ann Brown for the presence of Pelagian ideas in seventh-century Ireland.[10] The eschatological doctrines presented in this work incorporate Christian beliefs common in Late Antiquity and are especially interesting in view of later developments.[11]

---

7 Smyth (2003–2004), 23–39.
8 DOC 5.11.
9 DOC 4.1–3, DOC 11.1–2. See Smyth (1996), 104–13 and 271–93, especially 276–79.
10 Herren and Brown (2002), 87–97.
11 Smyth (2003).

Summary Review of the Evidence for the Origin and Dating of DOC

Already in the Middle Ages the treatise was commonly attributed to Isidore of Seville, and this misconception lasted well into the twentieth century.[12] In 1953, Manuel Díaz y Díaz, the Spanish expert on medieval Spain, spelled out why *De ordine creaturarum* cannot be ascribed to Isidore though it makes extensive use of the *Differentiae*, and he demonstrated that it was almost certainly written in Ireland.[13] A key element in his argument was the dependence of DOC on *De mirabilibus sacrae scripturae*, a text written in Ireland *c.* 655 by an author now known as Augustinus Hibernicus (or the Irish Augustine).[14] Credit for first noticing the relationship between these texts must go to Pierre Duhem who, already in 1915, eliminated the possibility of Isidorian authorship by pointing out that the tidal data in DOC was derived from that in *De mirabilibus*.[15] The relationship is clear from passages such as:[16]

De mirabilibus 1.7 (PL35:2159) Haec namque quotidiana inundatio bis in die a tempore ad tempus, *per horas uiginti quatuor semper peragitur*, et per alternas hebdomadas *Ledonis et Malinae uicissitudo* commutatur. Sed Ledo sex horas inundationis, et *totidem* recessus habet; Malina uero grandis per *quinque horas* ebullit, et *per septem horas* littorum dorsa retegit. Quae tantam concordiam cum luna ostendit, *ut* antequam *luna nascatur*, tribus diebus et duodecim horis semper incipiat; et post nascentis lunae principia alios tres dies et duodecim horas consuescit habere: similiter et ante plenilunium tribus diebus et duodecim horis incipit, et post totidem temporis cursus sui terminum consumit. Sex uero uniuscuiusque temporis Malinas, ueris scilicet et aestatis, autumni et hiemis, secundum lunarem supputationem, hoc est, *simul omnes uiginti quatuor unusquisque communis annus habet*, exceptis uidelicet	DOC 9.4–7 Quantam uero concordiam cum *lunae* cursibus inundatione et recessu suo oceanus habeat, intuentibus diligenterque animaduertentibus perspicue patet. Qui cotidie ad terram bis uenire ac recedere *per horas XXIIII indesinenter uidetur*; cuius cursus tota conuenientia in *ledonis et malinae* diuisas *uicissitudines* partitur. Sed *ledonis* adsissa *sex* semper *horas* incrementi sui inconmotata consuetudine conplet, et per *totidem* horas ipsa spatia quae texerat *retegit; malinae* autem adsissa *quinque horas* suae inundationis agit et *per septem horas* eiusdem recessae *litora* quae conpleuerat uacua reddit. *Quae tantam concordiam cum luna* habere uidetur, *ut* in eius medio semper *luna nascatur*, quae per VII dies et XII horas et quartam diei partem diligenti exploratione perseuerare uidetur. Et ita fit ut, cum iterum plena luna minuitur, etiam malina rursus tenebrosa demedietur; *interpositis uero spatiis ledo* deprehenditur,

---

12 For more information on previous scholarly work on DOC, see Smyth (2003–2004), 2–16.
13 Díaz y Díaz (1953), 159–65.
14 PL 35:2149–00; for an edition of both the long and the short versions, see MacGinty (1971). See n. 3, above, for the precise internal dating to AD 654. More generally, see Esposito (1919); Herren (1998), 401–04; Ó Cróinín (2000), 212–16; Wright (2000), 130–31, 147.
15 Duhem (1913–1959), 3:14–16.
16 Italics and translations are mine.

embolismis, qui uiginti et sex Malinas retinent: et uniuscuiusque de praedictis temporibus mediae duae uidelicet aequinoctiales, et aliae quando uel dies uel nox cursus sui terminum consumit, solito ualidior ac inundatione altior fieri consuescit. Interpositis uero spatiis iterum tantumdem semper Ledo intermittitur.

quia nec plenilunium nec nascentis lunae initium unquam adire cernitur. Et per hanc uicissitudinem efficitur, ut *per omnem communem annum XXIIII malinae* et totidem ledones inueniantur; *in embolismo autem XXVI malinae* et eiusdem numeri ledones inueniuntur, quia per omnia cum lunae cursu inseparabiliter marinus comitatur. Quatuor uero ex his, hoc est *temporum quatuor mediae, duae scilicet aequinoctiales malinae et aliae* duae *cum aut dies aut nox* incrementi et detrimenti sui finem faciunt, *solito ualidiores*, sicut oculis probare licet, *ac adundatione altiores fieri* uidentur et maiora litorum spatia tegere cernuntur.

For this daily flooding always occurs twice daily at different times throughout the twenty-four hours, and on alternate weeks there occurs the interchange of *ledo* and *malina*. The *ledo* has six hours of flood and the same for its ebbing. The great *malina* on the other hand, surges forth for five hours, then pulls back from the slopes of the coastline for seven hours; and it shows such agreement with the moon that it begins three days and twelve hours before the new moon, and usually lasts another three days and twelve hours after the new moon has appeared. Likewise, it begins three days and twelve hours before the full moon, and after completing its course it comes to an end after an equal length of time. There are six *malinae* in each season — namely, spring, summer, autumn and winter — that is, following lunar computation, each common year has altogether twenty-four of them, but embolismic years have twenty-six *malinae*. And at the middle of each one of the aforesaid seasons, that is, at the two equinoxes and when either the day or the night reaches the end of its course, the *malina* is habitually stronger and higher than usual. The *ledo* always occurs in the very same way in the intervening periods.

The remarkable agreement between the course of the moon and the ebb and flow of the Ocean is perfectly obvious to those who observe and pay careful attention. For every day the Ocean is seen incessantly to approach the land and then retreat twice in twenty-four hours; and the regularity of this pattern is divided into the distinct alternations of *ledo* and *malina*. While the incoming tide of the *ledo* invariably rises for six hours, and for the same number of hours pulls away from the area it has covered, the incoming tide of the *malina*, on the other hand, floods for five hours and then for the seven hours of its ebbing it vacates the shores it had submerged. And the *malina* is observed to be in such great agreement with the moon, that the moon is always born in the middle of it; and diligent investigation shows it to last for seven days and twelve hours and the fourth part of a day. And this happens in such a way that as the full moon begins to wane, the gloomy *malina* is divided in half. The *ledo* is observed in the intervening periods, and is never seen to occur either at the full moon or at the beginning of the new moon. And by this alternation, there occur twenty-four *malinae* and as many *ledones* in each common year, while in an embolismic year there are twenty-six *malinae* and as many *ledones*, for the sea follows the course of the moon inseparably in all things. Four of these, those occurring at the middle of the seasons, that is, the two equinoctial *malinae* and the other two when either the day or the night ends its increase or its decrease, are seen to be stronger — as can readily be checked by observation — and to rise more than usual and cover a greater area of the shore.

This is all very technical, and it is not surprising that these texts share specialized vocabulary and information. What is more interesting is that they share the same misinformation that the spring tides at the solstices are higher than most spring tides, whereas if the author of DOC were truly observant, he would have seen that, if anything, they are normally lower than most spring tides.[17] The other noteworthy common feature is the claim that the *malinae* tides flow for five hours but ebb for seven, a claim most likely derived from Philippus Presbyter's *Commentary on Job*.[18] It should also be noted that both authors go on to end their discussion of the tides with the observation that nobody knows where the water of the receding tide actually goes. Both assert that this will remain a mystery so long as we are in this world, where *we know in part, and prophesy in part* (1 Cor 13:9), and the only way to find out for sure is to hasten to the Kingdom of Heaven.

The evidence presented here, and earlier by both Duhem and by Díaz y Díaz who adduced several other closely related passages in his 1953 study, shows that *De mirabilibus* and DOC are closely related. Establishing the direction of the relationship is complicated by the practice common to both authors of appropriating and reformulating the information in their sources, rather than quoting them. To understand that DOC is dependent on *De mirabilibus* one must compare the structure and purpose of the texts. Augustinus Hibernicus is doing his best to explain how, despite appearances to the contrary, created nature is not disturbed when a miracle occurs, whereas DOC is giving a description of the universe. Explanations formulated with great care and effort by Augustinus Hibernicus in answer to specific problems arising from the Bible are simply taken over by the author of DOC and incorporated into his orderly account. The discussion of the tides, for instance, occurs when Augustinus Hibernicus is trying to figure out the origin of the water of the deluge. In DOC, it occurs unsurprisingly in the chapter on the sea.

Another example of such borrowing involves the section of *De mirabilibus* dealing with the miracle of the 'bitter' water at Mara 'sweetened' at the touch

---

17 Duhem (1913–1959), 3:16, is too general on this point, since so much depends on location and prevailing conditions. See, for instance, Cartwright (1999), 8–9.
18 Philippus Presbyter, *Commentarium in Iob* 38, PL 26:752D; Smyth (1996), 256–57.

of Moses's staff (Ex 15:23–25).[19] After eliminating the possibility that the wood of the staff somehow sweetened the water, Augustinus Hibernicus settles on the following explanation: the nature of water is both sweet and salty, and the mutation from one to the other takes place commonly through the action of some external material agent; it follows that a divine command performing this mutation instantaneously is not interfering with nature.

De mirabilibus 1.22 (PL35:2168) Aquas igitur amaras uel etiam ipsas salsissimas *in dulcem saporem* uerti posse, *frequenter nautae comprobant*, qui illas *per humum* optimae *terrae infusas*, et hoc artificio etiam indulcatas, saepe *sitim* temperant. Nubes quoque de marinis finibus uapores leuant salsi liquoris, sed easdem dulces, quando pluunt, terrenis usibus ministrant. Quoniam salsuginis uitium quod in semetipsis aquae insitum capiunt, *per infusionem terrae* aut nubium deponunt. Similiter quoque et dulces aquae, cum eas homines *per marinorum olerum cineres* hauriunt, salsum et plusquam Oceani saporem reddunt. Hanc ergo immutationem insitam sibi naturaliter aquae habent; sed celerius per praeceptum Conditoris illam quam per efficaciam humanae diligentiae et ipsarum rerum ministrationis exhibent… Ipse uero creaturarum conditor et gubernator naturam occultam quae per aliam rem manifestanda fieret, in re ipsa sola denudat. Sicut et nunc amara aqua dulcedinem quam in occulto suae naturae continuerat, per humum aut nubem ab amaritudine purgata ostenderet, ita iussu gubernatoris potentissimi naturarum per se solam absque alterius rei iuuamine exhibet.

That it is possible to change bitter or even very salty water into sweet-tasting water, is made clear by sailors who frequently quench their thirst after straining salt water through a layer of the best soil, making it sweet by this device. And the clouds also pull up the vapours of salty waters from the

DOC 7.8 *qui suspendit aquas in nubibus suis ut non erumpant pariter deorsum* (Job 26:8). Attamen illas aer aquas ad terram et ad mare demittit quas ex hisdem inferioribus partibus ante sustulit, et quamuis de salsa pelagi latitudine eas traxerit pluuialis conceptio, per aerem indulcescit, quemadmodum et cum salsa profundo maris unda propinata *per humum terrae infunditur* — *sicut nautis est frequens consuetudo* — in *dulcis aquae saporem* statim motatur. DOC 9.2–3 Imbres qui de nubibus cribrati per aerem defluunt, ut aptius ad fructiferam uim et sedandam *sitim*, sicut ante diximus, subuenirent, sapidi fiunt… Sed utrum sapidum an salsum saporem naturalius an aequaliter utrumque aquae habeant, pro certo deus uiderit, quamuis et plerique salsuginem naturalem esse aquarum saporem putant, dulciorem uero terrae ac aeris natura condiri aestimant; sed tamen quemadmodum salsa aqua *per humum defusa* dulcescit, ita et dulcis aqua *per marinorum olerum cineres infusa* salsi protinus saporis fit, unde uterque sapor naturalis esse suo modo non est difficilius credi, dum alterutro in alterumque potest refundi.

Who suspends the waters in His clouds, so that they break not out and fall down together (Job 26:8). And yet the air returns to the earth and to the sea those waters which it had carried up from these lower regions, and though the process of formation of rain pulled them up from the salty expanses, it

---

19 Smyth (1996), 229–35.

expanse of the sea, but administer them as sweet water to nourish the earth when it rains. For these waters shed by infusion through the earth or through the clouds that defect of saltiness which they contained. Similarly, when sweet water is drained through the ashes of seaweed, it acquires a taste more salty than the Ocean itself. For waters have within themselves, by their very nature, this ability to change into one another and they show it much faster at the command of the creator than through the careful efforts of men or even through ministration by things... Now the creator and ruler of all creation can reveal in all things that hidden nature which would normally be manifested through the agency of some other thing. Just as bitter water, when cleansed of its bitterness by the earth or the clouds, reveals the sweetness which it contained hidden within its nature, thus, at the command of the most powerful Ruler of natures, it can display it on its own, without assistance from some other thing.

now sweetens them through the air, just as, when salt water collected from the depth of the sea is strained through the soil of the earth — as is the common practice of sailors — it immediately changes to the taste of sweet water. Showers scattered from the clouds and flowing down through the air become sweet so as to be more fruitful and refreshing — as we said earlier. But God alone knows whether water is by nature sweet-flavoured or salt-flavoured, or whether it contains both flavours equally. Many believe that the salty taste is natural to water, and that it is the nature of earth and of air which brings about the sweetness, and yet, just as salt water becomes sweet when filtered through earth, thus sweet water strained through the ashes of sea-plants quickly acquires a salty flavour. It is thus not at all difficult to believe that both flavours could be natural each in its own way, since each one can be transformed into the other.

Bearing in mind that the author of DOC is arguing in Chapter 7 that air has solidity and 'earthy density', it is clear that when the author of DOC asserts that *the air* is the agent of the mutation from the salt water drawn from the sea into the sweet water of rain, he has gone a step further than Augustinus Hibernicus who had assigned this function to the clouds.

The explanation of why man can potentially be saved whereas the devil is forever doomed is a further illustration of the dependence of DOC on *De mirabilibus*. The rationale developed by Augustinus Hibernicus has been reduced to its essential elements in DOC.

De mirabilibus 1.2 (PL 35:2153–54) Homo uero *adhuc in terra positus generandi officio destinatus, ciborumque esui deputatus, immutationem in sublimiorem et meliorem spiritualemque uitam sine morte reciperet, si quamdiu in hac conuersatione positus esset, in mandati custodia permaneret*. Hunc antequam ad statum ueniret sublimiorem, delictum praeripuit. Et *ideo de inferiori illo suo ordine*, id est, immortalitate sui corporis

DOC 8.5–6 Humanum autem genus redemptionem a suo conditore accipere idcirco promeruerit, quia *de inferiore adhuc sui ordinis gradu corruit*; cum *adhuc in paradiso terreno* esset *positus, generandi officio distinatus, ciborumque esui deputatus, inmotationem in meliorem sublimioremque et spiritalem uitam sine morte reciperet si, quandiu in hac conuersatione positus esset, in mandati custodia homo permaneret.*

confestim *ruit*, dicente Domino '*Terra es et in terram ibis*' (Gen 3:19). *Clementia ergo Conditoris* homo *ad illam* beatitudinem *ad quam peccans adhuc non peruenit, per passionem Domini reuocatur*; qui *si inde cecidisset sicut angelus, nunquam iterum reuocaretur*, quoniam ad illum ordinem, id est, immortalitatem sui corporis nunquam iterum peruenit, nisi peracta omnium morte, illa beatitudo ad quam reuocamur per resurrectionem restauretur. *Non ad illum* tamen *ordinem* aut ad statum *unde primus homo ceciderat, sed ad alium sublimiorem quem sperauit restitutio fiet, dicente Domino 'Erunt sicut angeli Dei in coelo'* (Mt 22:30).

As for man when still set on this earth destined for the task of procreation and intended to eat food, he would have been granted a transformation without death into a higher, better, and spiritual life if he had kept well what had been commanded while he was in that abode. But he committed his crime before he reached that higher state. And thus, he immediately fell from that lower order, that is, from his body's immortality, as the Lord said: *You are earth and you shall go to the earth* (Gen 3:19). And the clemency of the Creator has called him back through the passion of the Lord to that blessedness to which he could no longer reach once he had sinned. And if he had fallen from there as the angel did, he would never be called back again, because he could never return to that order, that is, to his body's immortality, unless after all men have perished, that blessedness be restored to which we are called back through resurrection. Restoration, however, will not be to that level and state from which the first man fell, but to that higher condition for which he hoped, as the Lord says: '*They will be like the angels of God in heaven*' (Mt 22:30).

Clementia ergo conditoris ad illum statum *ad quem adhuc peccans non peruenerat, per passionem domini reuocatur; quem si inde cecidisset sicut angeli nunquam iterum reuocaret, quia non ad illum* gradum uel ordinem unde primus homo ceciderat, sed ad illum sublimiorem quem sperauit restitutio fiet, dicente domino: 'Erunt sicut angeli in caelo' (Mt 22:30), scilicet quia non sicut homines in paradiso.

The human race, on the other hand, merited to receive redemption from its Creator because it fell from a lower level of its nature. For when it was still set in the earthly Paradise, destined for the task of procreation and intended to eat food, it would have been granted a transformation without death into a better, higher and spiritual life, if man had kept well what had been commanded while he was in that abode. And the clemency of the Creator has called him back through the passion of the Lord to that condition which he could no longer reach once he had sinned. And if he had fallen from there, like the angels he would never be called back again, because restoration will not be to that level and condition from which the first man fell, but to that higher condition for which he hoped, as the Lord says: '*They will be like angels in heaven*' (Mt 22:30), that is, not like men in Paradise.

This is but one example showing that it was not only for information on cosmological matters that the author of DOC turned to *De mirabilibus*.

Since *De mirabilibus sacrae scripturae* has been dated from internal evidence,[20] it follows that AD 654 is the earliest possible date of composition for DOC.

The earliest borrowing from DOC is slightly later than has previously been claimed. A connection between DOC and the *Liber scintillarum* of Defensor of Ligugé was first noted in Díaz y Díaz's review of the edition (in CCSL 117) of Defensor's remarkable compendium of *c.* 700.[21] He claims that Defensor borrowed the last sentence of DOC:

> Deo enim placare curantes, minas hominum penitus non timemus
>
> > When we endeavour to please God, we have nothing to fear from the threats of men (DOC 15.14).

This claim was repeated in the introduction to the 1972 edition of DOC.[22] Defensor was correct, however, in ascribing the statement to St Jerome, and the two medieval authors were borrowing independently from the Introduction to the Book of Esther in the Vulgate. As this is the sole link that has ever been claimed between DOC and the *Liber scintillarum*, it can no longer be said that Defensor's collection of excerpts provides the first evidence for use of DOC, nor indeed evidence that the treatise was known on the Continent at this early date.[23]

The first known use of DOC was in fact in Northumbria, where Bede cited it extensively in his early work *De natura rerum* (DNR),[24] written *c.* 703. The following passages show this dependence, proving that Bede's use of DOC provides a firm *terminus ante quem*. In the discussion of the relative position in the universe of the proper places of the four elements, the basic components of all matter,[25] we read:

DOC 4.5 terram etenim omnium creaturarum corporalium *grauissimam* esse non minus ostendunt quam dicunt, atque illam ideo *humillimum in creaturis locum* tenere aiunt *quia natura aliqua nisi se ipsa sufferri non ualet; aquam uero quanto*	Bede, DNR 4.2–5 *Terra enim, ut grauissima* et *quae ab alia natura sufferri non possit, imum in creaturis* obtinet *locum. Aqua uero quanto leuior terra tanto* est *aere grauior*

---

20 See n. 3, above.
21 Díaz y Díaz (1958), 4.
22 Díaz y Díaz (1972), 36.
23 See Smyth (1996), 19, n. 96. The relevant passage occurs in *Liber scintillarum* 72.19 (CCSL 117, 215; SC 86, 256).
24 CCSL 123A, 173–234. See Smyth (2003–2004), 17–19; Jean-Michel Picard (2005) discussed Bede's use of Irish sources, in particular DOC at pp. 51–55.
25 See e.g., Smyth (1996), 47–87. Bede's use of *sufferri* confirms that this is the correct reading in DOC 4.5 (Smyth (1996), 49, n. 12 and the note to DOC 4.5, below). This makes better sense in the context of the four-element theory, replacing *sufferre* in the 1972 edition [Translations and italics are mine].

leuiorem terrae uidimus *tanto grauiorem aere* deprehendimus

They affirm and demonstrate that earth is the heaviest of all corporeal creations, and say that it holds the lowest place among created natures because it is held up by no other nature than itself. And in as much as we see water to be lighter than earth, so we perceive it to be heavier than air	For earth, since it is the heaviest nature and cannot be held up by another nature, holds the lowest place among all created natures. As for water, in as much as it is lighter than earth, so it is heavier than air

In both cases the section continues with a discussion, using similar terms, of air rising to the surface of water, and fire striving to rise to its proper place above the layer of air, though it is dispersed by the mass of the air through which it must ascend.[26]

Bede introduces his section on the supercelestial waters of Gen 1:7[27] with a summary of the account in DOC:

DOC 3.1–4 Ex quo intellegitur *aquas illas quae supra firmamentum sunt* locali spatio ex *omni corporali creatura esse superiores* … per quod demonstratur inter utrosque caelos esse collocatas, id est *caelis spiritalibus humiliores* et caelis corporalibus superiores	Bede, DNR 8.1–2 Aquas super firmamentum positas, caelis quidem spiritalibus humiliores sed tamen omni creatura corporali superiores
We see thus that those waters above the firmament are located in the highest place among all corporeal creation… This shows that the waters are located between these two heavens, that is, they are lower than the spiritual heavens, and higher than the corporeal heavens.	The waters set above the firmament, which are lower than the spiritual heavens, but higher than all corporeal creation

Bede's section on the layer of turbulent air has clear echoes of DOC in the discussion of the fallen angels:

DOC 6.7 in inferiorem et ipsi *aer*is huius obscurioris et turbulentiorem locum *deturbati* de *super*ni et puri *aer*is suaeque	Bede, DNR 25.4–5 Vbi etiam potestates aereae superna sede deturbatae cum

---

26 DOC 4.5–6, DNR 4.5–9.
27 Smyth (1996), 94–103; O'Loughlin (1992) and (1995). While Bede's statement (combining language occurring in two distinct statements in DOC) suggests otherwise, Bede believed that the supercelestial waters were part of the created world, as spelled out by the author of DOC in DOC 3.4.

dignitatis felicissima *sede*, misere et infeliciter sub exspectatione futuri examinis in quo *durius damna*buntur uiuere aestimant.

cast down from the happy seat of the higher and pure air and of their dignity, to the lower and more turbulent place of this same darker air, [they] are believed to be living miserably and unhappily in the expectation of the future judgement in which they will be mercilessly damned.

tormento diem iudicii *durius* tunc *damnan*dae praestolantur.

Where even the aerial powers cast down from a higher seat are awaiting in anguish the day of judgement when they will be mercilessly damned.

Bede's explanation of thunder and lightning is drawn from DOC:

DOC 7.9–10 et tamen *ae*ris natura utraque *in se trah*it, id est *aquam uaporaliter de imis et ignem caumaliter de super*ibus, ipsa duo contraria sibi elementa *confl*igunt ... in quo conflictu ignis et aquae confusi *sonus horr*ibilesque frangores suscitantur; *et si ignis uictor fuerit*, terrae atque arborum *fructibus* non mediocriter nocet; *si uero aqua uicerit*, fructiferam uim tam in arboribus quam in his, quae olerum diuersis speciebus nascuntur, non perdit.

Bede, DNR 29.5–8 Quidam dicunt, dum *aer in se uaporaliter aquam de imis et ignem caumaliter de superioribus trah*at, ipsis *confl*igentibus *horrison*os tonitruorum crepitus gigni; et *si ignis uicerit fructibus obesse, si aqua prodes*se.

The nature of air nonetheless draws both within itself (that is, water as vapour rising from below, and fire radiating from above), and these two opposing elements thus enter into conflict... In this conflict between fire and water there arise confused rumbles and dreadful crashes. And if fire wins out, it does great damage to the crops of the earth and of the trees. If water wins, however, it does not destroy the fruitful vigour either in the trees or in the produce of all the various sorts of plants.

Some say that whenever the air draws together within itself water rising from below as vapour and fire radiating from above, the dreadful sounding crashes of thunder arise from their conflict. And if fire wins out, this is harmful to crops; if water wins, it is beneficial.

Bede's account of other meteorological phenomena is also influenced by DOC, but even more striking is the similarity in the treatment of the bizarre doctrine of the dual nature of water:

DOC 9.2–3 Imbres qui de nubibus cribrati *per aerem* defluunt ut *aptius* ad *fructi*feram uim et *sedand*am *siti*m, sicut ante diximus, subuenirent, sapidi fiunt... Sed utrum sapidum an salsum saporem *naturali*us an aequaliter utrumque aquae habeant, pro certo deus uiderit ... sed tamen quemadmodum salsa aqua *per humum defusa* dulcescit, ita et dulcis aqua *per marinorum olerum cineres infusa* salsi protinus saporis fit, unde uterque sapor *naturalis* esse suo modo non est difficilius credi, *dum alterutro in alterumque* potest *refundi.*

Bede, DNR 38.3–8 et *aere dulces aptius alendis fructibus sitique sedand*ae congruunt. Sed quae harum *naturalis* sit quaeritur. Vtraque autem deprehenditur *dum in alterutrum refundi* — haec *per marinorum holerum cineres*, illa *per humum diffusa* queant.

This is also why showers scattered from the clouds and flowing down through the air become sweet so as to better increase the fertility [of plants] and the quenching of thirst — as we said earlier... But God alone knows for certain whether water is by nature sweet-flavoured or salt-flavoured, or whether it contains both flavours equally... And yet, just as salt water becomes sweet when filtered through earth, thus sweet water strained through the ashes of sea-plants quickly acquires a salty flavour. It is thus not at all difficult to believe that both flavours could be natural each in its own way, since each one can be transformed into the other.

... they [water vapours drawn from the sea] gather as sweet water in the air in order to better nourish crops and quench thirst. But it remains an open question which is natural to them. Each one can be discerned since they can be transformed into one another — the one when strained through the ashes of sea-plants, the other through earth.

Bede then closes this section with the topos of the utility of the sea borrowed from DOC 9.4. The author of DOC was reluctant to endorse the doctrine of the complete mutability of the two types of water — sweet and salt — which Augustinus Hibernicus had formulated in order to explain the miracle of the bitter waters at Mara (Ex 15:23–25).[28] Bede shared his hesitation.

Since both the earliest extant manuscripts of DOC (**B** = Basle, Universitätsbibliothek F.III.15b and **P** = Paris, Bibliothèque Nationale, MS lat. 9561)[29] originate from eighth-century Anglo-Saxon England, and perhaps even from Northumbria, Bede's use of DOC combines with the manuscript tradition to suggest that the treatise was composed in Northumbria. This was the view

---

28 See Smyth (1996), 229–36.
29 The manuscripts of DOC are described in the Appendix below.

expressed by Ch.W. Jones in private communications to several scholars, pointing to Lindisfarne or Whitby as likely places of composition.[30] And indeed, we know that towards the end of the seventh century, thanks to the efforts of Benedict Biscop and of his successor abbot Ceolfrith, the library of Wearmouth-Jarrow contained a substantial number of manuscripts,[31] both of Irish and Continental origin, so that the sources of DOC might have been available there.

Nonetheless, the close association of DOC with *De mirabilibus sacrae scripturae* written in Ireland during the third quarter of the seventh century, and for which there is no evidence in Northumbria at that time, argues for Irish rather than Northumbrian origin.

A number of paleographical features, especially in the earliest extant manuscripts, point in the same direction. Cogent paleographical comments by Manuel Díaz y Díaz have been recorded below in the description of the manuscripts (Appendix). Charles Wright commented specifically on the paleography of **M** = Munich, Bayerische Staatsbibliothek, MS clm 6302 (Freising, late eighth century according to Bischoff, though Lowe thought it could have been a little later; see the Appendix below), in which DOC occurs together with a group of texts which have been associated with early medieval Ireland (CLH 37, BCLL 777; CLH 38, BCLL 1258; CLH 71, BCLL 770; excerpts from CLH 559, excerpts from BCLL 345).[32] Daibhí Ó Cróinín remarked on the typically Irish abbreviations (*autem, com-, eius, est*) in manuscript **P** written in uncial script, which he considered the oldest extant copy of DOC.[33]

As regards orthography, applying the strict criteria for Hibernicisms formulated by Michael Herren[34] to the three earliest extant manuscripts of the treatise — **B** and **P** which originate from Anglo-Saxon England, and **M** copied in Freising — shows that they were almost certainly copied or derived from exemplars written by Irish scribes.

Class I. Spelling Influenced by the Irish Language

ea <*ē*, a characteristic hibernicism: *censeatur* (for *censetur*) 6.8 (**B**) and *mereantur* (for *merentur*) 8.4 (**B, P**) are the only two cases of which I am confident that they are not erroneous subjunctives.[35]

---

30 See MacGinty (1971), 132*, footnote, Cross (1972), 133, n. 5, and Ó Cróinín (1983), 41, n. 1, all citing private communications from Ch.W. Jones.
31 Colgrave and Mynors (1969), xxv–xxvi.
32 Wright (2000), 145–46.
33 Ó Cróinín (2000), 218; Wilmart (1926). See also E. A. Lowe, *Codices latini antiquiores. Part 7: Switzerland* (Oxford, 1956), 2, no. 844.
34 Herren (1982).
35 Herren (1982), 432. See Thurneysen [transl. Binchy and Bergin, 1975], 36–37.

The voiced fricative *v* does not exist in Irish and when it occurred in Latin words, it was pronounced *f*, and often so written.[36] There are several occurrences: *faticinium* (for *vaticinium*) 11.4 (**P**), *festibus* (for *vestibus*) 13.5 (**B**), *fiunt* (*sic* for *uiuunt*) 9.9 (**B, M**).

The spelling of *cherubin* was a problem since *ch* at the beginning of the word does not occur in Old Irish.[37] Our early manuscripts deal with this in various ways: *hirubin* 2.1, 2.2 (twice) (**B**), *cyruphin* 2.2 (but *chyruphin* a little later in 2.2) (**P**); the spelling *cerubin* was adopted by Díaz y Díaz in his edition at 10.12 (twice), which suggests that it occurred as such in the text of Gen 3:24 cited in both the **B** and **P** manuscripts. The probably more derivative manuscript **M** has *hyrubin* and *hyrubyn*, respectively.

As noted by Bengt Löfstedt,[38] the Irish pronounced *ii* as *i*, which led to the frequent use of a single *i* instead of *ii* and, conversely, to the hypercorrect use of *ii* for *i*. In **B**, we note *i* <*ii*: *aduersari* (for *aduersarii*) 8.14; *aeri* (for *aerii*) 6.3; *dilicis* (for *deliciis*) 6.6; *fornicari* (for *fornicarii*) 13.3; *iudici* (for *iudicii*) 13.1 and *ii* <*i*: *iniiquam* (for *iniquam*) 12. 2; *soliis* (for *solis*) 5.9. In **P**, *i* <*ii*: *abit* (for *abiit*) 11.6; *ali* (for *alii*) 4.8; *aeri* (for *aerii*) 6.3; *imperis* (for *imperiis*) 7.8; *impissimum* (for *impiissimum*) 8.10; *iudici* (for *iudicii*) 8.2; *propri* (for *proprii*) 8.18; *radis* (for *radiis*) 5.9 and *ii* <*i*: *fruguferiis* (for *frugiferis*) 6.10.

Class II. Words with Characteristic Spellings Occurring Frequently in Hiberno-Latin Texts, but Comparatively Rarely in Other Contexts

The three most common examples referred to by Herren as '*Lieblingsgraphien* — favourite spellings' of Irish scribes[39] are well represented in the early manuscripts of DOC: variants of *mot-* for *mut-* (numerous cases), *commonis* for *communis* — *commone* 1.3 (twice), 1.4; *conmonem* 9.6 (**B**); *commone* 1.3, 1.4 (twice) (**P**) — and *cremina* for *crimina* 13.1, 13.3, 13.4, 14.11 (**B**). Perhaps we can also add *crebratus* (for *cribratus*; see 2 Sam 22:12) 9.2 (**B, M**), since *crebrari* also occurs in *Liber questionum in euangeliis*[40] and in *Altus prosator*.[41]

---

36 Löfstedt (1965), 103, agrees that this is an Irish phenomenon, but questions whether it is exclusively Irish.
37 See Rittmueller, in the Introduction to her edition of *Liber questionum in evangeliis* (CCSL 108F, 97*, n. 122).
38 Löfstedt (1965), 94–95; see also Stotz (1996), 45, § 35.2 and 47, § 36.5.
39 Herren (1982), 432. Already in 1963, Bieler (*The Irish Penitentials*, pp. 29–30) identified the spellings in the group *cremina, commonis, excommonis, commotauerit* as characteristically Irish. See also Löfstedt (1965), 107, n. 3.
40 See *Liber questionum in euangeliis* 2.21 (CCSL 108F:214 and 93*: *Siue quia cinis in saccum solet crebrari*).
41 *Altus Prosator*, strophe 11 (L), line 1: *Ligatas aquas nubibus/Frequenter crebrat Dominus*, cited from the 1908 edition by Clemens Blume 'based primarily on the relatively early continental manuscripts' (see Stevenson (1999), 326, n. 4). Note: the edition by Howlett reads *cribrat* (Howlett (2015), 366).

INTRODUCTION 21

There are several cases of *i* inserted before a vowel:[42] *equianimiter* 5.11 (**P**), *limpiaticum* 7.4 (**B**), *pluuiant* 7.6 (**P**; for *pluant*), *uicinia* 6.4 (**P, B**), *chiemisferiorum* 6.2 (**B**), *hiemisperiorum* 6.2 (**P**), *lugientes* 11.7 (**M**), *miserie* 6.7 (**B**).

Summing up, solid indications in the orthography of these early manuscripts argue for exemplars written by Irish scribes. Indeed, Michael Winterbottom, Andrew Orchard and David Howlett have examined various aspects of the Latinity of DOC and concur in identifying the treatise as an early Latin work from Ireland.[43]

Reinforcing the likelihood of Irish composition, a number of features in DOC are characteristic of an Irish environment. Díaz y Díaz had already noted instances of a practice symptomatic of Hiberno-Latin texts, namely latching on to very precise, but relatively unimportant information in patristic sources. For example, both the notion borrowed from St Jerome that there are precisely 153 types of fishes, and the claim — this time following St Augustine — that the name ADAM is derived from the Greek names for the four cardinal directions, are among favourite Irish themes identified by Bernhard Bischoff.[44]

The prominent position assigned to the apostle John is characteristic of seventh-century Ireland: in DOC 15.6, John is even given the epithet *potens*, 'powerful.' Among the original apostles he is mentioned three times,[45] twice with explicit reference to his resting his head close to the heart of the Lord at the Last Supper, while Peter is mentioned but twice and James only once.[46] During the seventh-century Easter controversy, at Whitby for instance, the Irish appealed to the authority of John, the apostle who had been so close to Christ, and at the end of the seventh century, an Hiberno-Latin commentary on the Gospels, the *Expositio IV euangeliorum*[47] explains that John acquired his great wisdom essentially through osmosis when he was so close to the heart of the Lord at the Last Supper. There is evidence already from the eighth century for the Irish designation *Eoin Bruinne* (John of the Breast), which persisted through the Middle Ages.[48]

As often occurs in texts with Irish connections, the devil is referred to as *seruus fugitiuus*, 'the fugitive slave',[49] and the lengthy treatment of the nine orders of

---

42 Stotz (1996), 46, §§ 36.1 and 36.2.
43 Winterbottom (1977), 71–73 and 54, n. 4; Orchard (1987–1988), 181–82; Howlett (1997), 64–66.
44 Bischoff (1954; repr. 1981; transl. 1976).
45 DOC 2.6, 13.4, 15.6.
46 DOC 11.6, 15.5 and DOC 13.4, respectively.
47 CLH 65; BCLL 341 (e.g., PL 30:531–90, at 588D–589A). For a list of the manuscripts of the various recensions of this text, see Kavanagh (1999), 129–31.
48 Smyth (2003–2004), 36.
49 DOC 8.8. See also Bischoff (1966–1981), 1:219. In his commentary on Mt 8:28–32, Jerome, *In Matthaeum* 1.8.29 (CCSL 77, 53) said that at the sight of Jesus, the devils possessing the two men were as terrified as fugitive slaves encountering their master. This comparison tends to be repeated in later commentaries on the text of Matthew, including those with Irish connections, such as *Liber questionum in euangeliis* 8.29 (CCSL 108F, 169) and the *Würzburg Glosses on Matthew* (CLH 394; BCLL 768), both from the eighth century. Jerome's analogy was especially popular among Irish authors and was used in commentaries on other gospels. It occurs, for instance, in the commentary

angels[50] combined with the author's emphasis on the eventual transformation of the elect at the end of time so that they will be *sicut angeli*, 'like angels',[51] brings to mind the medieval Irish cliché that man was created 'the tenth order.'[52] There are also examples of the enumerative style to which the Irish were very partial. One of the attempts to describe the eternal happiness of the elect is a list of things not found in this world, a well-known formulation which in this case contains nine elements: 'light will not be ended by darkness, nor life by death, nor health by pain, nor happiness by sorrow, nor youth by old age, nor love by the absence or desertion of the loved ones, nor beauty by any vileness, nor strength by illness, nor righteousness by sin.'[53] We are also told that 'as men fell in three ways in the transgression of the first man, so their children are affected by three wounds, that is, suffering, old age and death.'[54] There is no hint of how the threefold nature of original sin might have been understood, suggesting that this was a well-known topos: the Irish triad of 'thought, word and deed' comes to mind,[55] but perhaps the interpretation was rather in terms of the three components of sin analysed by St Augustine in his commentary on the Sermon on the Mount:

---

on Luke in the eighth-ninth century manuscript Vienna, Nationalbibliothek 997 (CLH 84; BCLL 773). In that text, the comment *more serui fugitiui* is twice immediately followed by: *Fugit enim diabulus de caelo in terram*, thereby suggesting that the devil himself was a *seruus fugitiuus*; see *Commentarius in Lucam* 4.34 and 8.28 (CCSL 108C, 37–38 and 69). Bede will copy Jerome's passage twice, once in *In Marcum* 1.1.23–24 (CCSL 120, 447) and again in *In Lucam* 2.4.33–34 (CCSL 120, 110). In DOC, the use of *seruus fugitiuus* is especially interesting: completely detached from the gospel episode, it has become an alternate name for Satan.

50 DOC 2.1–13.
51 DOC 15.1–2.
52 The assumption that humans are 'the tenth order' was derived from the early Christian belief that the saints will replace the fallen angels in heaven, combined with the conviction that there are nine orders of angels. St Gregory expressed this idea in his Sermon 34 (the main source for DOC 2), where the story of the woman who lost one of her ten drachmas (Lk 15:8–10) is interpreted in terms of the nine angelic orders and *ut compleretur electorum numerus, homo decimus est creatus*; see Gregory, *Hom. in Ev.* 34.6 (CCSL 141, 304). Isidore in *Sententiae* 1.10.13 (CCSL 111, 33) was even more explicit: *Bonorum angelorum numerus, qui post ruinam angelorum malorum est diminutus, ex numero electorum hominum subplebitur*. For evidence of this concept in medieval Irish vernacular literature, see Carey (1987), 3–4. *Commemoratorium*, a Latin commentary on the Apocalypse (CLH 98; BCLL 781) associated with Ireland and dated to the second half of the seventh century was probably originally a set of glosses. One of these reads: *ET OMNEM CREATURAM QUAE EST IN CAELO, id est nouem ordines angelorum, decimus sanctorum*; see *Commemoratorium* 5.1 (CCSL 107, 207 and 181–82). The idea is also clearly present in the *Cosmography of Aethicus Ister*, that puzzling eighth-century work with Irish connections. Thus § 4, after referring to the nine orders of angels, states: *Ordo idem decimus futurum cum hominibus sanctis*; see Herren (2011), 4 and 58. There was some confusion on the number of the fallen angels: the Irish *Liber de numeris* asserts that they formed one tenth of the entire angelic population (CLH 577; BCLL 778; PL 83:1297B), whereas the *Saltair na Rann* claims they were a third of the total (Carey (1998), 124).
53 DOC 15.7. See also *Collectanea Pseudo-Bedae* § 177 (Bayless and Lapidge (1998), 142 and 239–40); Wright (1989), 72–73.
54 DOC 12.2.
55 Sims-Williams (1978), 78–111; Wright (1989), 31–35, further elaborated in the chapter 'The "Enumerative Style" in Ireland and Anglo-Saxon England', in Wright (1993), 79–83.

delectatio, suggestio, consensus, 'desire, persuasion, assent.'[56] Gregory the Great and, following him, Isidore added the fourth element *defensionis audacia*, 'the boldness of denial',[57] but St Augustine's triad kept recurring in Hiberno-Latin texts.[58] Whichever triad was intended in DOC, a tendency to attach great significance to numbered lists, especially to triads, was characteristic of Irish thought, as further exemplified by the triad *dolor, senectus, mors*, 'suffering, old age, death', which occurs no less than four times in the treatise.[59]

The eschatological scheme described in DOC reveals yet another theme characteristic of Irish religious speculation: the theme of the fourfold division of mankind — which recurs as a refrain in later Irish texts with their allusions to the *non ualde boni* and the *non ualde mali* — is clearly expounded here.[60] *At death*, according to DOC, the soul leaves the body and joins one of *three groups*, depending on behaviour in life: the very good go immediately to the 'Paradise' of which Jesus spoke to the Good Thief, the very bad go straight to Hell, and those in between, who have committed only minor sins, must await the final resurrection. Nothing is said of the whereabouts or disposition of their souls in the meantime, and it is only at the end of time that they will know their ultimate destiny.[61] *At the general resurrection at the end of time*, souls and bodies will be joined again and there will be a further subdivision of mankind at the Last Judgement when Christ will judge the members of the middle group *only*, and this *only* according to the criteria outlined in Mt 25: 'Did you feed me when I was hungry? Did you clothe me when I was naked? etc.' Those moderate sinners who have performed good works *will be called* to the right hand of Christ,[62] but they must first be subjected in their bodies to the *iudicii ignis* or *ignis purgatorius*, that is, to the purgatorial fire of judgement, before they can join the elect.[63] In contrast, those moderate sinners who have failed to perform works of mercy will be damned at this time.[64] This is an unexpected verdict since they have committed no serious offences. Nonetheless, the treatise *De duodecim abusiuis saeculi* — now accepted as an Irish composition[65] — confirms that this was the normal view in Ireland during the third quarter of the seventh century: we are told in that treatise that the miserly

---

56 Augustine, *De sermone domini in monte* 1.12.34 (CCSL 35, 36–38).
57 Gregory, *Moralia* 4.27.49 (CCSL 143, 193), and Isidore, *Sententiae* 2.17.2 (CCSL 111, 130).
58 Bracken (2002), 158–60.
59 See DOC 10.10, 10.16, 12.2, 12.3. The closest I have come is the parallel of the *five likenesses of hell* in the *Catechesis Celtica*, in a passage cited and translated in Wright (1989), 66, or (1993), 96–97: V *inferni sunt: I dolor, II senectus, III mors, IIII sepulcrum, V pena*.
60 This concept was transmitted by the *Moralia* of Gregory the Great, as shown by Biggs (1989–1990).
61 DOC 13.5; 14.4.
62 DOC 14.4–5.
63 DOC 14.5–12.
64 DOC 13.5–6.
65 CLH 576; BCLL 339; Breen (2002).

rich man will be sent to Hell *at the Last Judgement*, though there is nothing to indicate he was guilty of serious sins.[66]

The emphasis in DOC on the *uocatio*, 'the call' by which the Lord will summon some of those in the middle group of moderate sinners to go and join the elect, is another indicator of an Irish milieu. When the author said that some possess the Kingdom of Heaven while they are living on this earth and *sine uocatione*, 'without being called', he was assuming that his audience knew which call was meant.[67] Later in the text, the account of the Last Judgement explains that the elect among those in the middle group must *be called* because they are still somewhat far away from Christ as they are undergoing the cleansing fire to remove the soil of their sins, and therefore Christ must *call* out to them: '*uenite*.'[68] Now emphasis on the *call* of some sinners at the Last Judgement is another theme recurring in Irish texts. There is a parallel, also from the third quarter of the seventh century, in the *Man* glosses of the *Gospel of Máel Brigte*. The main text dates from 1138, but the *Man* glosses are attributed to Manchán of Liath Manchaín who died in 665.[69] Manchán's elaboration on the words of Christ at the Last Judgement are another example of the emphasis on the Last Judgement in Irish works before the last quarter of the seventh century, but in addition, when commenting on Mt 25:34, Manchán speaks explicitly of the Lord's merciful call: *uocatio illorum cum misericordia dicendo*: '*uenite*.'[70]

There is no reason to make DOC dependent on the Eleventh Council of Toledo held in 675. I have shown elsewhere that the credal formulations present in the first chapter of DOC were common during the seventh century.[71] The belief that there was a connection between DOC and that particular Spanish council took hold at a time when it was still assumed that Isidore was the author of DOC. Since many statements formulated at that council were drawn from works by Isidore, it was then reasonable to assume that borrowings also occurred from DOC.[72] When Isidorian authorship of DOC was disproved, the alleged link with the Toledan council persisted in the scholarship. There is, however, no reason to affirm that DOC was written after 675 and I believe it was written earlier. In fact, I would

---

66 On the other hand, it must be said that the *Lorica* which Michael Herren attributes to Laidcenn of Clonfert-Mulloe (d. 661), suggests that the author is hoping that his good deeds will erase his sins so that *immediately at death* he may rise to the celestial Paradise: *Ne de meo possit uitam trudere/pestis febris langor dolor corpore/donec iam deo dante seneam/et peccata mea bonis deleam/Ut de carne iens imis caream/et ad alta euolare ualeam*; Herren (1987), 88 and 42–45.

67 DOC 14.2 and 14.4.

68 DOC 14.5.

69 Rittmueller (1983), 186 and 200–14; (1984), 215–18. For further examples, see Smyth (2003–2004), 35–36, n. 176.

70 I thank Jean Ritmueller for making her transcriptions available to me and allowing me to cite from them.

71 Smyth (2003–2004).

72 Smyth (2003–2004), 23–29. See Madoz (1938), 33, 79, 99, 104, where other sources are also proposed; see also the summing up at 112–18.

set 675 as the latest likely date, since DOC exhibits no awareness of the more 'Roman' ideas on the state of the soul after death introduced to the Insular world with the arrival of Theodore of Tarsus at Canterbury in 669.[73]

Reception

As we have seen, the parallel passages in Bede's early work *De natura rerum* (c. 703) are the earliest evidence for the influence of the treatise. Manuscript **B** was copied in Northumbria in the early eighth century, followed soon after by manuscript **P**, which was written somewhere in England, not necessarily Northumbria. The text remained influential in England through the Anglo-Saxon period. James Cross discovered that many statements in the sections of the ninth-century *Old English Martyrology* dealing with Creation (Days 2–6, 19–23 March) are simply translations from DOC.[74] The presence of Anglo-Saxon glosses, albeit to another text copied in manuscript **P**, suggests possible interest in DOC in tenth-century England. The treatise also influenced the twelfth-century Belfour Homily XI (*On the Transfiguration*) copied in Bodley 343.[75] Moreover, in addition to the five manuscripts of English origin mentioned in the Appendix below (**O, I, D, X** and Oxford, Bodleian Library, MS Laud. Misc. 345), it is clear from the very useful *List of Identifications* provided by the *British Medieval Library Catalogues* project[76] that at least three Benedictine libraries in Britain had manuscripts of the work before the end of the thirteenth century[77] and that many other monastic houses owned a copy later in the Middle Ages.

There is no manuscript evidence for the text in medieval Ireland, but some of its ideas have been identified in later vernacular compositions. Most striking is the appearance in the ninth-century vernacular poem *Saltair na Rann* of the analogy of the firmament to the shell of an egg surrounding the yolk on all sides or with the hide bounding the body of an animal. What was merely an option in DOC 4.1–3 had become a certainty. John Carey conjectured that DOC was a source for a now lost treatise written in the first half of the eighth century by an Irish scholar who accepted the common late-antique view of a spherical universe surrounding a spherical earth.[78] The egg image was taken over from the *Saltair* into a prose

---

73 Smyth (2003–2004), 29–34.
74 Cross (1972), 133–38; (1981), 185–86; (1985), 242.
75 Cross (1972), 139–40.
76 https://www.history.ox.ac.uk/british-medieval-library-catalogues#tab-266421.
77 DOC is listed as a work of Isidore in the 1123 catalogue of Rochester, whereas in the late twelfth-century catalogue of Bury St Edmunds, it is attributed to St Augustine. There is also a copy recorded in the 1247 catalogue of Glastonbury.
78 Carey (1985), 51–52.

Tract on Creation which was partly copied in the introduction to the *Senchas Már* in British Library, Harley 432.[79]

Díaz y Díaz observed that the early surviving manuscripts from continental Europe are all associated with the Irish and Anglo-Saxon missionary activity of the early Middle Ages (Freising, Fulda, Lorsch, Auxerre, Burgundy, Rheims).[80]

The first continental evidence for the influence of DOC comes from Freising, where manuscript **M** was copied, most likely at the end of the eighth century (see the Appendix, below). Moreover, in what is now known as the *Florilegium frisingense*,[81] DOC 1.2–4 was copied in Freising by the Northumbrian scribe Peregrinus as the most substantial part of a section entitled *Fides senodi cartaginiensium*.[82]

Also around the end of the eighth century and probably at the monastery of Flavigny, a codex of DOC was used to compose the collection of credal statements and conciliar materials in manuscript **N** (see Appendix). This contains only the first chapter of DOC, with the title *de fide trinitatis Isidori epi*. In the middle of the ninth century, Aeneas, bishop of Paris, incorporated DOC 1.3–4 into his treatise *Liber aduersus Graecos*, attributing the passage to Isidore.[83] Manuel Díaz y Díaz noted that the phrase *quia nullus anterior et nullus posterior, nullus inferior et nullus superior* in the ninth-century Stavelot commentary to the *Quicunque* as it is found in London, British Library, add. 18043, may be drawn from DOC 1.2.[84]

It is likely that a copy of DOC, or at least DOC 9.10 on the conjectured origins of the different types of birds, was available to the author of the *Commentary on Genesis* (CLH 40; BCLL 1260) in the eighth-ninth century manuscript Sankt Gallen, Stiftsbibliothek, MS 908, probably from Northern Italy.[85]

When describing the end of time, Haimo of Auxerre (fl. 850) paraphrased DOC 5.4–6 in his *Commentary on Isaiah*[86] clearly giving his source: *Dicit enim beatus Isidorus in libro creaturarum...* It is therefore likely that a manuscript attributing DOC to Isidore was available at Auxerre in the mid-ninth century. Haimo added the curious explanation that the glorified sun and moon will remain

---

79 Carey (1986), 5, § 5: *uair amail bís a blaesc im ogh, is amlaidh atá in firmamindt im thalmain* — 'for as its shell is around the egg, so the firmament is around the earth' (p. 8, § 5). See also Smyth (1996), 109.
80 See the Appendix, below, for more information on the manuscripts of DOC. Since the archbishop of Rheims in the middle of the eighth century was Abel *de eadem Anglorum gente* who remained in close contact with Boniface, Díaz y Díaz suggested it was more likely that a manuscript of DOC was directly transmitted to Rheims from England, rather than from Péronne or some other Irish centre on the continent; see Díaz y Díaz (1972), 68.
81 *Florilegium frisingense (clm 6433)* (CCSL 108D, 3–4).
82 Lehner, Introduction to his edition of the *Florilegium frisingense* (CCSL 108D, p. xiii). On Peregrinus, see Wieland (1994 for 1991), 184–85. See manuscript **M2** in the Appendix, below.
83 PL 121:721B–C.
84 *Stavelot commentary* 24 (Burn (1898), 17 and xlviii–l). See Díaz y Díaz (1972), 85, n. 3.
85 See the notes to DOC 9.10 and 9.11, below; also, Wright (1987).
86 PL 116:869D–870A and also PL 116:1041A. See Cross (1972), 140; Stegmüller (1951), 7, no. 3066 & 11, no. 3083. See the convenient table of authentic works by Haimo of Auxerre in Shimahara (2007), 275–77. See also Savigni (2005), 229; Iogna-Prat (1991), 163–64.

stationary *ne claritate solis sive lunae illi qui apud inferos erunt perfruantur* — so that those who will be in Hell will not enjoy the brightness of the sun or of the moon.[87] The glosses to Bede's *De temporum ratione* now known as the B glosses because they were attributed to Byrhtferth of Ramsey (fl. 1000) in the edition published by Johannes Herwagen (d. 1564) from a now lost manuscript, were most likely assembled at Auxerre in the last quarter of the ninth century.[88] This section of Haimo's commentary[89] is cited essentially verbatim in the B glosses, including the explicit reference to DOC and the attribution to Isidore:

> Omnia quae omnipotens Deus per spatia sex dierum operatus est, propter hominem facta sunt, in cuius lapsu omnia elementa detrimentum sustinerunt. Nam terra antea spinas et tribulos non proferebat. Aer iste non tantae crassitudinis erat sed purus erat. Sic sol et luna et sidera detrimentum sui luminis sustinerunt. In die autem iudicii determinato illo examine cum fuerint omnes reprobi una cum diabolo in inferno conclusi, sustollet se dominus Iesus pariter cum corpore suo, quod sunt omnes electi in caelum, et tunc mutuabit sibi luna splendorem solis et sol septempliciter lucebit quam modo sicut lux septem dierum, hoc est multipliciter, et recipiet lumen et splendorem solis quem amisit peccante primo homine. Dicit etiam beatus Isidorus in libro creaturarum quod neque sol neque luna ad occasum uenturae sint postea, sed in loco quo creata sunt sine fine manebunt, iuxta illud Abacuc: *Sol et luna steterunt in habitaculo suo*, pro eo quod est stabunt. Et quare hoc? Ne claritate solis siue lunae illi qui apud inferos erunt perfruantur (PL 90:479B–C).

Note how Haimo emphasized that even though the prophecy was set in the past,[90] it actually referred to the future, the very point made in DOC 5.6. The last detail about depriving Hell of light, however, is not to be found in the text of DOC as edited by Díaz y Díaz, nor is it mentioned in the apparatus to his edition.

Because of the inclusion of the comment that the damned will have no light, I suspect that a marginal gloss to Is 60:19–20 in the *Glossa ordinaria*, though attributed explicitly to Isidore and his *liber creaturarum*, is a summary of Haimo's

---

87 This must have been an attempt to reconcile two contradictory passages in Scripture, namely Is 30:25–26 prophesying that at the end of the world the moon will shine like the sun and the sun will be seven times brighter than it is now — the basis for DOC 5.2–7 — as opposed to Mt 24:29 asserting that the sun will darken on Doomsday and the moon will no longer shed its light. This inconsistency was registered in the ninth-century *Old-English Martyrology*; see Cross (1972), 135–36.
88 The B glosses to *De temporum ratione* were copied from the Herwagen edition in PL 90:297–518, and at PL 90:685–98 and 699–702. See Contreni (2005), 252–59; Jones (1939), 21–38. Gorman in (1996a) and, more recently, Lapidge in (2009), xxxiii–xxxvi, have argued that there is no reason why Byrhtferth could not have assembled earlier continental glosses. But see Contreni (2011–2012).
89 Specifically, PL 116:869D–870A.
90 See Hab 3:11.

paraphrase or of the Auxerre text cited above rather than derived from DOC itself.[91]

> Isidorus in libro creaturarum. Post iudicium sol laboris sui mercedem recipiet; unde propheta: *Lucebit septempliciter*, et non veniet ad occasum nec sol nec luna, sed in ordine quo creati sunt stabunt, ne impii in tormentis positi sub terra fruantur luce eorum. Unde abacuch: *Sol et luna steterunt in habitaculo suo.*

This gloss in turn was cited by Peter Lombard (c. 1100–1160), just a few paragraphs after what is probably a summary of DOC 5.3–5 (though that content could have been derived from patristic sources):

> unde Isidorus, illud Isaiae quasi exponens, ait: "Post iudicium sol laboris sui mercedem suscipiet; unde Propheta: *Lucebit septempliciter.* Et non veniet ad occasum nec sol nec luna, sed in ordine quo creati sunt, stabunt, ne impii in tormentis sub terra positi fruantur luce eorum. Unde Habacuc: *Sol et luna steterunt in ordine suo.*"[92]

Both Lombard and the *Glossa ordinaria* assign the statement to Isidore, so that this information was now broadly available. Martín de León (d. 1203) used the above statement twice, mentioning Isidore but not DOC:

> Unde Hispaniarum doctor Isidorus illud Isaiae quasi exponens, ait: "Post judicium sol laboris sui mercedem percipiet. Unde propheta: *Sol lucebit septempliciter*, et non ueniet ad occasum, nec luna, sed stabunt in quo creati sunt ordine, ne impii in tormentis sub terra positi fruantur eorum luce. Unde Habacuc: *Sol et luna steterunt in ordine suo.*"[93]

The use by Martín de León of this passage derived at several removes from DOC cannot therefore be seen as evidence for direct knowledge of DOC in Spain during the twelfth century.

Clairvaux itself (manuscript **C**) seems to be at the origin of the spread of DOC throughout Cistercian houses in continental Europe, starting in the twelfth century. Three related manuscripts were copied at the end of the twelfth century in southern France (**F**) and in Spain (**T** and **E**), the latter being the earliest known manuscripts from Spain.[94]

Díaz y Díaz summed up the transmission of *Liber de ordine creaturarum* as follows: Irish mission, Anglo-Saxon mission and Cistercian circles, these are the

---

91 Gloss to Is 60:19–20. See the left-hand margin of p. 89 of volume 3 of the 1992 facsimile reprint of the 1480/81 Strasbourg edition the *Biblia Latina cum glossa ordinaria.*
92 Peter Lombard, *Sententiae* 4.48.5, in *Magistri Petri Lombardi Parisiensis episcopi Sententiae in IV libris distinctae*, 3rd edn (1971–1981), 2:547.
93 Martin of León, *Sermo secundus in adventu Domini*, PL 208:56C–D; see also *Sermo vicesimus quintus de resurrectione Domini*, PL 208:929D–930A.
94 The manuscript evidence and the lack of evidence for the influence of DOC in early medieval Spain do not support Michael Gorman's claim that *De ordine creaturarum* was composed in 'Visigothic Spain at the end of the seventh century': Gorman (1996b), 266; see also (1996a), 219.

routes by which the treatise spread throughout Europe from the early eighth century — with the curious exception of Italy and partly of Spain — to reach Bohemia in the fifteenth century.[95]

Division into Chapters and Chapter Headings

DOC is divided into fifteen sections of unequal length. Díaz y Díaz deduced from the conventional phrases preceding each one and from internal allusions to the progress of the exposition, that the separation into chapters was the work of the author.[96] In most codices the chapters are given the headings preceding them in the 1972 edition, though some variations have been carefully analyzed by Díaz y Díaz.[97] The main differences in the treatment of the chapters are as follows:

1. No chapter headings at all, as in codex **B**.
2. A full table of chapter headings immediately after the title of the work, as in manuscripts **M** and **H** = Bamberg, Staatsbibliothek, MS B.V.18 (Patr. 102), Bavaria, early ninth century.
3. The chapter heading immediately precedes the content of each chapter, but in codex **P** from Chapter 5 onward the assigned heading agrees each time with the content of the next chapter.[98]
4. The chapters are assigned numbers in **B**.
5. In some manuscripts the chapter headings are accompanied by the relevant chapter numeration.
6. Most manuscripts have no chapter numeration.

It seems that the archetype separated and differentiated the chapters, perhaps only by an initial capital letter. The lack of numeration in almost all codices argues for the absence of numeration in the original. The *capitulatio* at the beginning of the text was created later, from which the titles were then distributed among the corresponding chapters, occasionally giving rise to errors such as those in manuscript **P**. Díaz y Díaz believed the *capitula* might even go back to the time

---

95 Díaz y Díaz (1972), 66–72.
96 Chapter 2: *De creatoris uero inmensitate tantulo praemisso...*; Chapter 3: *Verum quoniam de ordine creaturarum sermonem sumpsimus...*; Chapter 4: *post illas aquas ... secundo loco...*; Chapter 5: *... sermo in ordine locali ... solem et lunam ... describat*; Chapter 6: *sermone de firmamento et luminaribus dicto...*; Chapter 7: *dehinc inferius spatium...*; Chapter 9: *post aeris spatia cum suis habitatoribus decursa, nunc...*; Chapter 10: *et quia post aquam terra ... statuta est, prius...*; Chapter 11: *porro*; Chapter 13: *sed quia*; Chapter 14: *at uero*; Chapter 15: *de illa autem uera beatitudine*; Sometimes it is the end of the preceding chapter which is the best indicator of the transition: end of Chapter 6 *his utcunque explanatis ad subsequentia festinemus*.
97 Díaz y Díaz (1972), 44–46.
98 The proper heading for Chapter 5 is not given in **P**. In that codex, Chapter 12 bears the title *de diuersitate peccantium*, the first half of the title corresponding to Chapter 13, which in turn bears the second half as its title: *de loco poenarum*. Chapters 14 and 15 have the correct titles.

of the author, and certainly to the beginning of the eighth century, when **P** was copied.

Given the importance of the symbolism of numbers in the Middle Ages, it is legitimate to consider whether the author of DOC made the conscious decision to divide the treatise into *fifteen* sections. I believe he did, because the number fifteen had particular eschatological associations at that time.[99] Thus, in the discussion of Noah's ark in his *Quaestiones in Vetus Testamentum* — a context which invited a show of numerological expertise — Isidore of Seville had interpreted as the combination of seven and eight, the fifteen cubits height to which the flooding water rose, covering up all the mountains. In his view, seven signifies 'repose' since God rested on the seventh day, eight refers to 'resurrection' since Christ rose on the eighth day, and these are combined in the number fifteen to refer to the deep mystery of baptism and of the 'repose of the resurrection' which surpasses human understanding.[100] Again, in the *Moralia* — a text available in Ireland in the second half of the seventh century[101] — Gregory the Great associated the number fifteen with the passage from this life to the next, as symbolized by the fifteen steps of the temple. This explanation also depends on the sum of seven and eight, but this time seven represents this life on earth which unfolds in weeks of seven days, whereas eight represents eternal life which Christ made manifest by his resurrection on the eighth day:

> The entire duration of this present life unfolds in groups of seven days... It is made even more clear that the number seven refers to the entirety of the present life when the number eight is mentioned afterwards. For when that number follows the number seven, this very increase shows that the end of time is bounded by eternity... The number eight refers to eternal life, which the Lord revealed to us through his resurrection... It is fitting that you should take care to do good deeds in this life, since you do not know how great is the tribulation of the future judgement. This is why one ascends to the temple by fifteen steps, so that we might learn from this ascent through seven and eight that we should be careful of our temporal actions and prudently strive after the eternal dwelling place.[102]

When viewed in this perspective, it is no accident that the systematic treatment of the physical world in DOC is interrupted at Chapter 8 with a lengthy discussion of Satan and the other fallen angels, complete with an explanation of why it is impossible for them to be saved. To be sure, since the lower zone of air discussed in Chapter 7 was assumed to be the dwelling place of these

---

99 See H. Meyer and R. Suntrup (1987), 654–58.
100 PL 83:233ABC.
101 Lathcen mac Baith, whose death is recorded in the Irish annals for the year 661, compiled brief selections from the *Moralia* (SLH 566). This collection has been edited as *Egloga quam scripsit Lathcen filius Baith de Moralibus Iob quas Gregorius fecit* (CCSL 145). See Paul Grosjean (1955).
102 Gregory, *Moralia* 35.8.17 (CCSL 143B, 1784–1785). The translation is mine.

demons after their Fall, it was not out of place to elaborate at this point on their current status and prospects. Nonetheless, this is a surprising digression from the matter-of-fact, scientific approach in the surrounding chapters. Chapter 9 resumes the overall plan of treating the layers of the universe in descending sequence and deals with the expanses of water on the surface of the earth. Chapter 8 must have been intended as a hinge inviting the reader to move on from the seven days of this material world in which his attention had just been immersed and to be ever mindful of the eternal dimension of all human destiny.

The use of the number fifteen in the very organization of DOC was thus a clever way of incorporating time into the account of the created universe. There is much explicit discussion of eschatological matters, but the approach revealed in the structure of the treatise is far more subtle. The author was keen to ensure that he provided not only a careful spatial account of this world and of the next, but he also took every opportunity to remind the reader that this temporal world will transform into eternity.

Text and Translation

Liber de ordine creaturarum

1. De fide trinitatis

1. Uniuersitatis dispositio bifaria ratione debet intellegi, in Deo uidelicet et rebus, hoc est in creaturis et creatore; non quod Deum in parte ponamus aut aequiperare creatorem creatura possit, sed quia omne quod est aut factum intellegitur aut infactum, aut potens aut subiectum aut aeternum aut temporaneum; factum ergo et subiectum et temporaneum ipsa est creatura, infactum autem et potens atque aeternum ipse est Deus.

2. Sancta utique trinitas, Pater et Filius et Spiritus Sanctus, per omnia inseparabilis, in substantia una diuinitas et in personarum subsistentiis inconiuncta trinitas, in qua nihil inferius nihil superius, nihil anterius nihil posterius in natura diuinitatis esse credendum est, nihil seruiens, nihil subiectum, nihil loco comprehensibile, nihil temporaneum, nihil infirmum, nihil adcrescens, nihil ad sexum habitumue pertinens, nihil corporeum sentire fas est, sed unus Deus sine initio sempiternus, sine loco ubique totus, sine sui motatione omnia motabilia disponens, creaturarum tempora praeterita praesentia futura pariter cernens, cui nihil est praeteritum, nihil restat futurum, sed cuncta praesentia sunt; cui nihil displicet quod bonum est, nihil placet quod malum est, a quo nihil naturaliter malum creatum est, quod per se nihil nisi creati boni uitium est; bonus ergo sine qualitate, magnus sine quantitate, aeternus sine tempore, praecipuus sine situ, qui omnibus creaturis infunditur, cum non sit illi locus, et circumfunditur omnibus creaturis; quem nulla capit creatura, nulla comprehendit intellegentia.

3. Deus unus omnipotens, sancta trinitas, Pater et Filius et Spiritus Sanctus: Pater ergo Deus omnipotens ex nullo originem ducit et ipse origo diuinitatis est, a quo Filius Deus omnipotens genitus sine tempore est: non quippe creatus est, quia Deus est, cui praeter quod Filius est in diuinitate totum est commune Patris in aeternitate, in uoluntate, in potestate, in sapientia; sic et Patri praeter quod Pater est totum est commune Filii.

A Treatise on the Ordering of Creation

1. The Doctrine of the Trinity

1. The compass of the All should be understood to be twofold, consisting of God and of things, that is, of the created* and of their Creator. Not that we can put God to one side, nor that the Creator can be set at equality with the created, but because everything that exists should be understood to be either made or not made, either full of power or subordinate, either eternal or temporal. Thus, that which is made and subordinate and temporal is created, while that which is not made and full of power and eternal, is God Himself.

2. The Holy Trinity, the Father, the Son and the Holy Spirit, is truly inseparable in all things, one divinity in substance, but a trinity differentiated in the subsistences of persons,[1] * in which it must be believed that nothing is lower, nothing is higher,[2] * nothing is prior and nothing is posterior in the divine nature, and it should be thought that nothing is subservient, nothing is subordinate, nothing can be contained in space, nothing is temporal, nothing is weak, nothing is increasing, nothing pertains to sex* or appearance, nothing is corporeal. But it is one God, eternal without beginning, wholly everywhere without occupying space, ordering all mutable things without Himself changing,* seeing simultaneously the past, the present and the future of all creatures, to Whom nothing is past, nothing remains future, but all is present, Whom nothing that is good displeases and nothing that is evil can please, by Whom nothing has been created evil by nature — for evil is in itself nothing but a defect of a created good.[3] * For God is good without quality, great without quantity, eternal without time, eminent without position, present in all creatures while in no way localized, and embracing all creatures.[4] * No creature contains Him, no intelligence comprehends Him.

3. One* all-powerful God, Holy Trinity, Father and Son and Holy Spirit: the Father, all-powerful God, draws His origin from nothing and is Himself the source of divinity,* by whom the Son, all-powerful God, was begotten outside of time. He was certainly not created since He is God and, apart from the fact that He is Son, He has everything in common with the Father in divinity, in eternity, in will, in power, in wisdom; in the same way, the Father has everything in common with the Son, except that He is the Father.

---

1 Cf. Columbanus, *Instructio* 1.2 (SLH 2, 60).
2 Cf., e.g., Rufinus, *Expositio Symboli* 4 (CCSL 20, 137–39), Ps.-Rufinus, *Liber de Fide* 1 (PL 21:1125), the *Quicunque uult* (Pelikan and Hotchkiss (2003), 1: 673–77), and *De ecclesiasticis dogmatibus liber* 4 (PL 83:1229C).
3 Cf., e.g., Augustine, *De natura boni* 4 (CSEL 25/2, 857), *Enchiridion* 3.11 (CCSL 46, 53), *De civitate Dei* 11.22 (CCSL 48, 341).
4 Cf., e.g., Augustine, *De Trinitate* 5.1 (CCSL 50, 207).

4. Spiritus Sanctus est omnipotens Deus: nec genitus est quia non est Filius, nec creatus quia non est creatura, sed ex Patre processit et Filio, cui praeter quod Spiritus Sanctus est totum est commune Patris et Filii, quia non qui Pater est Filius aut Spiritus Sanctus in persona hic est, nec qui Filius est Pater aut Spiritus Sanctus hic est nec qui Spiritus Sanctus est Pater aut Filius hic est; sed in essentia quod Pater est, Filius et Spiritus Sanctus hoc unum est, et quod Filius est, Pater et Spiritus Sanctus hoc est, et quod Spiritus Sanctus est, Pater et Filius hoc est: sed non triplex in illa trinitate deorum numerus est: salua enim separatione personarum totum commune diuinitatis est.

5. Filius ex tempore carnem sumpsit humanam quae omne uitio caret, humanitatis naturam habuit, animam prudentem, intellectualem, sapientem excepto diuina natura habens ut humanitas integra fieret; quam ideo Filius qui sine tempore Dei Patris est adsumpsit, ut qui in diuinitate erat Dei Filius in humana natura idem esset hominis filius. Qua humanitate natus est de Spiritu Sancto et Maria semper uirgine, non quia Spiritus Sancti sicut et Mariae filius esse credendus sit, sed quod ex uirtute et opere Spiritus Sancti conceptus ex uirgine natus sit. 6. Passionem crucis carne non diuinitate sustulit, mortem pro nostra redemptione et salute sustenuit, tridui tempore sepulcro conditus diuina uirtute in eadem carne surrexit, et postquam ecclesiam unam sanctam catholicam uerbo instruxit, exemplo solidauit, gratia firmauit, pace uniuit, adsumpta tota humana natura excepto eo quod corruptione obnoxia non est, ad Patrem rediens unde nunquam defuit, sedit in dextera Patris, unde resurgentibus cunctis hominibus ad iudicium uiuorum et mortuorum adfuturus in gloria Patris impiis aeternas poenas, iustis aeterna praemia reddit.

7. Haec est catholica fides; hanc credere et confiteri quam discutere plus proficit: quam non prudentia saecularis, non mundana philosophia, rerum potius imagines quam ueritatis intellegentiam sequens, agnoscere potuit, sed apostolica fides tradidit, ecclesiastica uigilantia custodiuit.

4. The Holy Spirit is all-powerful God, neither begotten since He is not the Son, nor created since He is not a creature, but He proceeded from the Father and the Son.* He has everything in common with the Father and the Son except that He is the Holy Spirit, for He who is the Father is neither the Son nor the Holy Spirit as to person, He who is the Son is neither the Father nor the Holy Spirit, nor is He who is the Holy Spirit either the Father or the Son. But what the Father is in essence, the Son and the Holy Spirit are at one with, and what the Son is, the Father and the Holy Spirit are this also, and what the Holy Spirit is, the Father and the Son are this also. There is, however, not a threefold number of Gods in the Trinity, since while maintaining the separation of persons, the entirety of divinity is common to all.

5. Within time, the Son took on a flawless human flesh. He had human nature, having a prudent, intellectual and wise soul apart from his divine nature, so that his humanity was complete. He who is the Son of God the Father beyond time, assumed humanity so that He who was the Son of God in divinity would also be the Son of Man as to human nature. In this humanity he was born of the Holy Spirit and of the ever-virgin Mary, not that he should be thought to be the son of the Holy Spirit as he is of Mary, but rather that he was born of a virgin after being conceived through the power and the action of the Holy Spirit. 6. He bore the passion of the cross in His flesh, not in His divinity, He endured death for our redemption and salvation, and after being laid away for three days in a tomb, He rose again in this same flesh by the power of God, and after He had instructed the one, holy catholic Church by his words, strengthened it by His example, confirmed it by His grace, and united it with His peace, having assumed full human nature though not subject to corruption, returning to the Father from whom He was never absent,* He sits at the right hand of the Father, whence He will return in the glory of the Father, when all men resurrect to the judgement of the living and of the dead, to give eternal punishment to the impious and eternal reward to the righteous.

7. This is the catholic faith, which it is better to believe and confess than to analyse. It can neither be known by secular discernment nor by worldly philosophy which pursues the images of things rather than the understanding of truth, but it was transmitted by the faith of the apostles and preserved by the watchfulness of the Church.[5]

---

5 Cf. 1 Cor 2.

2. De creatura spiritali

1. De creatoris uero inmensitate tantulo praemisso, ad creaturarum ordinem paulisper aspiciamus; in quo non nostrae intentionis quae nulla per se est inuentionem, sed sanctae scripturae et maiorum explanantium uestigia uel tenui aliquo relatu sequimur.

Omnis ergo creatura aut spiritalis aut corporalis est, sed quia spiritalis creatura in intellectualibus spiritibus, qui carne non tenentur, et animabus hominum, quae carne cluduntur, constat, prius de distinctis gradibus supernorum spirituum dicendum est, quorum gradus uel differentiae nouem esse per scripturas diuinas deprehenduntur: syraphin scilicet et chirubin, troni, dominationes, principatus, potestates, uirtutes, arcangeli, angeli.

2. Syraphin etenim super solium Domini excelsum stare Esaias uidit et cantare audiuit, et uno ex his ad se misso purgari de sui oris pollutione promeruit. Chirubin uero in oraculo testimonii propitiatorium figurati et arcam tegebant, et in templo Domini cum bouibus et leonibus per Salomonem depincti erant; Ezechiel quoque in uisionibus Dei quadrigam chirubin uidisse se describit, quam quatuor scripturae utriusque testamenti rotis famine mistico coniungit; ad Colossenses uero Paulus apostolus scribens thronos et dominationes et principatus siue potestates conmemorat dicens: *siue thronos siue dominationes siue principatus siue potestates*. Ipse etiam ad Ephesios de uirtutibus enarrat ita inquiens: *supra omnem principatum et potestatem et uirtutem et dominationem*. Arcangelorum et angelorum ostensionibus et nominationibus diuinorum uoluminum prata referta sunt.

3. Horum quoque nouem ordinum supernorum ciuium significationem nouem pretiosi lapides apud Ezechiel ostendunt, ubi sub persona principis Tyri super summum illum qui lapsus est angelum sermones prophetae planctum diregunt, ubi dicitur: *omnis lapis pretiosus operimentum tuum, sardius, topasius,*

2. On Spiritual Created Beings

1. After dealing thus briefly with the immensity of the Creator, let us examine for a while the order of the created world. In this somewhat superficial account, we will not be led by the findings of our own inquiry which is nothing of itself, but rather follow in the footsteps of Holy Scripture and of earlier expositors.

All creatures are either spiritual or corporeal, but because spiritual creation consists of spirits with intellect not bound by flesh, and of the souls of men which are confined by flesh, we should first speak of the various levels of the higher spirits, of which the divine Scriptures show that there are nine orders or divisions, namely, Seraphim and Cherubim, Thrones, Dominations, Principalities, Powers, Virtues, archangels and angels.[6]*

2. And indeed Isaiah saw Seraphim standing above the high throne of the Lord, and he heard them sing, and he obtained* that one of them be sent to him to cleanse him of the impurities of his mouth.[7] As for the Cherubim represented in the oracle of the covenant, they covered the propitiatory and the ark,[8] and they were depicted also by Solomon in the temple of the Lord, together with oxen and lions.[9] And Ezekiel described how he saw in visions God's chariot of Cherubim, which he joined by mystical speech to the four wheels of the two Testaments of Scripture.[10]* And indeed, the apostle Paul, when writing to the Colossians, refers to the Thrones and Dominations and Principalities or Powers when he says: *whether thrones, or dominations, or principalities or powers.*[11] And to the Ephesians he speaks also of the Virtues when he says: *above every principality and power and virtue and domination.*[12] The meadows* of the Holy Books are filled with appearances and namings of archangels and of angels.

3. The nine precious stones mentioned in the book of Ezekiel signify the nine orders of these celestial citizens, when, in the person of the prince of Tyre, the words of the prophet utter the lament for that supreme angel who fell, saying: *every precious stone was your covering, sardius, topaz, jasper, chrysolite, onyx, beryl,*

---

6 Cf. Gregory the Great, *Homily 34 on the Gospels* 34.7 (CCSL 141,305).
7 Cf. Is 6:2–7; Gregory, *Homily* 34.12 (CCSL 141,312).
8 Cf. Ex 25:16–20 and Ex 37:6–9.
9 Cf. 1Kgs 6:23–35 and 1Kgs 7:29.
10 Cf. Ez 10:1–22.
11 Col 1:16. Cf. Gregory, *Homily* 34.7 (CCSL 141,305).
12 Eph 1:21.

iaspis, crisolitus, onix, berillus, saphyrus, carbunculus, zmaragdus; quibus nouem lapidibus opertus idcirco dicitur, quia nouem spiritalium officiorum ordinibus quibus praeerat ornabatur.

4. Sicut ergo de numero diximus sic etiam de distinctis officiorum gradibus aliqua pandamus. Syraphin igitur, id est "ardentes" uel "incendentes", dicti sunt quia Dei amore plus quam omnis rationabilis creatura speciale quadam diuini muneris largitione inardescunt, et quanto omnibus creaturis excellunt tanto diuinae caritatis priuilegio creatori adpropiant, et in tanto excelsitatis honore sublimati consistunt ut inter se ac Dominum nulli alii spiritus sunt. 5. Secundo quoque ordine chirubin inter supernos ciues numerantur, cuius ordinis uocabulum "scientiae multitudo" interpretatur; quorum intellectus, dum Dei contemplatione prope haerendo reficitur, plus omnibus quae subiacent creaturis intellectualibus scientiae multitudine dilatatur. Qui enim diuinae claritatis speculum perspicacius intendunt, ab his abdita creaturarum occulta fieri qualiter possunt? 6. Tertio uero ordine intellectualium spirituum tronorum agmina constituta sunt qui sedes nuncupantur: in his etenim dum speciale munere Dominus sedet, super hos iudicia sua in creaturis omnibus terribiliter et mirabiliter exercet; hinc per psalmistam dicitur: *sedisti super thronum qui iudicas iustitiam*; et in reuelatione Iohannis euangelistae loquitur: *qui sedet in throno defendet eos*. 7. Quarto etiam gradu officiorum caelestium dominationes consistunt, quia illorum qui infra scribentur quinque graduum ministeria alta dominatione praecellunt, et quanto aliis potentiae magnitudine praeponentur tanto his ceterorum subiectio per oboedientiam exhibetur. 8. Dehinc post illas, quinto ordine supernorum ciuium principatus uocantur, quibus, dum his bonorum spirituum iam principatus conmittitur, ad explenda Dei ministeria quae facere subiecti debeant principantur. 9. Sexto quoque statu in bonis spiritibus potestates sunt ordinatae, qui principari aduersis potestatibus Domini munere perciperunt; qui per potestatem nequitiam malignorum spirituum refrenant ne plus quam permittuntur saeuitiam exercere uel humanis sensibus inhae-

sapphire, carbuncle, emerald.[13] And he is said to have been covered by these nine stones, because he was adorned by the nine orders of spiritual attendants of which he was the leader.

4. As we have spoken of their number, let us now discuss a little the various levels of their functions. Thus, the Seraphim, that is, 'the flaming ones', or 'the burning ones',[14]* are so named because they burn more than all other rational creatures with the love of God by the grant of a special divine gift, and in as much as they excel all other creatures, so they are closer to the Creator by a special dispensation of divine love, and they stand elevated to such a high level of honour that there are no other spirits between them and the Lord. 5. The Cherubim are counted as the second order among the citizens above, and the name of this order means 'abundance of knowledge'[15]* and their intellect, as it is replenished by very close and constant contemplation of God, is more expanded by an abundance of knowledge than all creatures with intellect which are below them. For how can the secrets of creatures remain hidden from those who look most clearly into the mirror of divine brightness? 6. In third position among the spirits with intellect are the armies of the Thrones, who are called 'seats': for when the Lord sits upon them by special dispensation, he carries out his judgements on all creatures from upon them in a terrible and wondrous way. Thus the Psalmist says: *You sat upon the throne, You who judge justice.*[16] And in the Revelation of the evangelist John, we read:* *He who sits on the throne shall defend them.*[17]* 7. The Dominations form the fourth level of the celestial attendants, because they surpass with a high domination the ministries of the five levels described below, and in as much as they are set above the others by the greatness of their power, so the subjection of the others to them is manifested through obedience.[18] 8. After these, the fifth order of the celestial citizens are called Principalities; and since principality over good spirits is entrusted to them, they enjoin the things their subjects must do to carry out the service of God.[19] 9. The Powers are ranked in the sixth position among good spirits, they who received by divine gift full control over the adverse powers; through their power they restrain the malevolence of the evil spirits, lest they dare to exert their savagery or cleave to human senses more than is allowed.[20] 10. The seventh grade of

---

13 Ez 28:13. Cf. Gregory, *Homily* 34.7 (CCSL 141, 306).
14 Cf. Jerome, *Liber interpretationis* (CCSL 72, 121–22); Gregory, *Homily* 34.10 (CCSL 141, 309).
15 Jerome, *Liber interpretationis* (CCSL 72, 74 and 80); Gregory, *Homily* 34.10 (CCSL 141, 308).
16 Ps 9:5. Cf. Gregory, *Homily* 34.10 (CCSL 141, 308).
17 Cf. Apoc 7:15.
18 Cf. Gregory, *Homily* 34.10 (CCSL 141, 308).
19 Cf. Gregory, *Homily* 34.10 (CCSL 141, 308).
20 Cf. Gregory, *Homily* 34.10 (CCSL 141, 308).

rere audeant. 10. Septimus gradus spiritalium ministrationum uirtutes nominantur per quos spiritus uirtutes et signa et mirabilia in hominibus saepe faciuntur. 11. Octauus ordo arcangeli, id est "summi nuntii", uocantur, per quos maiora quaeque hominibus nuntiantur, et quanto angelis in ordinis summitate excellunt, tanto hominum notitiae Domini iussione excelsiora perferunt. 12. Nonus ministrorum caelestium ordo angeli sunt nominati, qui minora quaeque commonia ex Dei uoluntate hominibus nuntiant et suadent.

13. Porro in his sciendum est, quandocumque nominantur, ex officiorum proprietate quando ad homines ueniunt sumere uocabula, quia illa supernorum ciuium summa societas propriis nominibus non indiget. Unde et Michael dicitur, id est "qui sicut Deus?", eo quod in fine contra eum qui se aduersus Deum eregeret mittendus distinatur: et Gabriel, id est "fortitudo Dei", ad Zachariam et Mariam uirginem missus scribitur, ut, qui quod natura humana denegabat futurum esse praedixerat, fortitudo Dei diceretur. 14. Ad Thobiam quoque Rafael, id est "medicina dei", mittitur; nimirum enim qui diuina natura salutem ferebat non incongrue medicina Dei nuncupatur. Et quod in singulis hoc et in gradibus potest esse, ut cum unus alterius officium facit illius etiam nomine censeatur, sicut dicitur: *qui facis angelos tuos spiritus*, id est, cum uis, spiritus hos omnes angelos, id est "nuntios", facis. Et aliquando ex uicinitate aliorum graduum, alii gradus officia adsumunt, sicut ex thronorum uicinia etiam super chirubin sedere Dominum scripturae dicunt, sicut in psalmo scriptum est: *qui sedes super chirubin manifestare coram Effrem*.

15. Sed in illa superna societate quod in aliquo specialiter habetur, ab omnibus in commune possidetur, quia non minus unumquemque reficit quod in aliquo uidet quam quod in semetipso possidet. Et cum mittuntur nunquam ab eorum contemplatione Deus a quo reficiuntur abest; non quod illi spiritus

the spiritual ministries are called Virtues, and it is by these spirits that wonders and signs and marvels are usually performed among men.[21] 11. The eighth order are called 'archangels', that is, 'highest messengers', by whom all the greater things are announced to men. And in the same degree as they surpass the angels in the loftiness of their rank, so, at the Lord's command, they bring to men the knowledge of more lofty tidings. 12. The ninth order of the celestial ministers are called angels, who relay to men and urge upon them the lesser messages from God's will.[22]

13. It should also be known of all these that whenever they are given a name, they acquire this name from the nature of their services when they come to men — for this lofty society of the celestial citizens has no need of individual names. Thus Michael, that is, 'who is like God', is so called because he is destined to be sent at the end of time against the one who will rise up against God.[23] And it is written that Gabriel, that is, 'the strength of God', was sent to Zachariah[24] and to the virgin Mary[25] so that he who foretold that which human nature said could not possibly happen, should be called the strength of God.[26] 14. And again Raphael, that is, 'the healing of God', was sent to Tobias,[27] and truly, he who brought health from the divine nature was most fittingly called the healing of God.[28]* And that which is true of the individuals can also hold for the orders, so that when one performs the duties of another, it also acquires its name, as when it is said: *You who make your spirits angels*,[29] that is, when you wish, you make all those spirits into angels, that is, into 'messengers.'[30] And sometimes, because they are so proximate, some orders take on the functions of other orders. Thus, it is because of their closeness to the Thrones, that Scripture says that the Lord sits upon the Cherubim, as is written in the psalm: *you who sit upon the cherubim make yourself manifest to Ephraim*.[31]

15. But in this celestial society, that which can be found in a particular one is possessed in common by all, because that which he sees in another replenishes* any one of them no less than what he possesses himself.[32] And when they are sent, God by whom they are replenished is never absent from their contemplation, not because those spirits who are sent can be everywhere at the same time, but

---

21 Cf. Gregory, *Homily* 34.10 (CCSL 141,308).
22 Cf. Gregory, *Homily* 34.8 (CCSL 141,306).
23 Cf. Gregory, *Homily* 34.9 (CCSL 141,307); cf. Apoc 12:7.
24 Cf. Lk 1:19.
25 Cf. Lk 1:26–27.
26 Cf. Gregory, *Homily* 34.9 (CCSL 141,307).
27 Cf. Tob 3:25.
28 Cf. Gregory, *Homily* 34.9 (CCSL 141,307–08).
29 Ps 103:4.
30 Cf. Gregory, *Homily* 34.8 (CCSL 141,306).
31 Ps 79:2–3. Cf. Gregory, *Homily* 34.14 (CCSL 141,313).
32 Cf. Gregory, *Homily* 34.14 (CCSL 141,314).

ubique pariter possunt esse qui mittuntur, sed quod Dominus qui ubique est ab his qui discurrunt semper in omni loco sine sui motatione conspicitur, unde scribitur: *milia milium ministrabant ei et decies milies centena milia adsistebant ei.*

16. Utrumque enim supernae potestates pariter faciunt quia et ministrant dum mittuntur et adsistunt dum contemplantur. Aliquando autem qui mittuntur angeli illis ad quos ueniunt hominibus per se nuntiant, aliquando alios uelut subiectos per se adnuntiandi officium distinant, sicut apud Danielum scriptum legitur: *Gabriel fac istum intellegere sermonem,* quod ab aliquo uelut superiore dictum minime dubitatur.

because the Lord who is everywhere is always seen in all places and without any movement on their part by those who are on their way.[33] * Whence it is written: *thousands of thousands ministered to him and ten thousand times a hundred thousand stood before him.*[34]

16. The celestial powers do both at the same time: they minister while they are sent and stand before Him while they contemplate.[35] Sometimes the angels who are sent give the message themselves to those men to whom they come, and sometimes they delegate the role of announcing the message to others who are in some way subject to them, as we find written in the book of Daniel: *Gabriel, make him understand these words*[36] * — which must clearly be said by someone of higher rank.[37] *

---

33 Cf. Gregory, *Homily* 34.12 (CCSL 141, 312).
34 Dan 7:10. Cf. Gregory, *Homily* 34.12 (CCSL 141, 312).
35 Cf. Gregory, *Homily* 34.12 (CCSL 141, 312).
36 Dan 8:16.
37 Cf. Gregory, *Homily* 34.12–13 (CCSL 141, 312–13).

3. De aquis quae supra firmamentum sunt

1. Uerum quoniam de ordine creaturarum sermonem sumpsimus quod tuae propositionis continentia comprehenderat, post spiritalem creaturam de qua paulisper deseruimus de aquis quae supra firmamentum sunt quid auctorum intentio potuit excogitare proferre temptabimus.

Cum enim in principio prima die facta fuisset lux, quae spiritalis creatura esse dignoscitur, secunda die firmamentum quod diuidet inter aquas quae sunt supra firmamentum et aquas quae sunt sub firmamento esse factum scriptura testatur. Ex quo intellegitur aquas illas quae supra firmamentum sunt locali spatio ex omni corporali creatura esse superiores. 2. Quamuis enim in psalmo CXLVIII post firmamentum et solem et lunam et stellas aquae illae quae super caelos sunt positae inueniuntur, tamen ut illas omnibus esse corporalibus creaturis ostenderet altiores, iterum excelsarum uirtutum uelut recapitulans habitacula psalmista his anteponit dicens: *laudate eum caeli caelorum et aquae quae super caelos sunt laudent nomen Domini*. 3. Unde ostenditur post illa spiritalia spatia qualiacumque sunt, ubi spiritales de quibus diximus ordines conmorantur, quae caelorum caelos propheta nominat, ante hoc uisibile caelum aquas illas uelut initium corporalium rerum esse constitutas, quas tamen ne quis spiritali iungeret creaturae post caelos caelorum antequam de terra diceret propheta posuit; paulo post enim subinfertur: *laudate Dominum de terra*. 4. Ecce has aquas psalmista super caelos positas dixit, et tamen his caelos caelorum anteponit, per quod demonstratur inter utrosque caelos esse collocatas, id est caelis spiritalibus humiliores et caelis corporalibus superiores; et tamen corporalibus creaturis pertinere dicendae sunt, dum in secundi diei opere factae supra istud corporeum firmamentum consistunt.

5. Sed quid ibi utilitatis in rerum corporalium usibus agant, bina magistrorum intentione inuestigatur. Quidam namque illas ad terrarum orbis ablutionem in diluuio, quod sub Noe factum est sicut Geneseos historia narrat Dei praescientia reseruatas aiunt, sicut scriptura inquit: *et cataractae caeli apertae sunt*

3. On the Waters Above the Firmament

1. Since we have begun to speak about the order of created things, as proposed in your plan,* after saying a little about spiritual creatures we will now try to relate what the efforts of investigators were able to figure out about the waters above the firmament.[38] *

While light — which is understood to refer to spiritual creation[39]* — was created in the beginning on the first day, Scripture affirms that the firmament was made on the second day, dividing the waters above the firmament from the waters below the firmament. We see thus that those waters above the firmament are located in the highest place among all corporeal creation. 2. Even though we find in Psalm 148 that the waters set above the heavens are mentioned after the firmament, the sun, the moon and the stars, the Psalmist, wishing to show that these waters are the highest of all corporeal creatures, recalls again the dwelling places of the higher powers, mentioning them before these waters and saying: *Praise him ye heavens of heavens; and let all the waters that are above the heavens praise the name of the Lord.*[40] 3. Whence it is clear that these waters set below those spiritual spaces, whatever they may be, where dwell the spiritual orders of which we have just spoken — spaces which the prophet calls 'heavens of heavens' — are set above the visible heaven as the beginning of corporeal things. And lest someone should connect them with spiritual creation, the prophet mentions them after the heavens of heavens, before he speaks of the earth. For he adds a little later: *Praise the Lord from the earth.*[41] 4. Thus, while the Psalmist says that these waters are set above the heavens, he speaks first of the heavens of heavens. This shows that the waters are located between these two heavens, that is, they are lower than the spiritual heavens, and higher than the corporeal heavens. And yet they must be said to belong among corporeal creatures, since they were set above the corporeal firmament during the work of the second day.

5. As regards their purpose there among corporeal things, scholars have approached this question in two different ways. Some say that these waters were intended by the foreknowledge of God for the cleansing of the entire world by the flood which took place at the time of Noah, as the Genesis account relates.[42] * For Scripture says: *And the floodgates of heaven were opened and there was rain for forty*

---

38 Cf. Aug. Hib., *De mirabilibus* 1.6 (PL 35:2156med).
39 Cf. Augustine, *Gen. litt.* 2.8 (CSEL 28/1, 43).
40 Ps 148:4.
41 Ps 148:7.
42 Cf. Aug. Hib., *De mirabilibus* 1.6–7 (PL 35:2157med-2158in).

et facta est pluuia XL diebus et XL noctibus. Sed quia et nubes, de quibus pluuiarum imbres terreni soli fertilitatem inrigant, atque etiam aer, in quo hemisperia omnia et aurae[1] concipiuntur, caelorum nomine per scripturas diuinas saepe censentur, — quemadmodum dicitur: *et pluit illis manna ad manducandum et panem caeli dedit eis,* et in alio loco: *et caeli dabunt imbrem et terra dabit fructum suum* — quibusdam doctoribus placet ex illo inferiore nubium caelo tantarum aquarum abundantiam fuisse defusam ut secundum illam consuetudinem qua per omne tempus agitur etiam tunc pluuiarum copiam nubes effunderent; in quibus tamen cataractas apertas scriptura conmemorat, eo quod plus solito aquarum defusio inmissa fuerat. Ceteri uero easdem aquas supra firmamentum positas idcirco adserunt ut igneum qui in luminaribus ardet et sideribus calorem temperarent, ne plus quam sufficit inferiora spatia aestate torrerent.

---

1 Replacing *ex aere* in the 1972 edition.

days and forty nights.[43] But because the clouds from which rain showers irrigate the fertility of the soil of the earth, and even the air in which all hemispheres* and winds* are formed, are often given the name 'heavens' by the divine Scriptures — as when it says: *and he rained manna onto them to eat and gave them the bread of heaven,*[44] and elsewhere, *and the heavens will give rain and the earth will give its fruit*[45]* — some teachers prefer to think that a vast amount of such waters was emitted from that lower heaven of the clouds, so that in the very same way as is customary at all times, the clouds also then shed an abundance of rain. And Scripture says that the floodgates opened within them because an unusually great downpour of water was sent down.[46] Others affirm that these waters were put above the firmament to moderate the fiery heat burning in the luminaries and in the stars, so that they should not scorch the spaces below more than necessary during the summer.*

---

43 Gen 7:11–12.
44 Ps 77:24.
45 Aug. Hib., *De mirabilibus* 1.6 (PL 35:2157); Jer. 14:22, Ps 66:7, Ps 84:13.
46 Cf. Aug. Hib., *De mirabilibus* 1.6 (PL 35:2157).

4. De firmamento caeli

1. Post illas aquas creaturarum corporalium ordine secundo loco uidetur esse firmamentum, quod in secunda die ut praediximus factum inter utrasque diuidit aquas; de cuius etiam statu, utrum uelut discus terram desuper operiat an ut testa oui omnem introclusam creaturam undique cingat, utriusque aestimationis non desunt putatores. 2. Nam et illud quod de hoc psalmista conmemorat cum dixit: *extendens caelum sicut pellem*, utriusque aestimationis assertionibus non contrafacit quia cum animalis carnem cuiuscumque sua pellis uestiat omnia sua membra aequaliter undique circundat, cum uero excisa de carne seorsum extenditur siue rectam siue curuam cameram uestire posse non dubitatur. 3. Utrum ergo terram desuper uelut extensa pellis tabernaculum tegat an sicut animalis membra corio conteguntur mundi molem undique firmamentum cingat, utrique adsertioni non difficulter suffragatur.

4. De huius quoque firmamenti situ utrum inane ac penetrale an solidum ac firmum sit, diuersi auctores suas aestimationes uelut quid se ad has deducat protulerunt; quorum sententias utilius quam nomina ponere curabo.

Eorum enim illi qui firmamentum inane ac penetrale fieri plus diligunt ad confirmationem sententiae suae omnium elimentorum naturas conferunt: 5. terram etenim omnium creaturarum corporalium grauissimam esse non minus ostendunt quam dicunt, atque illam ideo humillimum in creaturis locum tenere aiunt quia natura aliqua nisi se ipsa sufferri[2] non ualet; aquam uero quanto leuiorem terrae uidimus tanto grauiorem aere deprehendimus. Aer namque sub aqua per se subsistere non ualet sed ad sua spatia, etsi aliqua necessitatis ui[3] aquis subductus fuerit, statim uadit; 6. ignis quoque natura supra aerem esse deprehenditur quod etiam in illo igne qui in materia terrena ardet facile conprobatur, quia statim ut accensus fuerit flammam ad superna quae super aerem sunt spatia, ubi illius est habundantia et locus, diregit sed circumfusione crassi aeris exstinctus in mollem aerem cito euanescit, ut ad suae naturae locum peruenire non possit; in quo tamen ostenditur ignis

---

2 Replacing *sufferre* in the 1972 edition.
3 Replacing *uim* in the 1972 edition.

4. The Celestial Firmament

1. After these waters, the firmament holds second place in the order of corporeal creation. It was created on the second day, as we have said, and divides the waters from one another. But as to its shape — whether it covers the earth from above like a disc, or whether, like the shell of an egg, it contains all creation enclosed within itself — both opinions have many proponents.* 2. And indeed, the words of the Psalmist: *stretching the sky like a skin*,[47] contradict neither of these claims. Indeed, while the skin of an animal when it covers the flesh surrounds equally from all sides all parts of the animal, when it has been cut away from the flesh and stretched, it can without a doubt cover either a plane or a curved vault.[48] *
3. For whether, like a stretched skin, a tent covers the earth from above, or whether the firmament surrounds the mass of the world from all sides, as the parts of an animal are bounded by its skin, both claims can easily be supported.

4. Concerning the substance of the firmament, whether it be fluid* and penetrable or solid and firm, various investigators have offered their opinions and their justification. It is more useful that I should present their opinions rather than their names.

Those who would rather the firmament be fluid and penetrable, adduce the very nature of all elements to support their claim. 5. They affirm and demonstrate that earth is the heaviest of all corporeal creations, and say that it holds the lowest position among created natures because it is held up by no other nature than itself.* And in as much as we see water to be lighter than earth, so we perceive it to be heavier than air. For air does not have the power to remain of its own accord under water, but immediately escapes to its own space though brought down under water by some constraining force.[49] * 6. Moreover, it can easily be shown from that very fire which burns in earthly materials, that the nature of fire is located above the air. For as soon as a fire is lit, it shoots a flame upward to the spaces above the air, the location of its fullness and its proper place.[50] * This flame is extinguished, however, by the disturbances of the dense air flowing about and quickly vanishes into the soft air, so that it can never reach its natural proper place. It

---

47 Ps 103:2.
48 Cf. Augustine, *Gen. litt.* 2.9 (CSEL 28/1, 45–47).
49 Cf. Augustine, *Gen. litt.* 2.2 (CSEL 28/1, 35).
50 Cf. Augustine, *Gen. litt.* 2.3 (CSEL 28/1, 36).

naturam qui ascendit aere esse leuiorem, sicut aquae naturam quae discendit monstratur fieri grauiorem. 7. Hac ergo ratione etiam firmamenti spatium quod supra igneum est leuius ac tenuius putant, quia excelsius his omnibus quas praediximus naturis constat. In quo spatio etiam stellarum fulgorantium lucem inaequalem esse idcirco aestimant, quod in illo tam amplo spatio ex illis aliae longius aliae propius currant.

Sed hanc putationem qui minus suscipiunt, supra illud aere atque igne subtilius et inanius ac penetrabilius spatium constare aquas minime posse dicunt, nisi forte, ut illi quos praediximus aiunt, omni uaporalitate tenuiores et subtiliores ibi consistunt. 8. Quibus etiam ab aliis contra respondetur quia unquam, quamuis tenuissima, aquarum uaporalitas firmamento leuior esset, quod igni qui aere leuior est subtilius et leuius ac penetrabilius fieret; propter quod ergo illi alii firmamentum uelut aere solidissimo fusum constare solide ac firmiter facilius putant, atque ideo firmamentum nominari existimant, quia tam solida quam inania, tam leuia quam grauia quae diximus cuncta spatia intra se concludat et supra se positas aquas qualescumque sunt susteneat. Uerum quia inter tantos uiros de tali et de tanta re uariatum est, nullius aestimationem alii praeponendam censemus, sed ad hos lectorem utrarumque partium arbitrum mittimus.

appears from this then, that since the nature of fire is to rise, it must be lighter than air, just as the downward-falling nature of water shows it to be heavier. 7. For this reason, they hold that the layer of the firmament above the fiery zone must be yet lighter and thinner since it is clearly located above all these natures of which we have been speaking. They think that the stars shine with varying brightness in this space because some run their course farther away in this vast expanse, and others nearer.

But those who reject this view say that it is impossible for the waters to remain above such a layer which is even more subtle, fine and permeable than air and fire, unless perhaps (as those of whom we have spoken claim) they are in that place more rarefied and subtle than any vapour.[51] * 8. Others however retort that if the vapour of the waters, however fine it may be, were lighter than the firmament, it would have to be more subtle, light and penetrable than fire, which is lighter than air. For this reason, they would rather think that the firmament stands in place firmly and solidly, as though cast of solid bronze.[52] * They believe that it is called firmament because it encloses all the spaces of which we have spoken — be they solid or fluid, light or heavy — and it sustains the waters set above it, whatever these may be. And indeed, when there are differences among so many about such matters of great importance, we do not feel we should set one opinion above another, but we refer the reader to them, to judge between the two sides.*

---

51 Cf. Augustine, *Gen. litt.* 2.3–5 (CSEL 28/1, 36–39).
52 Cf. Job 37:18.

5. De sole et luna

1. Quia uero in firmamento caeli licet post speciem maris et terrae formata duo luminaria magna in principio Geneseos mosaicae legis, immo diuina, scriptura pronuntiat, non est indecens si discendens de supernis sermo in ordine locali creaturarum solem et lunam statim post firmamentum describat, ita tamen ut in conditionis ordine post terram et mare duo haec luminaria et stellas cum scripturae uocibus animus ponat, quamuis omnia elimenta sine tempore facta fideli ratione catholica inuestigatio credat.

2. Sol ergo et luna duo luminaria in firmamento caeli constituta, unum quod est maius ut praeesset diei, secundum quod minus est statutum ut praeesset nocti; sed non eandem sui splendoris lucem quam cum in principio creata sunt habuerunt nunc per omne sui ministerii tempus dierum ac noctium decursionibus conseruant. 3. Haec enim, dum humanis usibus ministrare a Deo creatore destinata sunt, cum homines inculpabiliter uixissent et sub creatoris quo conditi sunt lege perseuerassent, etiam sui luminis plenitudine decorata ministrabant. Cum uero homines, quibus in ministerio sociata primitus rutulabant, propter transgressionem deiecti paradisi beatitudinem amiserunt, ipsa quoque luminaria, quamuis non sua culpa, sui luminis detrimenta non sine suo dolore pertulerunt, sicut apostolus Paulus contestatur dicens: *quia omnis creatura congemescit et dolet usque adhuc.*

4. Sed quia per redemptoris aduentum humano generi pristinae beatitudinis in melius restauratio promittitur, etiam creatura suum antiquum decorem accepta non dubitatur; unde propheta de sole specialiter et luna inlustratus spiritali famine inquit: *et erit in die illa cum ceciderint turres, erit lux lunae sicut lux solis et lux solis septempliciter motabitur in lucem septem dierum cum alligauerit Dominus uulnus populi sui et percussuram plagae eius sanauerit.* 5. Cum enim factum fuerit *caelum nouum et terra noua et non fuerint in memoria priora* quae corruptioni seruiunt, et peccati uulnus et percussuram plagae mortis in

5. The Sun and the Moon

1. Since Scripture affirms at the beginning of the Mosaic law, nay, of the divine law of Genesis, that the two great luminaries were formed in the celestial firmament[53] — though after the appearance of the sea and the earth — it is not unfitting for our discussion to descend from the higher things in the spatial order of creatures and to describe the sun and the moon immediately after the firmament, in such a way, however, that the mind follows the words of Scripture in setting these two luminaries after the earth and the sea in the order of creation, though catholic enquiry by reason full of faith believes that all created natures were created without time.[54] *

2. For the sun and the moon are two great luminaries set in the firmament of heaven, the greater one to rule over the day, the second smaller one to rule over the night.[55] But they do not now retain throughout the duration of their ministry of days and nights, that same splendid light they possessed when created in the beginning. 3. These two were intended by God the Creator to minister to the needs of man, and so long as men lived untainted by sin and obeyed with great constancy the law of the Creator by whom they came to be, they remained adorned with the fulness of their light as they performed this service. But when men — for whom they were glowing as colleagues in this ministry — lost their state of happiness on being cast out of Paradise for their disobedience, the luminaries themselves — though through no fault of their own* — endured a loss of brightness, and this not without suffering on their part. The apostle Paul testifies to this when he says: *For we know that every creature groans and suffers pain, even till now.*[56] *

4. But because through the coming of the Redeemer restoration into a state better than its original happiness has been promised to the human race,* it cannot be doubted that creation itself will receive its former beauty. Thus, with special reference to the sun and to the moon, the inspired Prophet says in spiritual speech: *And it shall be in that day when the towers shall fall, the light of the moon shall be as the light of the sun, and the light of the sun shall be changed sevenfold into the light of seven days, when the Lord shall bind up the wound of his people, and heal the injury from their blow.*[57] 5. When *a new heaven* * and *a new earth* shall be made *and the former things* which were subject to corruption *shall not be in remembrance,*[58] and the Lord

---

53 See Gen 1:14.
54 Cf. Augustine, *Gen. litt.* 4.33–35 (CSEL 28/1, 131–36).
55 Cf. Gen 1:14–18.
56 Rom 8:22.
57 Is 30:25–26.
58 Cf. Is 65:17.

corporibus resurrectorum Dominus sanauerit, et superbi spiritus ex inperio quod arripuerant depositi fuerint, tunc lux lunae in lucem solis motabitur et lux solis restaurabitur in lucem septem dierum quibus conditus fuerat, hoc est, in septuplum suum lumen restaurabitur. Nihil enim restauratur nisi quod amissum est aut corruptum. Quod igitur sol amisit et luna, hoc rursum accipient; 6. ex quo apparet septimam nunc sui luminis partem luminaria retinere quam septempliciter resument quando, sicut per Abacuc Spiritus Sanctus pro futuris praeterita ponens, ut prophetis mos est, inquit: *eleuabitur sol in ortu suo et luna stabit in ordine suo.*

Cessante namque motabilitate humani status cui seruiunt, et sui cursus motabilitas cessabit; quod enim inquit: *eleuabitur sol in ortu suo,* hoc indicat quod nunquam inclinabitur in occasu suo, et in et quod dicit: *luna stabit in ordine suo,* hoc insinuat quod motationes incrementi et detrimenti sui iterum non patietur, sed in suo ordine semper stabit. 7. Hoc autem erit *quando* — ut apostolus loquitur — *ipsa creatura liberabitur a seruitute corruptionis in libertatem gloriae filiorum Dei*; cum enim sancti pro mercede sui laboris, quod Deo seruierunt, inmotati fuerint et fulserint *sicut sol iustitiae, cuius in pennis est sanitas,* tunc et ipsi corporeo huic soli pro mercede sui ministerii quo seruituti corruptionis subiecta est, in septuplum sui fulgoris rutulatio restituetur; 8. interim uero cotidianis sui ministerii motibus quotiens solem sequitur luna sui incrementa luminis auget, quotiens autem solem antecedet detrimenta sui fulgoris auget.

De statu uero lunae uarie putatum est, utrum spera demedia sui parte nigra ac tenebrosa et demedia parte altera lucida sit et candida, et sic eius incrementa ac detrimenta agantur ut, cum paulatim pars illius lucida ostenditur, eodem modo tunc tenebrosa occultatur, similiter quoque dum lucida uertitur tenebrosa iterum manifestatur, 9. an etiam rota radiis solis inluminata, quae quandocumque soli siue ante siue post adpropiat uelut in ora radio luminis inlucescat; cum autem longius ac longius recedere uidetur, maius ac maius paulatim suum lumen a solis splendore augetur ut cum ad integrum aequiperato orbe facie ad faciem soli subposita consisteret, tunc plene in se imaginem solis habere possit.

has healed the wound of sin and the injury from the blow of death in the bodies of those resurrected, and the proud spirits will have been deposed from the rule they seized, then the light of the moon will be changed into the light of the sun and the light of the sun will be restored to the light of the seven days when it was created, that is, into seven times its present brightness. For nothing is restored except what was lost or corrupted. The sun and the moon will thus receive again that which they had lost. 6. From which it is manifest that the luminaries now retain the seventh part of their brightness, which they will recover sevenfold when, as the Holy Spirit says through Habakkuk, setting past events for future ones as is customary for prophets: *the sun shall be raised in its rising and the moon shall stand in its proper state.*[59] *

With the end of the mutability of the human condition which they served, the mutability of their course will also cease; for when it is said: *the sun shall be raised in its rising*, this shows that it will never decline in its setting, and when it is said: *the moon shall stand in its proper state*, this suggests that it will no longer endure the changes of its increase and decrease, but will always remain in its proper state.*
7. This will be — as the Apostle says — *when creation itself shall be delivered from the servitude of corruption into the liberty of the glory of the children of God,*[60] for when the saints will have been transformed as the reward for their labour with which they served God, and will shine *like the sun of justice, in whose rays there is health,*[61] then the brightness of its glow will be restored sevenfold to the corporeal sun itself, in recompense for its service through which it was subjected to the servitude of corruption. 8. In the meantime, through the daily movements of its ministration, in as much as the moon follows the sun, so it increases its light, and in as much as it precedes the sun, so it decreases its brightness.*

There are conflicting opinions on the shape of the moon.[62] Is it a sphere which is half black and dark and half bright and white, and its increases and decreases are caused when by gradually revealing its bright side it simultaneously conceals its dark one, and similarly when the bright side is turned away, the dark one appears again? 9. Or is it a disc* illuminated by the rays of the sun, which, whenever it comes close to the sun, either in front of it or behind it, is illuminated as though at the rim by a beam of light.* When however, it is seen to recede further and further, it gradually increases its light more and more from the splendour of the sun, until it stands face to face with the sun with fully equal orb, and can hold the full image of the sun within itself.*

---

59 Cf. Hab 3:11.
60 Rom 8:21.
61 Mal 4:2.
62 Cf. Augustine, *Gen. litt.* 2.15 (CSEL 28/1, 56–57) and, ultimately, *In psalmum* 10.3 (CCSL 38, 75–76).

10. De cursibus autem solis et lunae nec temporis nec istius est breuitatis deserere, quos idcirco in hoc opusculo neglegentius adsequor, quia et ipsius conpendiosa breuitas non patitur et in usum paene omnibus lectoribus dierum festorum conpotandorum gratia conuersi sunt.

11. Haec uero lucis organa nonnulli insensibiles creaturas opinantur, sed quae diximus usitatius a catholicis auctoribus frequentantur; in his ambiguis sententiarum aestimationibus intendendum est cui plus sanctarum scripturarum auctoritas suffragatur, et si haec desit, hoc etiam amandum est quod multitudo catholicorum in fidem traxit; deuersae autem aestimationes, quae tantundem a catholicis adsertae sunt et quibus utriusque canonis sacri dicta non contrafaciunt uel ad quas aequanimiter currunt, haec arbitris lectoribus in ambiguo relinquendae sunt.

10. Time does not allow for discussion of the courses of the sun and of the moon in this brief treatise. I have neglected them in this little work, on the one hand because the very brevity of this summary does not permit this, and on the other because they are known in practice to almost all readers* for the purpose of computing the dates of feast days.

11. Some are of the opinion that these instruments of light are insensible creatures,[63] but we have given the view most commonly held by catholic authors.* When confronted with such difficult assessments of opinions, one should first examine which opinion is best supported by the authority of the holy Scriptures. If this fails, one should prefer the views which most catholic believers have reconciled with their faith. As for the differing opinions put forward by catholic believers and which either do not contradict the words of both the holy canons of Scripture or are equally congenial with them, they should remain uncertain in the judgement of readers.*

---

63 Cf. Jerome, *Comment. In Esaiam* 9.30.26 (CCSL 73,395).

6. De spatio superiore et paradiso

1. Sermone de firmamento et luminaribus dicto, sequitur inane longum quod a caelo firmamenti usque ad terram deducitur et in duo spatia esse diuisum a nonnullis scriptoribus explanatur; sed superius spatium ad caelum pertinere dicitur, inferius autem terrae fieri coniunctum non dubitatur. 2. Etenim excelsum spatium, quod caelo pertinere diximus, purissimum ac subtilissimum, nec nubium tumores nec uentorum inflationes nec pluuiarum aut imbrium humidas conspirationes nec niuium uel grandinum gelidas coagulationes nec aeris ullas motationes nec tempestatum et tonitruorum fragores, sed nec ipsum etiam aerem qui uolantium auium corpora et ipsarum nubium spissionis aeris ipsius molem sufferre ualuisset et animantium diuersarum uitas aerei spiritus reciproca inflatione reficeret atque alitu animaret nec ullas omnino diuersorum hemisperiorum perturbationes omnimodis habet;

3. sicut Olimpi montis altissima terrarum et ob id ceteris incognita hominibus iuga conscendentibus conprobatur et eorum relatione refertur, qui aceto umectas spongias ad conseruandum aeri spiritus inflationem et respirationem ori ac naribus circumponentes anniuersaria consuetudine, nescio qua superstitione ducti, conscendunt et nec ibi ullam auem nec nubem nec pluuiam nec uenti aliquem motum uidisse se confirmant. Consumatis sacrificiorum quorum gratia uadunt officiis, ibidem signa quaedam ac notas arenis inprimentes redeunt quas etiam illic post annum iterum conscendentes inlaesas atque intemeratas inueniunt; 4. ex quo perspicue demonstratur nihil ibi perturbati aeris consistere, praesertim cum in eodem loco nihil quod ad uirorem olerum pertineat aut arbustorum reperiri aut uideri nequeat, sed tamen non ipsud esse de quo superius diximus purissimum illud ac subtilissimum supernum spatium putandum est, ad quod nulla terra pertinere uel accedere potest, sed hic locus ad extrema huius spatii inferioris et uicina illius superioris confinia pertinet, in quo tamen loco eorum qui carne uestiuntur uita nequaquam potest conmotari.

6. The Higher Space and Paradise

1. We have spoken about the firmament and the luminaries. Then follows a great empty space stretching from the heaven of the firmament to the earth. Some authors say it is divided into two spaces: the higher is said to belong to heaven, while the lower one is unquestionably associated with the earth. 2. And, indeed, the higher space which we have said is associated with heaven, is most pure and most subtle, and it contains neither the swelling of clouds, nor the breath of winds, nor the blowing together* of rains or moist showers, nor the frozen coagulations of snow or hail, nor any movements of air, nor the crashes of storms or of thunder. It does not even contain that air which can bear up the bodies of flying birds and the mass of this same air compacted into clouds, and which also sustains the life of various living beings by the alternating blowing of an airy flow, animating them with breath, nor does it contain any at all of the disturbances of the various hemispheres.[64] *

3. This has been confirmed by those who have climbed to the summit of Mount Olympus,* the highest place in all the world and for that reason unknown to most people. Those who climb it every year because of some religious superstition, say that they must press sponges which have been soaked in vinegar[65] against their mouth and nostrils to maintain the inhaling and exhaling of a flow of air. They affirm that they have seen neither bird nor cloud there, nor rain, nor any movement of the wind. After completing the rituals of the sacrifices for which they came there, they inscribe some signs and letters in the sand before descending. When they climb up there again the following year, they find these signs intact and undisturbed.[66] 4. Which shows clearly that the air there does not move at all, all the more so that nothing like green plants or shrubs* can ever be found or seen in this place. And yet one should not think that this is that same most pure and most subtle higher space of which we spoke earlier, which contains no earth at all, nor can earth ever reach there. But this space extends on the one hand to the highest parts of the lower space and on the other to the neighbouring limits of the higher space.[67] And in that space, the life of those who are clothed in flesh cannot be sustained* in any way.

---

64 Cf. Augustine, *Gen. litt.* 3.10 (CSEL 28/1, 73–74).
65 Cf. Jn 19:29, Mt 27:48 or Mk 15:36.
66 Cf. Augustine, *De Genesi contra Manichaeos* 1.15.24 (PL 34:184); *Gen. litt.* 3.2 (CSEL 28/1, 64–65).
67 Cf. Augustine, *Gen. litt.* 3.6–7 (CSEL 28/1, 68–70).

5. Unde perspicuum est, illud superius purissimum tranquillissimumque spatium, de quo paulo ante deseruimus, non carnalium habitationi neque mortalium corporaliumque rerum usibus esse praeparatum, quapropter plurimi catholicorum auctorum illud spatium primitus angelis qui lapsi sunt cum suo principe adserunt ad habitandum fuisse distinatum, eo quod de supercaelestibus angelis neminem cecidisse arbitrantur, subcaelestes uero quamdiu in angelica beatitudine fuerant, in qua tamen per tempus non steterant, 6. — quia, ut scriptura inquit, *ipse diabulus ab initio mendax est et in ueritate non stetit* — hunc locum habitationis sorte putant percipisse, quem paradisum caelestem scriptura pronuntiat, quae sub persona principis Tyri ad summum illum angelum apostatam ita loquitur: *perfectus decore in deliciis paradisi Dei fuisses.*

7. Quemadmodum enim homines post peccatum suum de terreni paradisi felicitate deiecti in huius terrae maledictione obnoxiae plagali modo habitationem trusi sunt, ut dum in terra peccauerunt in deterioris terrae mansione postea sub poena delicti uiuerent, ita et angelos, qui in superiore etiam aeris ipsius puriore spatio peccasse putantur, in inferiorem et ipsi aeris huius obscurioris et turbulentiorem locum deturbati de superni et puri aeris suaeque dignitatis felicissima sede, misere et infeliciter sub exspectatione futuri examinis in quo durius damnabuntur uiuere aestimant; ut dum aerea corpora habent et in aere nunc conmorantur, non inconuenienter aestimantur etiam priorem suae beatitudinis sedem in aere sed puriore et subtiliore pridem habuisse. 8. Qui tamen locus, dum caelo firmamenti ut praedixi pertinet, caeli nomine censetur sicut Dominus ipse perhibet dicens, *uidi Satanam sicut fulgor de caelo cadentem.* Ex ipsius enim loci perspicua ac pura beatitudine peccati sui merito deiectus, in inferioris spatii, hoc est nebulosi ac brumosi aeris huius, infelicem ac miseram habitationem distinatus est, sicut Paulus apostolus contestatur dicens: *non est conluctatio aduersus carnem et sanguinem sed aduersus principatus et potestates huius aeris, aduersus mundi rectores harum tenebra-*

5. From which it is clear that this higher very pure and very still space of which we have been speaking was not intended as the dwelling place of corporeal beings, nor for any purpose connected with mortal or corporeal things. Many catholic authors therefore claim that this space was originally intended as the dwelling place of those angels who fell with their leader.[68] They are of the opinion that none of the supercelestial angels lapsed, but that as long as the subcelestial ones enjoyed angelic beatitude — in which, however, they did not remain 6. since, as Scripture says, *the devil was a liar from the beginning and did not remain in the truth*[69]* — that dwelling place which Scripture refers to as the heavenly Paradise, was assigned to them. For Scripture is speaking about that highest apostate angel under the guise of the prince of Tyre, when it says: *you would have been* perfect in beauty in the pleasures of the Paradise of God.*[70]

7. In the same way as men, thrown out from the happiness of the terrestrial Paradise after their sin, were thrust as a punishment to inhabit this earth made hateful on account of a curse, so that having sinned on earth, they would live thereafter, as punishment for their crime, in the dwelling place of a worse earth,[71] so the angels who are thought to have sinned in that higher purer space of air, cast down to the lower and more turbulent place of this same darker air from the most happy seat of the higher and pure air and of their dignity, are thought to be living miserably and unhappily in the expectation of the future judgement in which they will be mercilessly damned. Since they have bodies of air and now dwell in the air,[72] it is not improperly thought that the earlier seat of their happiness was also in air, though more pure and more subtle. 8. And that space, since it borders on the heaven of the firmament as I mentioned earlier, is properly assigned the name 'heaven' as the Lord himself asserts when he says: *I saw Satan falling like lightning from heaven.*[73] * Cast out from the clear and pure beatitude of this place on account of his sin, he was destined for the unhappy and miserable dwelling of the lower space, that is, of this cloudy and moist air, as the apostle Paul confirms when he says: *For our wrestling is not against flesh and blood, but against the principalities and powers of*

---

68 Cf., e.g., Augustine, *Gen. litt.* 3.10 (CSEL 28/1,73); *Enchiridion* 9.28 (CCSL 46,64); *In psalmo* 148.9, in *Enarr. in ps.* (CCSL 40,2171).
69 Aug. Hib. *De mirabilibus* 1.2 (PL 35:2153*med*). Cf. Jn 8:44 and 1 Jn 3:8.
70 Ez 28:12–13.
71 Gen 3:17–19.
72 Cf. Augustine, *Gen. litt.* 3.10 (CSEL 28/1,72).
73 Lk 10:18.

rum qui etiam spiritalia nequitiae in caelestibus, [id est, Paulus Christum in semetipso denuntiat triumphasse].

9. Deiectis ergo malignis spiritibus cum suo principe diabulo ex illo quem praediximus limpidissimo subcaelestium spatiorum habitaculo et postmodum redempto ex Adae et proprio uniuscuiusque delicto per mediatoris aduentum humano generi eundem locum animarum sanctarum interim quieti, dum resurrectionem expectant futuram idem putatores opinantur, quem etiam caelestem paradisum autumant esse nominatum, de quo Dominus latroni in cruce confitenti responderat: *amen dico tibi, hodie mecum eris in paradiso*; 10. quia in illo paradiso arboribus consito et lucido fonte praepollente animae exutae corporibus non indigent, quia spiritalis homo carnalem usum corpore mortis liberatus non possedet nec refici terreni paradisi frugiferis arboribus necesse habet. Aeternus enim temporalibus non utitur sed aeterna et spiritalia contemplatur.

11. Haec non confirmantium sed aestimantium sensibus praestrinximus, praesertim cum et ipsam aestimandi de talibus perspicaciam nobis ipsis non adtribuimus; cum enim necessitas exigerit, harum omnium putationum[4] auctores in medium adducere poterimus, quibus aut fides aut dubitatio adscribi potest, quorum sententias referendo potius quam defendendo laboramus; nos enim alterius forte melioris, si adsit, adsertionis, cui plus uel scripturarum exempla uel catholicorum consensus sapientium suffragauerint, concordiam subire parati sumus.

Sed de superiore spatio his utcunque explanatis ad subsequentia festinemus.

---

4 Replacing *putationem* in the 1972 edition.

this air, against the rulers of the world of those dark places, who are the spirits of wickedness in the heavens[74] [that is, Paul affirms that Christ has triumphed in him].*

9. The evil spirits and their leader the devil having been cast out from that most clear residence of the subcelestial spaces of which we have spoken, and after this, the human race having been redeemed from the sin of Adam and from individual sin by the advent of the Mediator, these same scholars speculate that this place is for the repose of the holy souls as they await the resurrection to come. And they claim that this is the very celestial Paradise the Lord was referring to when he replied to the thief confessing on the cross: *Amen, I say to you, this day you shall be with me in Paradise.*[75] * 10. For in that Paradise planted with trees and adorned with a remarkable bright spring,* the souls stripped of their bodies want for nothing, for the spiritual man, freed from the body of death, has no need of carnal things, nor does he need to be restored by the fruit-bearing trees of the earthly Paradise. For that which is eternal has no use for temporal things, but contemplates eternal and spiritual things.

11. We have woven this presentation not with established views but with opinions, all the more so since we do not attribute to ourselves the discernment necessary for making a judgement on such matters. If it should become necessary, we could adduce the authors of all these theories,* to whom one might grant belief or doubt and whose views we strive to present rather than defend. For ourselves, if there should be some perhaps better claim, better supported either by the content of Scripture or by the consensus of catholic scholars, we are prepared to agree with it.

But after these explanations, such as they are, concerning the higher space, let us hasten on to the sequel.

---

74 Eph 6:12.
75 Lk 23:43; Isidore, *Differentiae* 2.12.32 (CCSL 111A, 23–24).

7. De spatio inferiori et hemisperis diuersis

1. Dehinc inferius spatium aer uocatur quem terrae sociari diximus et a quo uniuersae carnis quae in terra et aere uersatur uitam adiuuari et conteneri in nobis et per nos conprobamus. Qui et aliquando etiam terrae per scripturas nomine uocitatur, sicut per psalmistam dicitur, cum in Domini creatoris laudem ordine summo cunctae creaturae incitantur, et, cum consummatis hiis quae ad superiorem caelorum ordinem pertinent ad haec aeris spatia peruenitur, taliter subinfertur: *laudate eum de terra, dracones et omnes abyssi, ignis, grando, nix, glacies, spiritus procellarum qui faciunt uerba eius.* 2. Hucusque enim in aere sermo est qui terrae nomine uocitatur: postmodum namque de humo et inferioris terrae naturis scripturae uocibus imperatur: *montes et omnes colles, ligna fructifera.*

Idcirco autem hic aer terrae uocabulum saepe sortitur quia crassitudine et uelut soliditate quam in se habet uolantium auium quamuis maximarum corpora sustentantur; quae, uelut pisces et omnia paene aquatilia marinorum fluctuum recondita natando penetrant, sic uolucriter aerea spatia uolando pertranseunt. 3. Cuncta etenim quae aqua praestat ad conseruandam uitam aquatilibus, haec aer facit uolatilibus, quia sicut reciproco alitu auium et omnium qui in aere et terra uiuunt uita alitur et conseruatur, ita eorum qui in aquis degunt inspirandi respirandique tractu per aquam uitalis motus reficitur; 4. unde cum in aerem trahuntur, quia limpaticum spiramentum non habent, cito deficiunt, sicut et ea que in aere uiuunt, cum ab his aer excluditur, ultra uiuere non possunt.

Sicut autem illa aeris soliditate uolantia, ut dixi, corpora fulciuntur, ita et ipsa eadem terrena quam in se habet crassitudine — propter quam et terrae uocabulum saepe sortitur, — tumida nubium molis sustentatur et per illam soliditatem aerea crassitudo niues et grandines et glaciem, adnitente ui[5] frigoris, parit, quod ita efficitur. 5. Nam hoc aeris spatium suae naturae insitum habet ut fumali leuitate uapores aquarum de terra et maris facie contrahat et collegat, quos in sublime eleuans, quamdiu in minutissimis guttis consistunt, conglobatis in se

---

5 Replacing *uim* in the 1972 edition.

7. The Lower Space and the Various Hemispheres

1. The space below this is called air, and we have said that it is associated with the earth. We confirm in ourselves and by ourselves that it sustains and contains all corporeal life which dwells on earth and in the air. And indeed, Scripture itself sometimes calls it 'earth', as when the Psalmist calls on all creatures in descending order to enjoin them to praise the Creator. After naming those things which pertain to the higher order of the heavens, he goes on to these spaces of air and says: *Praise him from the earth, ye dragons, and all ye deeps, fire, hail, snow, ice, stormy winds which fulfill his words.*[76] 2. Thus far, things which are in the air have been called 'earth', and Scripture then goes on to address the soil and the natures of the lower earth: *Mountains and all hills, fruitful trees.*[77]

It is for the following reason that this air is often called 'earth', namely because it can sustain by its density and near solidity, the bodies of flying birds, however large.[78] For just as fish and almost all aquatic animals can swim into the secret recesses of the sea, so birds can fly in their birdlike manner through these spaces of air. 3. For all that water does to maintain the life of aquatic animals, air does the like for flying animals, since just as the life of birds and all those who live in the air and on earth is sustained and maintained by an alternating breath, thus the life and movement of those that live in water is refreshed by the process of inhaling and exhaling through water.[79] 4. Thus, when they are brought into the air, because they are deprived of their aquatic breath* they soon collapse, just as those who live in air can no longer live when air is taken away from them.

And so, just as the bodies of flying birds are borne up, as I have said, by this solidity of the air, thus the swelling mass of the clouds is borne by this same earthy density which it has within itself* — which is why it is often given the name 'earth.' And it is by means of this solidity and with the help of the power of cold, that the density of air can generate snow and hail and ice;[80] and these occur as follows.* 5. It is within the very nature of this layer of air that it draws together and gathers water vapours with the lightness of smoke from the earth and from the surface of the sea. After raising them, the air itself can keep them suspended as long as they remain in minuscule drops which the clouds have gathered within

---

76 Ps 148:7–8.
77 Ps 148:9.
78 Cf. Aug. Hib., *De mirabilibus* 1.23 (PL 35:2168).
79 Cf. Augustine, *Gen. litt.* 3.6–7 (CSEL 28/1,68–69).
80 Cf. Aug. Hib., *De mirabilibus* 1.23 (PL 35:2168).

nubibus, ipse per semetipsum aer suspendit; sed cum uexante uentu illae guttulae in maiores stillas coeunt, aeris amplius natura non ferente, pluuialiter imbres ad terram dilapsi cadunt. 6. Si uero ipsas quas praedixi stillas, uentu in maiusculas moles coagitante, conlatas antequam deorsum pluant gilu in nubibus arripuerit, in grandinis lapillos coagulatas frigoris uiolentia constringit; si autem paulo remissiores necdum densatos uapores in guttas idem gilu praeuenerit, in niuis speciem magna uis frigoris eosdem transmittit, et quod in se suspensa altius nebula taliter nutrit, non sufferente aere ac uentu dispergente, ad terram dimittit, 7. sicut de hoc eodem psalmista commemorans de Domino dicit: *qui dat niuem sicut lanam, nebulam sicut cinerem spargit, mittit cristallum suum sicut bucellas, ante faciem frigoris eius quis sustenebit*? Et, ut ostenderet siue in terra siue in nubibus niues in aquas iterum resolui consuescere, paulo post subiungit dicens: *emittit uerbum suum et liquefacit ea, flauit spiritus eius et fluent aquae.*

8. Ut autem perspicuum sit ipsas aquas hoc modo in nubibus suspendi in libro sancti Iob scriptum uidetur: *qui suspendit aquas in nubibus suis ut non erumpant pariter deorsum.* Attamen illas aer aquas ad terram et ad mare demittit quas ex hisdem inferioribus partibus ante sustulit, et quamuis de salsa pelagi latitudine eas traxerit pluuialis conceptio, per aerem indulcescit, quemadmodum et cum salsa profundo maris unda propinata per humum terrae infunditur — sicut nautis est frequens consuetudo, — in dulcis aquae saporem statim motatur.

Commotione uero aeris uentos et uehementiore concitatione ignes etiam ac tonitrua[6] occultis imperiis per angelos, quibus uisibilis regitur mundus, sicut et cetera, conditor facit. 9. Nonnulli uero de effectu tonitrui illud intendunt, quod cum circa aere duorum elementorum, hoc est ignis et aquae, sunt spatia, unum superius sicut diximus et unum inferius, et tamen aeris natura utraque in se trahit (id est aquam uaporaliter de imis et ignem caumaliter de superibus), ipsa duo contraria sibi elementa confligunt. 10. Inpossibile namque est absque humidis nubibus et fulgoribus tonitrua moueri, sicut intuentium oculis

---

6 Replacing *Commotatione uero aeris et uentus uehementiore, ignes etiam ac tonitrua* in the 1972 edition.

themselves. But when, tossed about by the wind, these small particles gather into bigger drops which can no longer be borne up by the nature of air, they fall to the earth as pouring rain.[81] 6. On the other hand, if those drops of which I spoke are tossed together by the wind into somewhat larger masses, and frost seizes them in the clouds after they have been brought together but before they pour down, the violence of the cold forces them to harden into the stones of hail. And if the freezing cold should find these vapours somewhat softer and not yet pressed together into drops, the great power of the cold transforms them into the texture of snow, and the mist suspended on high sends down to the earth that which it so produces within itself, when the air will no longer sustain it and the wind scatters it about.[82] *
7. The Psalmist is referring to this when he says of the Lord: *He who gives snow like wool, scattering the mist like ashes, sends his crystal like morsels: who shall stand before the face of his cold?*[83] And to show that snow is wont to melt back into water either on the ground or in the clouds, he then adds: *He sends out his word, and melts them: His wind shall blow and the waters shall flow.*[84]

8. So that it should be clear that these waters are suspended in this way in the clouds, we find written in the Book of the blessed Job: *Who suspends the waters in His clouds, so that they break not out and fall down together.*[85] However, the air returns to the earth and to the sea those waters which it had carried up from these lower regions, and though the process of formation of rain pulled them up from the salty expanses of the sea, it now softens them through the air, just as when salt water collected from the deep sea is strained through the soil of the earth — as is the common practice of sailors — it immediately changes to the taste of sweet water.[86] *

The Creator makes the winds by moving around the air and also lightning and thunder by agitating it more violently.* He does this, and all other things, by hidden commands carried out by angels, whereby the visible world is ruled.[87] *
9. Some hold the following view on the subject of thunder*: though, as we have said,[88] air is surrounded by the proper places of the two elements fire and water, one above and one below, the nature of air nonetheless draws both within itself (that is, water as vapour rising from below, and fire as heat radiating* from above), and these two opposing elements thus enter into conflict. 10. For it is impossible for thunder to occur in the absence of moist clouds and of lightning, as is obvious

---

81 Cf. Aug. Hib., *De mirabilibus* 2.18 (PL 35:2182).
82 Cf. Aug. Hib., *De mirabilibus* 2.18 (PL 35:2182).
83 Ps 147:16–17.
84 Ps 147:18.
85 Job 26:8.
86 Aug. Hib., *De mirabilibus* 1.22 (PL35:2168).
87 Cf. Augustine, *Gen. litt.* 3.10 (CSEL 28/1, 73).
88 Cf. DOC 4.5–6, above.

perspicue patet, in quo conflictu ignis et aquae confusi sonus horribilesque frangores suscitantur; et si ignis uictor fuerit, terrae atque arborum fructibus non mediocriter nocet; si uero aqua uicerit, fructiferam uim tam in arboribus quam in his, quae olerum diuersis speciebus nascuntur, non perdit.[7] 11. Illo enim praecipue tempore tonitrua sonant, quo arborum et terrarum fruges in ostensione adhuc fiunt, priusquam maturescere incipiant; per creaturas enim aliarum incrementa creaturarum aut detrimenta Domini conditoris inperio gubernantur.

---

7 Replacing *prodit* in the 1972 edition.

to all observers. In this conflict between fire and water there arise confused rumbles and dreadful crashes. And if fire wins out, it does great damage to the crops of the earth and the fruits of the trees.[89] If however water wins, it does not destroy the fruit-bearing vigour in the trees or in the produce from all the various sorts of plants. 11. For thunder is heard mainly at that time when the fruits of the trees and of the soil are just appearing, before they begin to ripen. And thus it is through creatures that the growth and decrease of other creatures are ruled at the command of the Lord, the Creator.

---

89 Cf. Wis 16.19–22, referring especially to Ex 9.24–25.

8. De diabulo et natura daemonum

1. In hac turbulenta ac nebulosa aeris huius mansione de sublimi felicitate, ut praediximus, angeli repulsi cum suo principe conmorantur; sed ille princeps Satanas et diabulus nominatur, reliqui uero spiritus ipsius principis ministri, qui prius angeli fuerant, nunc daemones dicuntur; quemadmodum etenim merita, sic et nomina motauerunt et loca. Sed tamen et nunc per scripturas, siue antiquo uocabulo siue quod isti nequitiae sunt nuntii, sicut boni spiritus nuntii iustitiae, saepe angeli uocantur; 2. sicut in euangelio legitur: *quem praeparauit pater meus diabulo et angelis eius*; et apostolus dicit: *datus est mihi stimulus carnis meae, angelus Satanae qui me colaphizat.*

Sed has etiam sedes usque iudicii tempus sub exspectatione terribilis Domini aduentus non sine timore et tremore licet infructuoso interim possedent, sicut apostolica dicta perhibent, quibus dicitur: *nam et daemones timent et contremescunt.* Et ut manifestum sit quod sub exspectatione temporis, in quo durius iudicabuntur uel potius perdentur, hunc locum aeris habitant inmundi spiritus, in praesentia saluatoris exclamabant: *quid nobis et tibi, Iesu, Fili Dei? Uenisti huc perdere nos ante tempus?* 3. In aduentu namque aeterni iudicis, quando commonis sanctorum omnium oratio conplenda est dicentium: *fiat uoluntas tua sicut in caelo et in terra*, et in tenebras exteriores serui inutiles eicientur, cum Dominus aduersarios suos, sicut reppulit caelo, sic expellit humo; quibus aeterni ignis, sicut et testatur ipse Dominus, a patre inremediabiliter praeparata est poena.

4. Qui ideo nec remissionem nec redemptionem recipere merentur, nec possunt, quia de sublimissimo statu sui ordinis ceciderunt, ac propterea nihil aliud in quod iterum remisso peccato reuocarentur habuerunt, dum omnem suam beatitudinem in qua constituti sunt, transgressione naturalis boni quo

8. Concerning the Devil and the Nature of Demons

1. It is in the turbulent and cloudy abode of this air, as we said above, that now dwell the angels who have been cast out from their supreme felicity, together with their leader.[90] That leader is called Satan and 'the devil', and those other spirits who are servants of this leader, though they were previously angels are now called 'demons.' As their merit changed, so did their name and location. But they are still frequently called 'angels' by Scripture, either on account of their former name or because they are messengers of wickedness, just as good spirits are messengers of justice. 2. Thus we read in the Gospel: *which my Father prepared for the devil and his angels*,[91] and the Apostle says: *there was given me a sting of my flesh, an angel of Satan, to buffet me.*[92]

But it is not without fear and trembling, however vain, that they dwell in this place till the time of judgement, in the expectation of the dreadful coming of the Lord, as shown by the words of the Apostle: *the demons also fear and tremble.*[93] * And so that it should be clear that the unclean spirits dwell in that space of air in the expectation of the time when they will be most harshly judged, or rather doomed, they called out in the presence of the Saviour: *what have we to do with you, Jesus, Son of God? Have you come to destroy us before our time?*[94] * 3. For at the coming of the eternal judge, fulfilling that prayer common to all saints when they say: *Thy will be done on earth as it is in heaven*,[95] the useless servants will be cast into outer darkness, when the Lord expels His enemies from the earth, just as He cast them out from heaven. And the punishment of an eternal fire was inexorably prepared for them by the Father, as the Lord Himself has testified.[96]

4. And they do not merit,* nor is it possible for them to receive either remission or redemption since they fell from the very highest position of their rank and therefore have nothing else to which they could be recalled were their sin forgiven, as they polluted all their happiness in which they were established by transgressing against the natural good in which they existed and against the law of the Lord in

---

90 Cf. DOC 6.7–8; Isidore, *Differentiae* 2.14.42 (CCSL 111A, 30); Augustine, *Gen. litt.* 3.10 (CSEL 28/1, 72–74).
91 Mt 25:41.
92 2 Cor 12:7.
93 Jas 2:19.
94 Lk 4:34.
95 Mt 6:10.
96 Cf. Mt 25:41.

erant et dominicae legis in qua conditi sunt, polluerunt; propterea nec poeniteri desiderant nec, etiam si poenituissent, ueniam recipere omnino possent.

5. Humanum autem genus redemptionem a suo conditore accipere idcirco promeruit, quia de inferiore adhuc sui ordinis gradu corruit; cum adhuc in paradiso terreno esset positus, generandi officio distinatus ciborum que esui deputatus, inmotationem in meliorem sublimiorem que et spiritalem uitam sine morte reciperet, si, quandiu in hac conuersatione positus esset, in mandati custodia homo permaneret. 6. Clementia ergo conditoris ad illum statum, ad quem adhuc peccans non peruenerat, per passionem Domini reuocatur; quem si inde cecidisset, sicut angeli, nunquam iterum reuocaret, quia non ad illum gradum uel ordinem unde primus homo ceciderat, sed ad illum sublimiorem quem sperauit restitutio fiet, dicente Domino: *erunt sicut angeli in caelo*, scilicet quia non sicut homines in paradiso. In illam enim inmortalitatem, quae generandae proli et ciborum esui deputata pro tempore est, quamuis redempti, homines redire non poterunt, sed post mortem resurgentes spiritalibus corporibus non crescendo, non senescendo, non moriendo angelicae felicitatis consortes erunt.

7. Tempus uero diabulicae transgressionis si requiritur, ante omne tempus uisibilium rerum diabuli peccatum fuisse originaliter deprehenditur. Omnia enim quae facta sunt, simul et sine tempore facta fuisse scriptura docet, quae dicit: *qui uiuit in aeternum creauit omnia semel*, in quibus omnibus infernalis ille ignis aeternus, de quo Dominus dicit: *mittite in ignem aeternum quem praeparauit pater meus diabulo et angelis eius*, simul factus fuisse minime dubitatur; in eo enim quod dicit: *creauit omnia semel*, nihil non simul factum in omnibus creaturis reliquit. 8. Cui ergo carcer in illa creaturarum conditione praeparatus est, illius peccatum originaliter ipsas creaturas praecessit; nequaquam enim adhuc innocenti poenam Dominus praeparasset, si non illius delictum praeparatam poenam praecessisset. Sed hoc etiam sine tempore fecit, qui illum et peccare prae-

which they were created. For that reason, they do not desire to repent,[97] nor, even if they did repent, could they possibly receive any mercy.

5. The human race, on the other hand, merited* to receive redemption from its Creator because it fell from a lower level of its nature. For when it was still set in the earthly Paradise, destined for the task of procreation and intended to eat food, it would have been granted a transformation without death into a better, higher and spiritual life, if man had kept well what had been commanded while he was in that abode.[98] 6. And the clemency of the Creator has called him back through the passion of the Lord to that condition which he could no longer reach once he had sinned. And if he had fallen from there, like the angels he could never be called back again, because restoration will not be to that level or condition from which the first man fell, but to that higher condition for which he hoped, as the Lord says: *they will be like angels in heaven*,[99] that is, not like men in Paradise. Though redeemed, men could not return to that immortality which was assigned temporarily for procreation and the eating of food, but resurrecting after death with spiritual bodies which neither grow, nor age, nor die, they will share in the happiness of the angels.[100] *

7. And if one looks for the time of the devil's transgression, one finds that the first sin of the devil occurred before time and all visible things.[101] * For Scripture teaches that all things which were made, were made simultaneously and without time, when it says: *He who lives for ever created all things together*,[102] and it cannot be doubted at all that the eternal fire of which the Lord says: *send them into the everlasting fire which my Father prepared for the devil and his angels*,[103] was created at the same time. For since it says: *He created all things together*,[104] there was not a single one among all created natures that was not created simultaneously. 8. And he for whom a prison was prepared in that creation of all created things, his first sin preceded those created things.[105] * For the Lord would never have prepared a punishment for someone who was still innocent, had his fault not preceded the prepared punishment. And the Lord did this without time: not only did He have

---

97 Cf. Isidore, *Differentiae* 2.15.45 (CCSL 111A, 32).
98 Cf. Augustine, *Gen. litt.* 6.23 (CSEL 28/1:196).
99 Mt 22:30; see also Mk 12:25.
100 Cf. Aug. Hib., *De mirabilibus* 1.2 (PL 35,2153-54).
101 Aug. Hib., *De mirabilibus* 1.2 (PL 35:2153).
102 Sir 18:1. Cf. Augustine, *Gen. litt.* 5.17 and *Gen. litt. imperf.* 1.3 (CSEL 28/1,160 and 461-65).
103 Mt 25:41.
104 Sir 18:1.
105 Aug. Hib., *De mirabilibus* 1.2 (PL 35:2153*med*).

sciuit, et cum eius peccato pariter damnationis eius poenam qua seruus fugitiuus cruciaretur effecit.

9. Iste autem angelus, cum a conditoris beatitudine recessit, omne suae naturae bonum quod in conditione sua habuit totum amisit; sed si ipsi malus, Deo bonus semper perseuerat, dum oboedienter dominicae iussioni, quamuis non sponte, propter potentiam tamen obtemperat. Ex omni enim naturae bono quod habuit, hoc nunc tantummodo habet: quod Deo creatori ad cuncta oboedit imperata. 10. Sed hoc bonum non in diabulo et ministris eius bonum est, qui idcirco oboediunt quod non oboedire non possunt, sed haec eorum oboedientia in Deo bona est, cuius bonae uoluntati inuita[8] diabuli mala uoluntas cum bene operare praecipitur, resistere non potest. Sed plerumque accidit, ut, cum Dei bona uoluntate aliquid facere imperatur, ipsius mala uoluntas in eodem opere pascatur; quemadmodum ad decipiendum Achab, impiissimum regem idolatram scilicet et prophetarum persecutorem, cum a Domino in quo deciperet interrogaretur, non solum se sponte paratum ad hoc opus obtulit, sed etiam quale consilio illud efficeret indicauit, ac respondit: *uadam et ero spiritus mendax in ore omnium prophetarum eius; et dixit Dominus: uade et fac ita et decipies.* 11. Ualde enim conuenerat ut qui ueros Domini prophetas neci dedisset, pseudoprophetarum falsiloquo ore seductus et deceptus periret. Ecce prumptissime daemon sua mala uoluntate cito ad istud decipiendi impii officium semetipsum obtulit, sed nisi a Domino permissus fuisset, hoc facere non potuit; in qua re bona Dei uoluntas sanctorum prophetarum iustam uindictam exercuit, sed malus minister in interitu impii et peccatoris malam suam uoluntatem cibauit.

12. Sed nec in hominibus nec in rebus quae hominibus subditae sunt, aliquid absque Dei permissione facere ualet, sicut euangelica ueritas perhibet, qua refertur: *si nos iecis, mitte nos in gregem porcorum.* Si enim in illis hominibus a quibus expellebatur, contra Domini praeceptum ultra permanere non potuit, sic et in porcos absque eius introire permissione non potuisse se ostendit; 13. quod et in beato Iob et rebus quas possederat et amiserat similiter manifestatur, in quibus inimici nequitia absque conditoris permissione nihil egisse probatur,

---

8 Replacing *in uita* in the 1972 edition.

foreknowledge of the devil's sin, but simultaneous to this sin He made the punishment of the damnation by which the fugitive slave* would be tormented.

9. For that angel, when he withdrew from the blessedness of the Creator, completely relinquished all the good of his created nature. But even if he is bad for himself, he remains good for God as he complies obediently with the commands of the Lord, not because he wishes to do so, but by the power of God. Of all the natural good he once had, he now retains this much only: that he obeys all the commands of God, the Creator. 10. But this good is not a good in the devil and his attendants, who obey because they cannot not obey, but their obedience is a good in God Whose good will the reluctant* bad will of the devil cannot resist when instructed to do good deeds. But it usually happens that when ordered by the good will of God to do something, his own bad will is gratified by that same deed. Thus, in the matter of deceiving Achab — a most impious and idolatrous king who persecuted prophets[106]* — when the Lord asked him in what way he would deceive Achab, the devil not only willingly presented himself as ready for the task but even indicated by which means he would accomplish it, when he answered: *I will go and be a lying spirit in the mouth of all his prophets. And the Lord said: Go and do this and you will deceive.*[107] * 11. For it was most fitting that he who handed over to death the true prophets of the Lord, should perish through treachery and deceit in the words of false prophets. Thus the demon offered most willingly, through his bad will, to perform the task of deceiving the impious king, but he could not have done this if the Lord had not allowed him. And thus the good will of God carried out the righteous vengeance for the holy prophets, but the wicked servant satisfied his bad will with the killing of the impious and the sinner.

12. But he can do nothing, whether among men or among things subject to men, without the permission of God, as is shown by the truthful word of the Gospel, where it is said: *If thou cast us out hence, send us into the herd of swine.*[108] This shows that while he could no longer stay against the command of the Lord, in those from whom he had been expelled, neither could he enter the swine without His permission. 13. Which is also clear in the case of Job and what he possessed and lost, where it is shown that the wickedness of the enemy could have done

---

106 Cf. 1 Kgs 16:31–33, 1 Kgs 18:4, 1 Kgs 19.1–2, 1 Kgs 22:26–27 (Cf. also 2 Chr 18:25–26).
107 Cf. 2 Chr 18:21 (also 1 Kgs 22:22). Cf. also Gregory, *Moralia* 2.20.38 (CCSL 143, 82–83).
108 Mt 8:31.

sicut dicitur: *nonne uallasti eum ac domum eius omnemque substantiam eius?*

Et cum a Domino maligni hostis potestati eius substantia permittitur, ita subinfertur: *ecce uniuersa quae habet in manu tua sunt; uerum tamen in eum ne extendas manum tuam.* Et haec ita esse sentiens, Iob, cum suarum rerum damna comperisset, ita respondet: *Deus dedit, Deus abstulit, quomodo uoluit Dominus fecit;* 14. non dixit 'Deus dedit, diabulus abstulit.' Certissime enim sciebat absque Dei permissione in rebus, aut in hominibus, nihil omnino facere posse aduersarium, sed saepe, ut dixi, in eodem ministerio eius aduersarii praua uoluntas per se pascitur et Domini beneuolentia aut iustae uindictae aut fructuosae probationis dispensatione ministratur; sub qua bifaria bonae et malae uoluntatis distributione et malos per uindictas trucidant et bonos per temptamenta probant. 15. Ad hoc namque ipsorum, quamdiu in hoc aere adhuc libere uolitant, usque ad tempus extremi iudicii poena a Domino defertur, ut praui ex hominibus eorum consortes et sceleris et punitionis appareant, et boni, per tribulationes eorum ab his inrogatas probati, manifesti fiant.

16. At uero isti inprobi et inpuri spiritus, uagi et subtiles, animo passibiles sunt et, aeris corporibus induti, nunquam senescunt et cum hominibus inimicitias exercentes superbia tument, fallacesque atque in fraude callidi hominum sensus conmouent, terroremque mortalibus inferentes, inquietudinibus somniorum et motibus et distortione membrorum uitam turbant, praestrigia atque oracula fingentes regentesque sortes, cupidinem inliciti amoris et cupiditatis humanis cordibus infundunt, et ueri similia mentientes in bonorum etiam angelorum habitum et lucem se transformant; 17. et quemadmodum nequitia ita et potestate gradibus distant, et sicut nunc boni spiritus, hoc est perfecti angeli, inpassibiliter aera penetrant, ita et hii, si non peccassent, ea quae nunc passibiliter loca possedent subiecta, si feliciter et beate uiuerent, haec eadem haberent. 18. Et hii quidem, quando sua nomina proferunt, ex officiis nequitiae et potestatibus uocabula sua sibi adsumunt, quemadmodum, cum a Domino de suo nomine in regione Gerassinorum aduersarius interrogatus fuisset, respondens inquit: *Legio*

nothing without the permission of the Creator, as it is said: *Did you not protect him on every side, and his house and all his substance?*[109]

And when his substance was surrendered by the Lord to the power of the evil enemy, He added: *Behold, all that he has is in your hand: but do not touch his person.*[110] And Job perceived this to be so, so that when he was apprised of the loss of all his possessions, he responded as follows: *God has given, God has taken away, the Lord has done as he wished.*[111] 14. He did not say: 'God has given, the devil has taken away', for he knew with certainty that without God's permission the Adversary can do nothing at all, whether to things or to men.[112] But often, as I have said, in the very same service the perverse will of the Adversary is gratified, and the benevolence of the Lord is carried out by means either of a just punishment or of a fruitful trial. And by this twofold combination of good and bad will, they torment the wicked with punishments and test the good with trials. 15. Their punishment for this, while they as yet fly freely in the air, is deferred by the Lord till the Last Judgement, so that the wicked among men should be seen clearly as their companions in crime and in punishment, and the good should become manifest from being tested by the tribulations called upon them by the demons.

16. These treacherous and impure spirits are inconstant and subtle, their passible souls clothed in bodies of air. They never age and they swell with pride at exercising their actions inimical to men. Deceitfully and by skillful fraud they disturb the senses of men and, bringing terror to mortals, they trouble their life by the worries of dreams and by the movements and distortions of their members. Contriving wonders and oracles, and presiding over lots, they fill human hearts with the concupiscence of illicit love and cupidity, and even, pretending to their likeness, they transform themselves into the appearance and the light of good angels.[113] * 17. And as they differ in wickedness, so do they also differ in the extent of their power, and as the good spirits (that is, the perfect angels) now remain impassible as they traverse the air, so they too — if they had not sinned and had lived happily and in beatitude — would have traversed in like manner those lower spaces where they now dwell as passible beings.* 18. And whenever they mention their names, they adopt names based on their wicked deeds and powers. Thus, when the Adversary was asked his name by the Lord in the region of the Gerasens,

---

109 Job 1:10.
110 Job 1:12.
111 Job 1:21.
112 Cf. Gregory, *Moralia* 2.18.31 (CCSL 143, 79) and *Moralia* 2.15.25 (CCSL 143, 75).
113 Cf. Isidore, *Differentiae* 2.14 (CCSL 111A, 29–30).

nomen est, quia multi sumus. Unde manifestum est, non proprii nominis quod non habuit, sed sui gradus ac potestatis uocabulum protulisse et requirenti Domino, quia aliter loqui non potuit, de semetipso quod erat uerum indicasse.

he answered saying: *My name is legion, for we are many.*[114] Whence it is clear that he was not giving a personal name, which he does not have, but the name of his grade and power and, since at the Lord's request he could not speak in any other way, he revealed truthfully what he was.

---

114 Mk 5:9.

9. De natura aquarum et cursu oceani

1. Post aeris spatia cum suis habitatoribus decursa, nunc ad aquae elimentum quod inter aerem et terram constitutum est, intentio deregitur, cuius congregatio, sicut Geneseos scriptura declarat, mare uocatur, cum dicitur: *et congregationes aquarum appellauit maria*. Quarum ea pars quae per fontes et flumina et stagna terris interfunditur dulcidinem habet, ut et sitientibus animalibus potamenti et ceterorum usuum solacia praeberet, et alendis fructibus terram fecunditas irrigaret; 2. propter quod et imbres qui de nubibus cribrati per aerem defluunt, ut aptius ad fructiferam uim et sedandam sitim, sicut ante diximus, subuenirent, sapidi fiunt; ea uero pars inmotata aquarum congregatio, quae per magna terrarum spatia dilatatur, et a qua ipsius fines occultantur, salsuginem et acriorem saporem insitum sibi naturaliter tenet, ut conuenientes humanis usibus fructus, quos sapidi liquoris non haberet unda, utilius nutriret. 3. Sed utrum sapidum an salsum saporem naturalius an aequaliter utrumque aquae habeant, pro certo Deus uiderit, quamuis et plerique salsuginem naturalem esse aquarum saporem putant, dulciorem uero terrae ac aeris natura condiri aestimant; sed tamen quemadmodum salsa aqua per humum defusa dulcescit, ita et dulcis aqua per marinorum olerum cineres infusa salsi protinus saporis fit, unde uterque sapor naturalis esse suo modo non est difficilius credi, dum alterutro in alterumque potest refundi.

4. Maris uero fretibus crebro terrarum spatia distinguntur, ut et gentium terminos intercluderet, et munificentia suorum fructuum omnes prouincias diuersorum populorum ditaret, et inter omnes patrias conmotata inuicem conmercia necessaria ministraret.

Quantam uero concordiam cum lunae cursibus inundatione et recessu suo oceanus habeat, intuentibus diligenterque animaduertentibus perspicue patet. Qui cotidie ad terram bis uenire ac recedere per horas XXIIII indesinenter uidetur; cuius cursus tota conuenientia in ledonis et malinae diuisas uicissitudines partitur. 5. Sed ledonis adsissa sex semper horas incrementi sui inconmotata consuetudine conplet, et per totidem

9. On the Nature of Water and the Behaviour of the Ocean

1. After discussing the layers in the air and their inhabitants, we now turn our attention to the element water which lies between the air and the earth. According to the scriptural text of Genesis, the gathering together of this water is called 'sea' when it says: *the gathering together of the waters he called seas.*[115] That part of these waters which flows through the land* in springs and rivers and expanses of standing water contains sweetness so that it can offer the comfort of drink and of other benefits to thirsty living beings, and so that its fecundity may irrigate the soil for the nourishment of crops. 2. This is also why showers scattered from the clouds and flowing down through the air become sweet so as to better increase the fertility [of the land] and the quenching of thirst — as we said earlier.[116] As for that gathering together of waters[117] which remains a stationary mass stretching over great expanses of the earth and hiding its very boundaries, it naturally contains within itself a salty and bitter taste, so as to better foster those products useful to man which sweet water does not provide. 3. But God alone knows for certain whether water is by nature sweet-flavoured or salt-flavoured, or whether it contains both flavours equally. Many believe that the salty taste is natural to water, and that it is the nature of earth and of air which brings about the sweetness, and yet, just as salt water becomes sweet when filtered through earth, so sweet water strained through the ashes of sea-plants quickly acquires a salty flavour.* It is thus not difficult to believe that both flavours could be natural each in its own way, since each one can be transformed into the other.[118] *

4. The land masses are separated from one another by the straits of the sea, so that it surrounds peoples with borders, and enriches all the provinces of these various peoples with the abundance of their produce; and since it lies between all countries it facilitates their mutual and necessary trade.*

The remarkable agreement between the course of the moon and the ebb and flow of the Ocean is perfectly obvious to those who observe and pay careful attention.* For every day the Ocean is seen to come to the land repeatedly and then retreat twice in twenty four hours; and the regularity of this behaviour is divided into the distinct alternations of the *ledo** and the *malina*.*[119] 5. While the incoming tide of the *ledo* invariably rises for six hours, and for the same number of hours

---

115 Gen 1:10.
116 Cf. DOC 7.8, above.
117 Cf. Gen 1:9–10.
118 Cf. Aug. Hib., *De mirabilibus* 1.22 (PL 35:2168); cf. DOC 7.8, above.
119 Cf. Aug. Hib., *De mirabilibus* 1.7 (PL 35:2159).

horas ipsa spatia quae texerat retegit; malinae autem adsissa quinque horas suae inundationis agit et per septem horas eiusdem recessae litora quae conpleuerat uacua reddit. Quae tantam concordiam cum luna habere uidetur, ut in eius medio semper luna nascatur, quae per VII dies et XII horas et quartam diei partem diligenti exploratione perseuerare uidetur. 6. Et ita fit ut, cum iterum plena luna minuitur, etiam malina rursus tenebrosa demedietur; interpositis uero spatiis ledo deprehenditur, quia nec plenilunium nec nascentis lunae initium unquam adire cernitur. Et per hanc uicissitudinem efficitur, ut per omnem communem annum XXIIII malinae et totidem ledones inueniantur; in embolismo autem XXVI malinae et eiusdem numeri ledones inueniuntur, quia per omnia cum lunae cursu inseparabiliter marinus comitatur. 7. Quatuor uero ex his, hoc est temporum quatuor mediae, duae scilicet aequinoctiales malinae et aliae duae cum aut dies aut nox incrementi et detrimenti sui finem faciunt, solito ualidiores, sicut oculis probare licet, ac adundatione altiores fieri uidentur et maiora litorum spatia tegere cernuntur.

Et quia impossibile est ut non aliqua, licet nobis incognita, spatia deserat, quando per nostrarum terrarum solum exundat, sicut eadem loca a nobis recedens implet, ut nostra adsissa ibi sit recessa et nostra recessa ibi sit adsissa, demedium maris ministerium ignorare fateri compellimur. 8. Sed in hoc et multis similibus nihil aliud nostrae conscientiae concedetur nisi creatoris potentiam atque inmensitatem clamare, qui *omnia in numero et mensura et pondere disposuit*, et interim cum insigni gentium magistro dicere: *ex parte cognoscimus et ex parte prophetamus; cum autem uenerit quod perfectum est, tunc cognoscam sicut cognitus sum.*

9. Ex hoc tamen limpatico elemento piscium et auium, hoc est omnium aquatilium et uolatilium, diuersa genera facta fuisse Geneseos scriptura pronuntiat. Sed piscium, id est omnium quae in aquis uiuunt animantium, CLIII esse genera philosophi

pulls away from the area it has covered, the incoming tide of the *malina* on the other hand, floods for five hours and then for the seven hours of its ebbing it vacates the shores it had submerged.[120] * And the *malina* is observed to be in such great agreement with the moon, that the moon is always born in the middle of it. Moreover, diligent investigation shows it to last for seven days and twelve hours and the fourth part of a day.* 6. And this happens in such a way that as the full moon begins to wane, the again dark *malina* is divided in half.* The *ledo* is observed in the intervening periods, and is never seen to occur at either the full moon or at the beginning of the new moon.* And by this alternation, there occur twenty-four *malinae* and as many *ledones* in each common year, while in an embolismic year* there are twenty-six *malinae* and as many *ledones*,[121] for the sea follows the course of the moon inseparably in all things. 7. Four of these, those occurring at the middle of the seasons, that is, the two equinoctial *malinae* and the other two when either the day or the night ends its increase or its decrease, are seen to be stronger — as can be easily checked by observation — and to rise more than usual and cover a greater area of the shore.[122] *

And because it is impossible that it should not be leaving some place — though it be a place we do not know — when it is flooding the land in our regions, and similarly filling that place when it retreats from us — so that what is flow* here is ebb there, and what is ebb here is flow there[123]* — we are forced to acknowledge that we know nothing of half the ministry of the sea.[124] * 8. But in this and many other similar things, nothing remains for our mind but to proclaim the power and greatness of the Creator, *who established all things in number and measure and weight*,[125] and for the time being to say with the great teacher of the pagans: *we know in part and we prophesy in part; but when that which is perfect has come*,[126] *then I shall know even as I am known.*[127]

9. Genesis declares that the various types of fishes and of birds, that is, all aquatic and flying animals, were made from this liquid element.[128] Philosophers who speak of the nature of things, on the other hand, count one hundred and fifty-three types of fishes, that is, of all animate beings living in water, and this is the

---

120 Cf. Aug. Hib., *De mirabilibus* 1.7 (PL 35:2159) and Philippus Presbyter, *Comment. in Iob* 38 (PL 26:752D).
121 Cf. Aug. Hib., *De mirabilibus* 1.7 (PL 35:2159).
122 Cf. Aug. Hib., *De mirabilibus* 1.7 (PL 35:2159).
123 Cf. Aug. Hib., *De mirabilibus* I.7 (PL 35:2157); Augustine, *Gen. litt.* 1.12 (CCSL 28/1,19).
124 Cf. Aug. Hib., *De mirabilibus* 1.7 (PL 35:2159*med & fin*).
125 Wis 11:21.
126 1 Cor 13:9–10.
127 1 Cor 13:12.
128 Cf. Gen 1:20.

qui de rerum naturis ratiocinantur enumerant, quem numerum apostolica sagina uelut ex omni genere piscium congregans contraxerat.

10. Aues uero, utrum et ipsae hunc suorum numerum generum habeant an maiorem an minorem, etsi sint aliqui qui aestimant, tamen quia grandi hoc auctoritate firmare non possunt, nec sequendi nec respuendi sunt. Sed cum de aqua omnium auium origo praecessit, unde tam diuersae earum consuetudines manendi seu uiuendi seu uolandi seu natandi exstiterunt, ut aliae in salsis undis supernatent et uictum habeant, aliae in dulcium aquarum stagnis et fluminibus conmorentur, aliae in terra sine ulla natandi consuetudine degunt (quarum aliae in campanis, aliae in siluis, aliae in montibus, aliae in palustribus locis fieri consuescunt), alias ad uolandum pinna non subleuat, ita aliae excelsa ac remota aeris spatia uolando penetrant, ut aestatis tempore etiam niuem de altissimis nubibus suis pinnis deferunt; 11. nisi forte has tam diuersissimas consuetudines originis, quamuis de aqua, diuersitas condicionis in omnibus auibus effecit, ut ex his aliae de salsa unda, aliae de dulci aqua, aliae de erbarum rore, aliae ex arborum constillatione, aliae ex paludium humore, aliae ex montium confluxione, aliae ex aereo uapore, aliae ex altissimarum nubium fluida conspiratione conditae sunt, atque illud etiam earum unaquaque naturaliter, quod suae conditionis origini pertineret, adsuesceret, ut ibi et inde quaeque auis uiueret, unde prius ut esset habuisset.

number gathered together in the net of the Apostles, as though selecting from every type of fish.[129]*

10. As for the birds, whether they also come in this same number of species — or whether the number be greater or smaller — though some think this is the case, yet because no such great authority confirms their view, they should be neither followed nor rejected. But since the origin of all birds is in water, why have they so many different habitats and ways of living or flying or swimming, that some swim in salt waters and have their nourishment there, some have their abode in the lakes and rivers of sweet water, some live on the ground without ever swimming — among these some are wont to live in fields, others in forests, others in mountains, others in swampy places? Why do feathers not raise some into flight, while others fly up to traverse the highest and most remote spaces of air, so that even in summer their wings carry back snow from the highest clouds?* 11. Unless perhaps creation from different original substances, different though still water, produced such very varied habits in all birds, so that some were created from salt water, some from sweet water, some from dew on the plants, some from drops in the trees,* some from swamp water, some from mountain streams, some from vapour in the air, some from moisture blown together in the highest clouds. And each one of them would by its very nature be accustomed to the surroundings corresponding to its origin at creation, so that each bird would live in that thing and from that thing whence it first obtained its being.

---

129 Cf. Jerome, *Comment. in Hiezechielem* 14.47.6-12 (CCSL 75, 717); cf. Jn. 21:11.

10. De paradiso ubi primorum hominum habitatio fuit

1. Et quia post aquam terra in elimentorum ordine statuta est, prius de paradiso, ubi primorum hominum habitatio exstiterat, quamuis conmorandi loco, sermo ponendus est, de quo plurimorum diuersae sententiae prolatae sunt:

Utrum ipsa inmortalis uita, qua homines ante peccatum donati sunt, paradisi nomine dicta est, an totus hic terrarum orbis tam commode innocenter uiuentibus dispositus fuerat, ut paradisus diceretur, quatinus quamdiu inculpabiliter sine ullo uitio possessores uixissent, etiam terrae huius habitatio hisdem cuncta feliciter absque ullo labore ministraret, ac postmodum ipsis peccantibus atque in deteriora motatis, etiam orbis eorundem uitio et uindictae sententia motatus atque obscuratus, quomodo de sole diximus et luna, et sui decorem et frugiferam uim etsi non totam, maxima tamen ex parte amisisset, ut quae beatitudine et felicitate beneuolentium opitulauerant, maleuiuentium uindictas cumularent,

2. an etiam specialiter aliquis locus huius terrenae felicitatis beatitudine plenus hominibus suae creationis meritum seruaturus dispositus erat, in quo nihil quod corporalem beatitudinem laederet, quamdiu mandati patientia seruaretur, inerat; cui sententiae scripturae Geneseos auctoritas non mediocriter suffragatur dicentis: *plantauerat autem Dominus Deus paradisum a principio in quo constituerat hominem quem formauerat*. A principio enim plantatus paradisus cum dicitur, principatum orbis specialiter hic locus tenere uidetur, in quo primus homo, statim post sui conditionem, constitutus fuisse non dubitatur. 3. Etenim omnibus modis conueniebat, ut caput et principium humani generis in capitale et principio poneretur orbis, ut inde omnium propago membrorum suorum incrementa sumeret, unde terrarum orbis quem inhabitat initium capiret. Cuius paradisi statum cum eadem scriptura enumerat, frugiferis arboribus consitum et fonte magno quo totius terrae facies irrigatur adornatum enarrat, dum ad positum ibi hominem ita inquiens loquitur: *ex omni ligno paradisi comede*; et mulier ait: *ex fructu*

10. On Paradise, the First Dwelling Place of Man

1. Since earth is situated below water in the ordering of the elements, we must now first speak of Paradise where the first men had their dwelling-place, albeit a temporary one. Different opinions have been put forward by many concerning this place:

Whether immortal life itself which was granted to men before sin is called by the name 'Paradise', or whether the entire orb of the earth was so conveniently arranged for those who lived in innocence that it was called 'Paradise.' So long as those dwelling there remained untainted by sin, this earthly habitation ministered to them* in complete happiness and without the slightest toil, and later, when they had sinned and were changed into a lower state, the orb itself was changed and obscured by their offence and by the sentence of their punishment, as we have said happened to the sun and to the moon.[130] Though it did not lose all its beauty and fertility, it nonetheless lost most of these, so that what had furthered the blessedness and happiness of those willing the good,* now heaped punishments upon those living badly.

2. Or was some particular place full of the blessedness of this earthly happiness especially established to preserve for men the benefit of its creation,* in which there was nothing that would damage corporeal blessedness, so long as the command was obediently observed? The Scriptural authority of Genesis supports this opinion more than a little, saying: *the Lord God planted Paradise from the beginning wherein he placed man whom he had formed.*[131] Since it is said that Paradise was planted from the beginning, it is clear that this place wherein the first man was set immediately after his creation, is first* among all places on the terrestrial orb. 3. And indeed it was fitting in all respects that the head and beginning of mankind should be placed at the top and beginning of the orb, so that mankind should spread out from that very place where the terrestrial orb which it inhabits also draws its beginning. When this same passage describes the appearance of this Paradise, it says that it is filled with fruit-bearing trees, and adorned with a great spring irrigating the entire surface of the earth.* Thus, speaking to man who was placed there, it says: *eat from every tree in Paradise;*[132] and the woman says: *we are*

---

130 Cf. DOC 5.2–7, above.
131 Gen 2:8.
132 Gen 2:16.

lignorum quae sunt in paradiso uescimur; et paulo ante praefertur: *et fons ascendebat de terra inrigans uniuersa super faciem terrae.* 4. In quibus rebus storialiter, absque ullis aenigmatibus, ipsius scripturae ueritatem seruare quid impediret, quomodo et de omnibus, quae de principio nascentis totius creaturae uisibilis continet corporaliter eius auctoritas elucet? Factum namque firmamentum et mare et terram et luminaria et stellas, aquatilia etiam atque terrena animalia, et hominem ipsum, sicut scriptura Genesis inuestigat, storialiter absque ullis aenigmatibus credimus; 5. an in hoc solummodo, quod paradisi locum fructiferis consitum arboribus et magno fonte inlustratum conmemorat, nisi aenigmate, non recipiemus? Sed hoc utroque modo potest intellegi, id est, secundum rerum gestarum storicam narrationem et secundum tropologiam, id est, iuxta moralem explanationem.

6. Scriptura enim sacra tripertita ratione intellegitur; cuius primus intellegendi modus est, cum tantummodo secundum litteram sine ulla figurali intentione cognoscitur, ut sanctus Hieronimus dicit: 'Actus Apostolorum nudam quidam mihi uidetur sonare historiam'; secundus modus est, cum secundum figuralem intellegentiam absque aliquo rerum gestarum respectu inuestigatur, ut prima et extrema pars Ezechielis, et Cantica Canticorum, et euangelii quarundam parabularum expositio, quae aliud loquuntur, aliud agunt; 7. tertius modus est cum, salua historicarum rerum narratione, mistica ratione intellegitur, sicut arca Noe et tabernaculum et templum storialiter facta sunt, et intellectualiter ecclesiae misteria per haec designantur. Sic nimirum et paradisus locus prioris Adae, qui est forma futuri, exstiterat et ecclesiae futurae, quae est terra sequentis Adae, misteria praefigurabat.

8. Dum uero ibi homo inmortaliter et beate uiueret, numquid et totius subiectio sibi non subiaceret? Quid enim illum ab ingressu orbis intercluderet, qui in creaturis nocere sibi aliquid non timeret, dum ignis non uriret, non aqua mergeret, non bestiarum fortitudo mactaret, non spinarum uel cuiuscumque rei aculei uulnerarent, non absentia aeris suffucaret, non omnia quae nocent mortalibus impedirent? 9. Corpus enim immortale

nourished by the fruit of the trees that are in Paradise;[133] and a little before this, we read: *and a spring rose from the ground, watering all things on the face of the earth.*[134] 4. What would prevent the truth of this passage from being preserved literally in these matters, without allegory, when its authority describes in corporeal fashion all the things it contains from the very beginning of the whole of visible creation. For we believe literally and without allegory that the firmament, the sea, the earth, the luminaries and the stars, the aquatic and the terrestrial animals, and man himself, were all created just as the text of Genesis explains. 5. And we should then not take literally this one thing only, namely that it relates that Paradise is a place full of fruit-bearing trees and adorned by a great spring?[135] But this can be understood in two ways, namely, according to the historical account of things that happened, and according to tropology, that is, with a moral explanation.

6. For Scripture can be understood in three ways*: the first of these modes of understanding is when something is known only according to the letter, without any figural meaning, as the blessed Jerome says: 'The Acts of the Apostles seem to me a purely historical account.'[136] The second way is when something is understood according to figurative meaning without any regard for the things that happened, as in the first and last part of Ezechiel and in the Song of Songs, and in the exposition of some parables of the Gospel, which say one thing and mean another. 7. The third way is when, while respecting the account of historical events, a mystical meaning should be understood. Thus, the building of Noah's Ark, of the tabernacle, and of the temple were historical events, and they are understood to designate the mysteries of the Church. It is clear then that Paradise, the dwelling place of the first Adam who is the form of the future Adam, was both a specific place and prefigured the mysteries of the future Church, the domain of the next Adam.[137]

8. While man was living there,* immortal and happy, was not the domination of all things in his hands?[138] * And what would prevent him from entering the rest of the Earth, he who had no cause to fear that anything in the created world would harm him, since fire would not burn, water would not drown, the might of beasts would not cause injury, the sharp point of thorns or of some other object would not cause pain, nor could the absence of air suffocate, when not one of all things

---

133 Gen 3:2.
134 Gen 2:6.
135 Cf. Augustine, *Gen. litt.* 8.1 (CSEL 28/1, 229–32); also, Jerome, *Epistula* 51.5 (CSEL 54, 404–05), *Contra Origenes*.
136 Jerome, *Epistula* 53.9 (CSEL 54, 463).
137 Cf. 1 Cor 15:45.
138 Cf. Gen 1:28.

et inuulnerabile et inlaedibile nihil quod mortem et uulnus et laesuram inferret in omnibus creaturis, quoadusque creatorem offenderet per inoboedientiam, inueniret. Paradisi ergo habitatorem lustrare omnia quae sibi fuerant subiecta quid prohibuit, cum et hoc facere Dominus eum non solum non interdixit, sed imperauit dicens: *crescite et multiplicamini et implete terram et subicite eam et dominamini piscibus maris et uolatilibus caeli*? 10. Sicut enim angelis in his quae sibi subiecta sunt a sede caeli discurrere liberum est et tamen in caelo habent sedes, quid et homines in paradiso constitutos, discurrere per omnem creaturam sibi subiectam cum libuissent sine suo labore inpediret? Quemadmodum namque a dolore et senectute et morte inmonia corpora possedebant, ita et omni labore et pigridine et fastiditate carentia habebant.

11. At uero cum paradisi colonus in loco suae terrenae felicitatis peccatum conmisisset, in maledictae terrae habitationem detrusus, protinus illa omnia quae prius possedebat, partim amisit, partim cum labore conseruauit; et illi excluso a sede beatitudinis possibilitas iterum redeundi interclusa est. Et ita factum est, ut quemadmodum angelus apostata cum suis de summa sui paradisi serenitate deiectus caliginosum aeris huius locum sortitus est, sic et homo de sui paradisi terrena beatitudine in maledictae terrae huius habitationem detrusus est; 12. sic etenim scribitur: *eiecit illum Dominus Deus de paradiso uoluntatis et proiecit in terram de qua sumptus est*, et: *constituit ante paradisum cerubin, flammeum gladium atque uersatilem, ad custodiendam uiam ligni uitae*, in quo demonstratur quod, quamuis uiam ligni uitae cerubin dicuntur custodire, ne tamen homines regredi possent, totum etiam paradisum iubentur deffendere, dum flammeum gladium non ante lignum solummodo uitae, sed ante totum paradisum indicat esse positum.

13. Non satis autem elucet de qua arbore specialiter Adam comederet, sed clarum est quod statim post peccatum nuditatem fici arbore texit, cui soli in tempore suae carnis Dominus Iesus, paulo antequam mortem pro Adae delicto susciperet, maledixit; et cito aruit, cum diceret: *numquam ex te fructus nascatur in aeternum*, hoc est, qui hominibus ultra, sicut supe-

that harm mortals stood in the way?[139] * 9. For his immortal, invulnerable and pain-free body would encounter nothing in all creatures that would inflict death or wounds or suffering, until such time as he offended the Creator by his disobedience.[140] * What then was to prevent the inhabitant of Paradise from surveying all things subjected to him, when the Lord not only did not forbid this, but actually commanded it, saying: *increase and multiply and fill the earth and subdue it and rule over the fishes of the sea and the birds of the sky?*[141] 10. For just as the angels are free to leave their seat in heaven to move about among things subjected to them, and yet retain their seats in heaven, what would prevent humans when in Paradise, from moving about without effort among all the creatures subjected to them if they so desired? For indeed, just as they possessed bodies immune from pain, old age and death, they also enjoyed complete lack of toil, sluggishness and boredom.*

11. But when the inhabitant of Paradise committed sin in the very place of his earthly felicity and was cast out into the dwelling-place of the cursed earth, from then onward he partly lost and partly retained with much effort all those things which he had previously possessed. Once he was cast out from his seat of happiness, the possibility of returning there was completely barred. And this happened in such a way that just as the rebellious angel was cast out with his companions from the highest serenity of his Paradise and assigned to the gloomy space of this air, so man was cast out from the happiness of his earthly Paradise into a dwelling place on this cursed earth. 12. For it is written: *The Lord God cast him out of the Paradise of pleasure* and sent him out into the earth from which he had been taken,*[142] and *He set Cherubim before Paradise, a fiery and moving sword, to guard the access to the tree of life,*[143] from which it is clear that though the Cherubim are said to guard the tree of life, they were in fact ordered to defend the whole of Paradise so that men could not return there, since the flaming sword is said to have been placed not before the tree of life only, but before the whole of Paradise.

13. It is not at all clear from what species of tree Adam ate, but it is clear that immediately after sinning he covered his nakedness with the leaf of a fig tree,[144] the only tree Jesus cursed when he was in the flesh — not long before he accepted death on account of Adam's fault. The tree immediately withered when he said: *henceforth no fruit will ever come from you,*[145] that is, it could no longer harm men as

---

139 Cf. Augustine, *Gen. litt.* 3.15–18 (CSEL 28/1, 80–84).
140 Rom 5:12. Cf. Augustine. *Gen. litt.* 6.22 (CSEL 28/1, 195).
141 Gen 1:28.
142 Gen 3:23.
143 Gen 3:24.
144 Cf. Gen 3:7.
145 Mt 21:19.

rius, nocere non possit. Ecce in hanc arborem, id est ficum, maledictum delicti Adae qui totam terram inficerat, priusquam sui sanguinis rore ipsam mundaret, Christus collegit. 14. Utrum tamen ab hac primitus homo culpam an de alia susciperit, pro certo Dominus uiderit;

attamen illa, quaecumque nunc est, quae tunc scientiae boni et mali arbor dicta fuerat, non est putandum quod nunc uescentibus ea tantum nocere possit quantum tunc in paradiso constitutis, ut etiam nunc uescentibus ea mortem inferre possit: non enim in arboris natura mortiferum aliquid inesse credendum est, aut etiam ut boni et mali scientiam facere ualeret, sed mandati Domini transgressio, quo praeceptum est ne de hoc ligno comederetur, mortem effecit. 15. Cuius oboedientia si esset, hoc erat scire bonum, et inoboedientia dum fuit, hoc est nosse malum; quorum tamen distantiam homo nisi transgressione intellegere non potuit: quando enim solummodo bonum possedebat, quod esset malum, quomodo sibi noceret, ignorabat. Ut autem manifestum sit quod in hoc ligno qualicumque praeter originalem inoboedientiam nihil inesse nociuum, ecce non huius sed ligni uitae uia excluditur, in cuius exclusione prioris delicti misericorditer remissio praeparatur.

16. Si enim homo post peccatum illud originale de ligni uitae fructibus comedisset, conmissi penitus maculam misere in aeternum et infeliciter in corpore senectute et doloribus obnoxio moriendo deponere non posset; nullo enim alio modo hoc facinus deleri nisi morte Dominus praeparauit quod per aduentum postea in carne Filii sui Iesu Christi futurum esse praesciuit et praedistinauit, ut per illius mortem nostra culpa moreretur, et per illius resurrectionem lex nostrae mortis euacuaretur, et per ipsius corporis ascensionem et in caelo mansionem nostrae humanitati inmortalitas donaretur, et angelicae et spiritalis uitae consortium, quod nobis in principio praeparatum est, donaretur, sicut in extrema futuri iudicii uocatione in dextera constitutis certum est a Domino dictum iri: *uenite, benedicti Patris mei, possedete regnum quod uobis paratum est ab origine mundi.*

it had done before. For Christ gathered in that tree, that is, in the fig tree, the curse of the sin of Adam which infected the whole earth until he cleansed it with the dew of his own blood. 14. For the Lord would have known for sure whether the first man received his guilt from this tree or from another.*

But that tree, whatever it is now, which then had been called the tree of knowledge of good and evil, we should not think that it can do as much harm to those who eat from it now as it did then to those who were in Paradise, so that it would even now bring death to those who eat from it. For we should not believe that there was anything lethal in the nature of the tree, nor even that it was able to give knowledge of good and evil, but it was the very transgression of the Lord's command that nobody should eat of that tree, which brought about death.[146] 15. For so long as there was obedience, this was knowledge of the good, and when there was disobedience, that was knowledge of evil. For man could not grasp the difference between these unless he had transgressed, since when he possessed only the good, he was completely ignorant of what evil is and of how much it would harm him. And so that it should be clear that there was nothing harmful in that tree, whatever sort it was, other than the original disobedience, it was not access to that tree but to the tree of life which was forbidden,[147] and this very exclusion most mercifully prepared the remission of the first sin.

16. For if man were to eat the fruit of the tree of life after that original sin, he could not — wretched forever and unhappy in a body subject to old age and suffering* — completely set aside the stain of the transgression by submitting to death.[148] For the Lord planned that this offence could not be wiped away except by death, which he foresaw and predestined would happen later with the advent in the flesh of his son Jesus Christ, so that our guilt* would die through his death, and the law of our death would be voided by his resurrection. By the ascension of his body and his dwelling in heaven, immortality would be granted to our humanity, as well as participation in the angelic and spiritual life which had been prepared for us in the beginning.[149] For it is certain that at the final call of the future judgement,* the Lord will say to those placed to the right: *come, blessed of my Father, take possession of the kingdom prepared for you from the beginning of the world.*[150]

---

146 Cf. Augustine, *Gen. litt.* 8.6 (CSEL 28/1, 239–40) and 8.13 (CSEL 28/1, 251–52).
147 Cf. Gen 3:24.
148 Cf. Gen 3:22–24.
149 Cf. Augustine, *Gen. litt.* 6.27 (CSEL 28/1, 198–99).
150 Mt 25:34.

11. De situ terreni orbis quem inhabitat humanum genus

1. Porro de terrarum orbis situ, quem inhabitat humanum genus, psalmista ad Dominum ait: *qui fundasti terram super stabilitatem suam, non inclinabitur in saeculum saeculi; abyssus sicut uestimentum amictus eius,* ex quo intellegitur non super alterius elimenti soliditatem, nisi super uim suam et stabilitatem et firmitatem terram esse fundatam.

Utrum uero sibi aliquid, sicut ipsa aquis, et aquae aeri, et aer spatio superiori, et ipsud firmamento, et firmamentum aquis superioribus substitutum sit, ipse nouit qui ubique et undique cuncta conspicit.

2. Ea ergo parte quae hominibus ad habitandum data est, quadrifarius orbis status esse multi prodiderunt auctores, quarum partium quattuor uocabula quattuor litteris nominis primi terriginae, hoc est Adam, incipere sapientes intellegunt: anatholae scilicet, disis, arctus, misimbria, id est, oriens, aquilo, auster, occidens. Conueniebat enim ut qui suo genere totam terram impleret, suo nomine quattuor quadrati orbis partium uocabula collegeret.

3. Quattuor quoque temporum articulis anniuersario ordine distinguitur atque, impleto anni spatio, terreni orbis dispensatio semper sine cessatione in circulum redigitur: ueris enim tempore, quo mundus fuerat institutus, semper uernat; aestate uero floret et fructificat; autumno maturescit et aptum suorum fructuum mortalibus usum tribuit, hieme uero decidit et arescit. 4. Sed hanc augmenti et detrimenti sui consuetudinem patitur, quamdiu seruituti corruptionis obnoxia mortalium officio mancipatur: cum enim nascendi et moriendi in hominibus condicio cessauerit, tunc etiam uiriditatis et ariditatis suae incrementa et damna ipsa terra non habebit, cum uaticinium Esaiae, immo Domini per Esaiam, conpletum fuerit: *ecce ego creo caelos nouos et terram nouam et non erunt in memoria priora, sed gaudebitis et exultabitis in his quae ego creo.* 5. Quoniam dum inmotatis corporibus homines spiritaliter uiuent, necesse est ut inmotata in melius habitandi loca, id est spiritalia, habitent. Hoc enim corpus, ut Paulus dicit: *seminatur in corruptione, surget in incor-*

11. The Disposition of the Terrestrial Orb Inhabited by Man

1. Speaking of the disposition of the terrestrial orb which the human race inhabits, the Psalmist says to the Lord: *Who hast founded the earth upon its own stability, it shall not be tilted for ever and ever. The deep like a garment is its clothing.*[151] From which it is understood that the earth is not resting upon the solidity of another element, but upon its own strength and stability and firmness.

As to whether there is anything below it, just as it is below the waters, the waters are below the air, and the air is below the higher space, and that in turn is below the firmament, and the firmament is below the higher waters, He alone knows this, who sees all things everywhere from all sides.

2. Concerning that part given to man as habitation, many writers assert that it is a fourfold orb. And wise men affirm that the names of these four parts begin with the four letters of the first earth-dweller, that is, Adam: to wit, Anatholia, Disis, Arctus, Misimbria,[152]* that is, east, north, south, west.* For it was fitting that he who was to fill the entire earth with his progeny, should gather within his name the names of the four parts of the fourfold earth.

3. In its yearly order, the disposition of the earthly orb is broken up into the four divisions of the seasons and, the duration of a year being completed, it always returns continuously in a cycle. In spring, the season in which the world was created,* the world is always green; in summer, it blooms and bears fruit; in autumn, it ripens and offers suitable use of its crops to mortals; in winter, it declines and withers.* 4. But it suffers this pattern of increases and decreases only so long as it is bound to the abject servitude of corruption by its service to mortals. For when birth and death will cease among men, the earth will no longer experience the increases and decreases of its greenness and dryness, when the prophecy of Isaiah, nay, of the Lord through Isaiah, will be accomplished: *Behold, I create new heavens* and a new earth, and the former things shall not be in remembrance, but you shall be glad and rejoice in these things which I create.*[153] 5. For when men will live spiritually with transformed bodies, it will be necessary that they have a dwelling place that is transformed for the better, that is, a spiritual dwelling place. For, as Paul says, this body *is sown in corruption, it shall rise in incorruption; it is sown a natural body, it*

---

151 Ps 103:5–6.
152 Cf. Augustine, *In Iohannis evangelium tractatus* 10.12 (CCSL 36, 1008).
153 Is 65:17–18.

ruptione; seminatur corpus animale, surget corpus spiritale; seminatur in contumelia, surget in gloria. Necesse est enim corruptibile hoc induere incorruptionem et mortale hoc induere inmortalitatem. Cum ergo corruptio et mortalitas in corporibus esse desinuerint, tunc mortalibus uti et inmortalibus homo necessitatem non habebit; 6. quod in dominici corporis resurrectione probatum fuisse euangelia sancta confirmant, dum linteamina, quibus inuolutum fuerat, post resurrectionem eius in monumento sola posita esse denuntiant, quemadmodum de Petro dicitur: *et uidit linteamina sola posita, et abiit secum admirans quod factum fuerat.* Nouis ergo corporibus non indigentibus his quae corruptibilis uitae usus requirit, noua terra cum nouo caelo ad habitandum creabitur, hoc est, huius terrae natura et superficies in spiritalem statum, qui spiritalibus conueniat, absque aliqua motabilitate instaurabitur.

7. Sed tunc hoc fiet, quando Hierusalem creata fuerit in terra et populus eius gaudium et exultatio; et quando sancti in his quae Dominus creat gaudebunt, quorum sol non occidet et luna non minuetur; cum redempti a Domino uenerint in Sion cum laude, et laetitia fuerit sempiterna super caput eorum, et obtinuerint gaudium et laetitiam, et fugerit dolor et gemitus, et repleti fuerint dies luctus eorum, et lugentes consolati fuerint, at abstergerit Deus omnem lacrimam ab omni facie sanctorum, et obprobrium populi sui deleuerit, et omnium lugentium in Sion moeror depositus fuerit, et acciperint coronam pro cinere, oleum gaudii pro luctu, pallium laudis pro spiritu moeroris, et uocati fuerint in ea fortes iustitiae; cum benedicti ad dexteram ueniunt et, sicut sol, fulgerint in regno Patris eorum.

shall rise a spiritual body; it is sown in dishonour, it shall rise in glory.[154] *For this corruptible must put on incorruption; and this mortal must put on immortality.*[155] Thus, when corruption and mortality will no longer be present in the human body, man will have no need for either mortal or immortal things.* 6. The holy Gospels confirm that this was shown in the resurrection of the body of the Lord, when the linen cloths in which he was wrapped are said to have been laid aside in the tomb after his resurrection, as it is said of Peter: *and he saw the linen cloths laid by themselves, and went away wondering at that which had come to pass.*[156] Since the new bodies will not need any of the things necessary for corruptible life,[157] a new earth with a new heaven will be created as habitation, that is, the nature and surface of this earth will be established in a spiritual state without mutability, as befits spiritual beings.

7. But when that happens, when Jerusalem shall be created on earth together with the joy and exultation of its people, and when the saints shall rejoice in that which the Lord has created, for whom the sun shall not set nor the moon decrease, when the redeemed of the Lord shall have come to Sion with praise, and everlasting joy shall be upon their heads, and they shall have obtained joy and gladness, and sorrow and mourning shall have fled away, and the days of their tears shall have come to an end, and the mourners shall have been consoled, and God shall have wiped away every tear from every face of the saints, and shall have taken away the reproach of his people, and the sorrow of all those who cry shall have been put aside in Sion, and they shall have received a crown for ashes, the oil of joy for mourning, a garment of praise for the spirit of grief, and they shall be called in it the mighty ones of justice, then the blessed will come to the right side and will shine like the sun in the kingdom of their Father.[158] *

---

154 Cf. 1 Cor 15:42 and 15:44.
155 1 Cor 15:53.
156 Lk 24:12.
157 Cf. Augustine, *Gen. litt.* 6.23 (CSEL 28/1,196).
158 Cf. Is 65:18 + Lk 1:14 + Is 35:10 + Jer 15:16 + Is 35:10 + Sir 48:27 + Is 25:8 + Jer 20:11 + Is 61:3 + Mt 13:43. Cf. also Apoc 21:1–4.

12. De natura hominum

1. Sed huius interim orbis habitationi post originale peccatum homines distinati, non totum quod in conditione sua habuerunt naturale bonum perdiderunt, sed uitiatum primitus delicto parentis prauis insuper moribus corrumperant. Et ita fit ut, sicut cum labore terrae maledictae fructus percipiunt, sic et bonum naturale quod in se habent non absque laboriosa cura custodire possunt, 2. et quomodo in protuplasti transgressione tripliciter ceciderant, pari modo tribus uulneribus afflicti omnes eiusdem filii, id est, dolore, senectute, morte deficiunt; et omne bonum quod in se insitum naturaliter a conditore susciperant, studioso labore ex parte aliqua inuentum magna animi uigilantia uix conseruant, et quodcumque per studium cum Dei munere quaesitum inueniunt, propter iniquam mammonam heredibus non relinquunt, et omnes artes quas singillatim in uita capiunt, in huius uitae defectu pariter dum spiritus funditur amittunt.

3. Parique infirmitatis condicione pauperes et reges, stulti et sapientes uexantur. Nam similiter omnes somno indigent, et cibo refici et uestibus indui necesse habent, passionibus uitiorum carnalium aut grauantur aut corrunpuntur; motibus animi, id est, ira et amore, concupiscentia et timore angustiantur; dolore et senectute et morte deficiunt; praeteritis cito exuuntur, de praesentibus modice utuntur de futuris incerta omnia praestulantur; 4. eodem modo auditu, uisu, tactu, gustu, odoratu sentiunt et uiuunt; eodem etiam nexu originalis peccati adstringuntur; eodem redemptoris munere ditati undis baptismatis et Spiritu Sancto abluuntur. Sed ex his aut redemptionis fidem aut opera fidei neglegentibus pariter cum transgressoribus angelis et diabolo suo principe poena debetur aeterna; seruantibus uero siue per scripturae documenta siue per naturae monimina primae conditionis iura redemptoris munere uita praeparata est futura.

12. On the Nature of Man

1. But men who were destined to dwell temporarily on this orb after the original sin did not lose all the natural goodness they had at the time of their creation, but by their evil habits they further corrupted that goodness which had first been tainted by the sin of their parents. And thus, just as they have to toil to obtain the fruits of the cursed earth, it is only with the most assiduous efforts that they can preserve the natural goodness they have in them.* 2. As they fell in three ways* in the transgression of the first man, so their children are all afflicted by three wounds, that is, suffering, old age and death.* And of every good embedded within themselves which they received from the creator as part of their nature, they can scarcely retain even with the greatest vigilance of soul, that small part which they could only find with great effort. And that which they find by the gift of God* after searching assiduously, they cannot pass on to their heirs with the wicked mammon,* and all the arts which they master one by one in life, they must relinquish as they pour out their spirit on departing this life.

3. Paupers and kings, fools and wise men, all are troubled in the same way by this wretched condition. For they all similarly need sleep, find it necessary to be restored by food and covered by clothes, and are either wearied or corrupted by the passions of carnal vices. All are disturbed by turmoil of the soul, that is, by anger and love, concupiscence and fear. All are brought down by pain and old age and death. As soon as they have freed themselves from the past, they scarcely use the present and expect uncertain things from the future.[159] * 4. They all sense and live in the same way by hearing, sight, touch, taste and smell. They are bound by the same fetter of the original sin.* Enriched by the same gift of the Redeemer, they are cleansed by the waters of baptism and by the Holy Spirit. But to those of them who are negligent either of the faith of redemption or of the works of faith, will be given eternal punishment together with the disobedient angels and their leader, the devil. On the other hand, life everlasting has been prepared through the gift of the Redeemer for those who have kept the commands of the first creation whether through the teachings of Scripture or through the precepts of nature.*

---

159 Cf. Isidore, *Differentiae* 2.14.43 (CCSL 111A, 30–31).

13. De diuersitate peccantium et loco poenarum

1. Sed quia peccatorum diuersa condicio est, sunt quaedam crimina quae igne iudicii purgari possunt, quaedam uero aeterni ignis poena complectenda sunt; et ex his quae aeterna poena digna fiunt, quaedam ad iudicium non perueniunt, quaedam post iudicii examinationem perpetuae damnationis sortem subibunt, sicut Paulus apostolus inquit: *quorundam hominum peccata* manifesta *sunt praeeuntia ad iudicium, quorundam autem subsequuntur.*

2. De his enim qui iudicio carent, Dominus ipse protestatur et dicit: *qui non credit in filio iudicatus est.* Unde intellegi datur quod qui fidei sortem subire non merentur, nec gratiam babtismi consequuntur, ad futurum non ituri sunt iudicium, sed ex hac uita euangelii sermone examinati ibunt, quo scribitur: *amen dico tibi, nisi quis renatus fuerit ex aqua et Spiritu Sancto non potest intrare in regnum Dei*; his etiam psalmistae uerba concordant, quibus ait: *ideo non resurgunt impii in iudicio.*

3. Qui autem post ablutionem babtismi peccatorum multitudine grauantur et ipsi in duas factiones diuiduntur: quidam namque ex ipsis priusquam ex hac uita exeunt, scripturae sacrae uocibus iudicantur, de quibus Paulus apostolus loquitur dicens: *nolite errare, neque adulteri neque fornicarii neque ebriosi neque maledici neque idolis seruientes neque auari neque molles neque masculorum concubitores neque fures neque rapaces regnum Dei possedebunt.* Qui enim haec et his similia capitalia crimina usque ad mortem absque poenitentiae medicamento faciunt, iudicati de hac uita ad perpetuas poenas exibunt; 4. de quorum reatu et conuiua pectoris Domini Iohannis loquitur: *est peccatum ad mortem, non pro illo ut roget quis.* Ad mortem enim peccatum deducit qui, licet in extremo uitae termino, de praeteritis criminibus poenitudinem agere neglegit. Et notandum iuxta Iacobum apostolum est quod: *qui in uno ex his offenderit,*

13. On the Different Kinds of Sinners and their Places of Punishment

1. There are different types of sins, and some offences can be cleansed by the fire of judgement, while others must be consumed by the torment of eternal fire. And among those offences deserving eternal punishment, some will not come to judgement while others will submit to their fate of perpetual damnation only after being examined at the judgement, as the apostle Paul says: *For some men their sins are manifest before going to judgement: and for some men they follow after.*[160] *

2. The Lord himself speaks of those who do not go to judgement, saying: *He who does not believe in the Son is already judged.*[161] This means that those who did not merit* the blessing of faith, nor sought the grace of baptism, will not come to the future judgement, but will depart from this life already judged by the words of the Gospel, where it is written: *Amen I say to you, unless a man be born again of water and the Holy Spirit, he cannot enter into the kingdom of God.*[162] The words of the Psalmist concur, when he says: *Therefore the wicked shall not rise again in the judgement.*[163]

3. As for those weighed down by a multitude of sins after the cleansing of baptism, they also are divided into two groups. Some are judged by the words of Scripture before they ever depart this life. The apostle Paul speaks of these when he says: *Do not be mistaken: neither adulterers, nor fornicators, nor drunkards, nor slanderers, nor idolaters, nor misers, nor the effeminate, nor sodomites, nor thieves, nor swindlers, shall possess the kingdom of God.*[164] Those who commit these and similar capital offences up until their death, without availing themselves of the medicine of repentance, will depart from this life already condemned to eternal punishment.

4. John who sat close to the bosom of the Lord* speaks as follows about their guilt: *There is a sin unto death: let no one ask for it.*[165] For he who neglects, even at the very close of his life, to repent for his past offences is committing a sin unto death. And, following the apostle James, it should be noted that *He who offends in one of these, has become guilty of all. For He who said: You shall not commit adultery, said also: You*

---

160 1 Tim 5:24.
161 Jn 3:18.
162 Jn 3:5.
163 Ps 1:5.
164 1 Cor 6:9–10.
165 1 Jn 5:16.

factus est omnium reus: qui enim dicit non moechaberis, ipse dixit non occides; quod si non moechaberis, occides autem, factus es transgressor legis.

5. Quidam uero ad extremum diuini examinis iudicium, qui his capitalibus criminibus non inuoluuntur, reseruati de hoc saeculo uadunt, et tamen sententia superni iudicis aeternae dampnationis sortem subibunt. Qui misericordiae opera condamnantes Christum in pauperibus nec cibo nec potu reficiunt, nec uestibus induunt, nec hospitio recipiunt, nec ullis infirmantibus et alligatis in metallis et carceribus uisitationis solacia ferunt, propter quod ab ipso audiunt: *ite maledicti in ignem aeternum, quem praeparauit pater meus diabulo et angelis eius.* 6. Non enim ad appetenda regna caelorum sufficit non agere mala, si quis non curauerit facere bona; per prophetam enim Esaiam pariter a Domino praecipitur: *quiescite agere peruerse, discite bene facere.* Per psalmistam quoque haec eadem uerba idem Domini Spiritus concinnat dicens: *declina a malo et fac bonum.* Ut et ostenderetur quod post terrorem tam terribilis huius quam diximus sententiae nulla poenitudine iudex flecteretur, in fine cunctae disputationis ita subinfertur: *tunc hi ibunt in ignem aeternum.*

7. De illius autem aeterni ignis loco, id est inferni ergastulo, multi dixerunt ut corporalis locus sit, ubi peccatorum corpora cruciabuntur; nisi enim ille ignis corporalis et locus esset, quomodo resurgentium corpora cruciata teneret? In quibus corporalitatis ueritas ita passibilis erit, ut stridoribus dentium et lacrimabilibus fletibus subiacebit, sicut ipsius Domini et iudicis uerba declarant dicentis: *seruum inutilem mittite in tenebras exteriores; illic erit fletus et stridor dentium, ubi uermes eorum non moriuntur et ignis non exstinguitur.* 8. De quo loco ad regem Babilonis per prophetam, ex persona eorum quos ipse ante se praeire ad eundem fecit, ita dicitur: *subter te sternetur tinea et opertorium tuum uermes.* De quo loco quidam etiam dicit 'sicut terra in profundo aquarum, sic inferna in profundo terrarum

shall not kill. Now if you do not commit adultery, but do kill, you have become a transgressor against the law.[166]

5. Some others, on the other hand, who have not been involved with these capital sins, when they depart from this life are set aside for the final decision of the Lord's judgement. And yet they will endure the fate of eternal damnation through the sentence of the celestial judge for they spurned the works of mercy and did not comfort Christ in the poor with either food or drink, did not clothe Him, nor provide Him with shelter, nor bring the comfort of a visit to the sick, or to those shackled in forced labour and in prisons.[167] * Because of this, these will hear him say: *Go, you cursed ones, into the everlasting fire which my Father prepared for the devil and his angels.*[168] 6. For in order to reach the kingdom of heaven it is not sufficient to avoid doing evil deeds: one must also strive to do good deeds.* The Lord instructs us of this through the prophet Isaiah: *cease to act perversely, learn to act well.*[169] The spirit of the Lord expresses these same words through the Psalmist when he says: *Turn away from evil and do what is good.*[170] And so that it should be clear that after the terror of the terrible sentence of which we have spoken, no amount of repentance will move the judge, the passage ends as follows: *and these shall go into the everlasting fire.*[171]

7. As for the location of this eternal fire, that is, the lower place of punishment, many say that it is a corporeal place where the bodies of sinners are tormented. For if that fire and that place were not corporeal, how could they hold the tormented bodies of those who are resurrected? Corporeality will be so capable of suffering there that this will be manifested by the gnashing of teeth and tearful wails, as the very words of the Lord and Judge declare: *cast the useless servant into the outer darkness; where there will be tears and gnashing of teeth,*[172] *where their worms will not die and the fire will not be extinguished.*[173] 8. The prophet spoke about this place as follows to the king of Babylon, in the person of those whom he sent ahead to him: *under thee shall maggots be strewn, and worms shall be thy covering.*[174] Someone also said about this place that 'just as earth lies beneath the waters, thus the regions of hell lie beneath the earth.'[175] *So that it appears to be about this place that it is writ-

---

166 Jas 2:10–11.
167 Cf. Mt 25:42–45.
168 Mt 25:41.
169 Is 1:16–17.
170 Ps 36:27.
171 Mt 25:46.
172 Mt 25:30.
173 Cf. Mk 9:45.
174 Cf. Is 14:11.
175 Philippus Presbyter, *Comment. in Job* 26.5.

sunt.' ut de illo loco scriptum uideatur illud quod scriptum est, quod *neque in caelo, neque in terra, neque subter terra inuentus est qui possit aperire librum et soluere signacula eius.* Unde perspicue patet hunc locum qualemcumque sub terra esse, qui infernus inferior et terra obliuionis uocitatur. 9. Sed hic ignis dum praeparatus diabolo dicitur et angelis eius, qualis corporalitatis esse putandus est qui angelos cruciare potest et animam diuitis exutam corpore — infernalis ille ignis cruciare describitur, dum dixit: *quia ualde crucior in hac flamma,* — nisi forte hanc uirtutem ille ignis et locus habent, ut angelos et animas et corpora eodem modo cruciare possit et retenere?

Uel certe dum de filiis resurrectionis et aeternae beatitudinis dicitur: *erunt sicut angeli in caelo,* 10. nimirum et filii aeternae damnationis, dum ad poenam ignis aeterni corpora resumunt, et ipsi erunt sicut daemones in inferno, ut filii bonae resurrectionis cum sint filii dei, bonorum angelorum consortium, et filii aeternae mortis, cum sint filii diaboli, consortium angelorum Sathanae, subeant; de quibus dicitur: *et congregabuntur congregatione unius fascis in lacum et cludentur ibi in carcere et post multos dies uisitabantur*; quod utrum ad augendas an ad minuendas poenas futurum sit ignoramus.

ten: *neither in heaven, nor on earth, nor under the earth, was anyone found who was able to open the book, and to loose the seals thereof.*[176] * Whence it is clear that that place, of whatever kind it may be, which is called 'lower hell'[177] and 'land of oblivion',[178] lies below the earth. 9. But since that fire is said to be prepared for the devil and his angels, what should be thought of the nature of its corporeality since it can torment angels and the soul of the rich man after it left his body? For he was clearly saying that the fire of hell was tormenting him when he exclaimed: *for I am tormented in this flame.*[179] Unless perhaps that fire and that place have the property that they can equally torment and detain angels and souls and bodies.[180] *

And surely, since it is said about the sons of the resurrection and of eternal blessedness: *they will be like angels in heaven,*[181] 10. it would not be surprising if the sons of eternal damnation, on recovering their bodies for the torment of the eternal fire, will similarly be like demons in hell. So that, as the children of the good resurrection, who are children of God, will enjoy the companionship of the good angels, so the children of eternal death, since they are children of the devil, will endure the company of the angels of Satan. Of these it is said: *And they shall be gathered together as in the gathering of one bundle into the pit, and they shall be shut up there in prison; and after many days they shall be visited.*[182] Whether this will be to increase or to decrease their torment, we do not know.*

---

176 Cf. Apoc 5:2–3.
177 Cf. Ps 85:13.
178 Cf. Ps 87:13.
179 Lk 16:24.
180 Cf. Augustine, *Gen. litt.* 12.32 (CSEL 28/1, 426–27) and *Civ. Dei* 21.2–10 (CCSL 48, 759–76); Gregory, *Moralia* 15.29.35 (CCSL 143A, 769–70).
181 Mt 22:30.
182 Is 24:22.

14. De igne purgatorio

1. At uero hii qui aeternae uitae solacia percipiunt, bino et ipsi modo largitoris munere regni caelorum beatitudinem sument.

Quibusdam namque ex his adhuc in terra positis, dum pro Christo pauperes efficiuntur, regnum caelorum promittitur; sed absens licet in labore et fatigatione perseuerantibus iterum donatur, cum dicitur: *beati pauperes spiritu quia ipsorum est regnum caelorum.* 2. Similiter et qui persecutiones hominum propter iustitiam sustinent, eadem mercedis retributione gaudent, dum subinfertur: *beati qui persecutionem patiuntur propter iustitiam quia ipsorum est regnum caelorum*; non dixit quia erit ipsorum ut uocationem futuram sperarent, sed cum a corporibus exibunt uelut per semetipsos recepturi sunt quod in corporibus conmorantes interim dono largitoris possedent; atque idcirco et his adhuc in terra positis dicitur: *quaecumque solueritis super terram erunt soluta et in caelis, et quaecumque ligaueritis super terram erunt ligata et in caelis.* 3. Ac si diceret: hoc intellegitur, quod regnum caelorum adhuc in terra conmorantium uestrum est, dum quemcumque peccatis solueritis, ut illius possessor esse possit, hoc possedebit, et quemcumque in massam perditionis distinatum excluderitis eodem regno exclusus erit. His igitur praecipit Dominus: *gaudete et exultate quia nomina uestra scripta sunt in caelis*; ac si diceretur: dum nomina uestra de terrenae hereditatis consortio causa regni caelestis deleta sunt et abiecta, uos aeternae patriae heredes interim scribi necesse est. 4. Ergo hi cunctas in hac uita pressuras et mala recipientes absque examinis aliqua tribulatione et, ut ita dicam, sine uocatione aeternum refrigerium intrabunt; quorum gratia et aliqui post purgationem uocabuntur, solacium sine fine possedebunt, quibus post examinationem dicitur: *uenite, benedicti Patris mei, possedete regnum quod uobis praeparatum est ab origine mundi*; propter solacia pauperum immo Christi in pauperibus, possedere merebuntur, dum esurienti cibum, sitienti potum, nudo uestitum, uaganti domum, infirmanti et in carcere posito Christo in suis fratribus minimis ministratio praebeba-

14. The Cleansing Fire

1. As for those receiving the solace of eternal life, they too will obtain the blessedness of the kingdom of heaven in either of two ways by the gift of the most gracious Lord.

To those who have become poor for the sake of Christ, the kingdom of heaven is promised while they are still on earth; though it may seem very remote to them, it is granted also to those who persevere in toil and weariness, for it is said: *Blessed are the poor in spirit, for theirs is the kingdom of heaven.*[183] 2. Similarly, those who have endured the persecution of men for the sake of justice rejoice in the recompense of this same reward, for it is also said: *Blessed are they who suffer persecution for the sake of justice: for theirs is the kingdom of heaven.*[184] He did not say that it shall be theirs so that they would hope for the future call,* but as they leave their bodies they will receive as though by themselves what they already possess by the gift of the gracious Lord while still in their bodies. And so it is said to them while they are still on earth: *whatsoever you shall loose upon earth, shall be loosed also in heaven and whatsoever you shall bind upon earth, shall be bound also in heaven.*[185] 3. As though it were said: this means that since the kingdom of heaven is yours while you are still dwelling on this earth, when you loose a person of his sins so that he may possess the kingdom, he will possess it, and whomever you exclude as destined for the throng of perdition, he will be excluded from that same kingdom. The Lord then instructs them thus: *rejoice and exult because your names are written in heaven,*[186] as if to say: when your names are barred from the enjoyment of your earthly inheritance and are cast down for the sake of the celestial kingdom, you will of necessity be written up in the meantime as heirs to the eternal homeland. 4. Therefore those who receive all burdens and evils in this life, will enter into eternal rest without the trial of being judged and, as I said, without being called. For their sake, others will be called after a cleansing, and will enjoy eternal solace, to whom will be said after the judgement: *Come, you blessed of my Father, take possession of the kingdom prepared for you from the beginning of the world.*[187] They will deserve to take possession of it since they gave solace to the poor, nay, to Christ in the poor, when they offered food to the hungry, drink to the thirsty, clothing to the naked, a roof to the wanderer, and attended to the sick and imprisoned Christ in the least of his brethren.

---

183 Mt 5.3.
184 Mt 5:10.
185 Mt 18:18.
186 Lk 10:20.
187 Mt 25:34.

tur. 5. In ipsorum autem uocatione manifestum uidetur quod nunc longiuscule a Christo, quamuis in dextera, fuerunt constituti, quibus postmodum dicitur a summo iudice: *uenite benedicti*, ac si diceret: qui hucusque in examinationis purgatione quamdiu aliquid habuistis inmunditiae, quod iudicii igni purgaretur, a salute longiuscule fuistis, nunc ad purum examinati ab omni uel modica culparum labe propius accedite et uenite.

6. Quasdam culpas in futuro remitti Dominus ipse non dinegat, cum dicit: *qui blasphemauerit in Spiritum Sanctum non habet remissionem neque in hoc saeculo neque in futuro sed reus erit aeterni delicti*; ex quo intellegitur quaedam esse peccata quae, etsi in hoc saeculo non remittuntur, in futuro tamen iudicio per ignem deleri possunt: si enim ita non esset, hanc districtionem Dominus nequaquam posuisset. 7. De quo igne Babtista Iohannis dominici praecursor aduentus, ita loquitur ad Iudaeos: *uenit post me cuius non sum dignus calciamenta portare; ipse uos babtizabit in Spiritu Sancto et igne*, hoc est: qui uestra quae praecesserunt peccata Spiritu Sancto per aquae babtismum abluet, et quaedam ex his, quae postea sequentur, criminibus per ignem purgatorium remittet. De illo enim igne qui non mundare iudicatos, sed perdere condamnatos accenditur, ab eodem Iohanne paulo post subinfertur: *cuius uentilabrum in manu sua et permundauit aream suam et congregauit triticum suum in horreum, paleas autem conburet igni inextinguibile*; 8. aliud est enim igne babtizari, aliud igne comburi inextinguibile; De quo etiam igni idem Iohannis ait: *omnis arbor quae non facit fructum bonum excidetur et in ignem mittetur*. De igne uero purgationis Dominus ipse in euangelio loquitur: *qui autem dixerit fratri suo fatue reus erit gehennae ignis*; non dixit ignis aeterni, quippe quia hoc delictum per ignem purgatorium potius quam perpetua flamma puniri credendum est.

9. De hac quoque deferentia eorum, quos ignis futuri laesura non tanget et eorum qui per ignis detrimentum salutem percipient, Paulus apostolus exponit ita dicens: *fundamentum enim aliud nemo potest ponere praeter id quod positum est quod est Iesus Christus: alius autem superaedificat aurum, argentum, lapi-*

5. From the very wording of their call, it is clear that they are now placed somewhat far from Christ, though at his right-hand side, those to whom the highest judge later says: *Come, you blessed*,[188] as if to say: 'you who were until now in the cleansing of judgement rather far removed from salvation as long as you had any filth to be cleansed by the fire of judgement, now that you have been tried until you were pure of all stain of sin — however small — draw near and come.'

6. The Lord himself does not deny that some sins shall be forgiven in the world to come,* when he says: *He that shall blaspheme against the Holy Ghost shall never have forgiveness, neither in this world nor in the world to come, but shall be guilty of an everlasting sin.*[189] This implies that there are some sins which, though not forgiven in this world, can nonetheless be wiped out by fire in the judgement to come. Were this not the case, the Lord would never have made this distinction.[190] 7. John the Baptist, the precursor of the coming of the Lord, spoke to the Jews as follows, concerning this fire: *He who comes after me, I am not worthy to bear his sandals; He shall baptize you in the Holy Spirit and in fire.*[191] That is, the One who will wash away your previous sins by the operation of the Holy Spirit through the baptism of water, will also wipe out some of the offences that followed thereafter by means of a cleansing fire. As for that fire which burns not to cleanse those who have been judged, but to destroy the condemned, that same John adds a little later: *Whose fan is in his hand, and he has thoroughly cleansed his floor and gathered his wheat into the barn; but the chaff he will burn with unquenchable fire.*[192] 8. For it is one thing to baptize with fire, another to be consumed by unquenchable fire. That same John also said of that fire: *every tree that does not yield good fruit shall be cut down and cast into the fire.*[193] But the Lord himself was speaking of the cleansing fire in the Gospel, when he said: *whosoever calls his brother 'fool' shall be in danger of the fire of Gehenna.*[194] He did not say 'of eternal fire', for surely it should be believed that this offence will be punished by a cleansing fire, not by everlasting fire.

9. The apostle Paul explains the difference between those who will not be injured by the fire to come and those who receive salvation by means of the destruction caused by fire, when he says: *For no man can lay another foundation but that which is laid, which is Jesus Christ. One man builds upon it gold, silver, precious*

---

188 Mt 25:34.
189 Mk 3:29.
190 Cf. Isidore, *De Ecclesiasticis Officiis* 1.18.12 (CCSL 113, 22–23).
191 Mt 3:11.
192 Mt 3:12.
193 Mt 3:10.
194 Mt 5:22.

des pretiosos; alius uero ligna, fenum, stipulam; si cuius opus manserit quod super aedificauit, mercedem accipiet; si cuius opus arserit, detrimentum patietur; ipse uero saluus erit, sic tamen quasi per ignem. 10. Per haec autem duo aedificia, id est, aurum, argentum, lapides pretiosos et ligna, fenum, stipulam perfecta et minus perfecta super fidem Christi aedificata opera designantur; sed illa quae per lignum, fenum, stipulam designantur quamuis fragilia non tamen polluta fieri demonstrantur: 11. unde intellegitur non principalia crimina quae maculant, quorum operarios a regno Dei Paulus exclusit, sed illa quae non multum nocent, quamuis minus aedificent, per haec posse designari, hoc est: inutiliter matrimonio legitimo uti, plus quam sufficit ciborum abundantiam uesci, inmoderate qualecumque laetari, ira usque ad uerba intemperata moueri, rebus propriis plus quam necesse est delectari, neglegentius orationi quam horarum expetit conuenientia insistere, uel tardius quam conpetit surgere, inmoderato risu uocem exaltare, somno plus quam necessitas exigit corpus indulgere, uerum reticere, otiose loqui, quod non ita in re sit opinari, falsum quod uerum putaueris in rebus quae ad fidem non pertinent approbare, bonum quod faciendum est neglegenter obliuisci, inordinatum habitum habere: haec et his similia peccata per ignem purgari posse non est denegandum, et eorum factorem, si maioribus non grauetur, sic tamen quasi per ignem saluandum putandum est.

12. Poenitentes autem in extremo uitae praesentis termino, utrum hic plene remissionem peccatorum accipiunt, an igni purgatorio eorum delicta delebunt, ipse scit qui renes et corda conspiciens poenitentiae dignitatem considerat, qui latroni in cruce paene iam sine tempore, sine opere poenitenti respondit: *hodie mecum eris in paradiso;* et ad Ezechielem inquit: *in quacumque die conuersus fuerit impius a uia sua mala, omnium iniquitatum suarum quas operatus est non recordabor.* Sed de illo purgatorio igne hoc animaduertendum est, quod omni, qui excogitari in praesenti potest, tormentorum modo et longior et acrior sit.

stones, another builds wood, hay, stubble.[195] *If a man's work abides, which he has built upon it, he shall receive his reward. If a man's work burns, he shall suffer loss; but he himself shall be saved, as though by fire.*[196] 10. These two buildings, that is, gold, silver and precious stones on the one hand, and wood, hay and stubble on the other, signify the perfect and less perfect works built on faith in Christ. Those signified by wood, hay and stubble, though fragile, are nonetheless shown not to be unclean. 11. Whence it must be understood that this does not refer to the principal offences which pollute, and whose perpetrators Paul has excluded from the kingdom of God, but to those which do not harm very much, though they build even less, to wit:* taking wanton advantage of the state of legitimate matrimony, consuming a greater amount of food than is necessary, rejoicing immoderately in anything, being moved by anger to the point of intemperate words, enjoying one's possessions more than necessary, attending to prayer more negligently than is required at different times of the day,* or rising later than is becoming, raising one's voice in immoderate laughter, indulging the body with more sleep than it requires, holding back the truth, speaking idly, saying something that is not true, or in matters which do not pertain to faith endorsing as false something which you believe to be true, negligently forgetting the good that should be done, or disorderly behaviour.* There is no doubt that these and other similar sins can be cleansed by fire, and we should think that their perpetrator, if not weighed down by more serious sins, will thus be as though saved by fire.

12. As for those who repent at the very end of this life, whether they then receive full remission of their sins or whether their offences are destroyed by the cleansing fire, this He alone knows who, seeing the loins and the hearts[197] can evaluate the worthiness of repentance, He who said to the thief on the cross, with almost no time left and no possibility of works of penance: *today you shall be with me in Paradise,*[198] He also said to Ezechiel: *on whatever day the impious man turns from his wicked ways,*[199] *I will not remember all his iniquities that he hath done.*[200] But as for this cleansing fire, it should not be forgotten that it lasts far longer and is far more painful than any kind of torment that can be imagined in this life.[201]

---

195 1 Cor 3:11–12.
196 1 Cor 3:14–15.
197 Cf. Jer 11:20, Jer. 17:10, Jer. 20:12, Apoc. 2:23.
198 Lk 23:43.
199 Ez 33:12.
200 Ez 18:22.
201 Cf. Caesarius of Arles. *Sermo* 179.5 (CCSL 104, 726–27), and also Augustine, *Enarr. in Ps.* 37.3 (CCSL 38, 384).

15. De uita futura

1. De illa autem uera beatitudine futurae uitae sancta exponit scriptura *quod oculus non uidit, nec auris audiuit, nec in cor hominis ascendit quae praeparauit Deus diligentibus se*; de quibus Dominus ait: *erunt sicut angeli in caelo*.

Et eiusdem Domini excelsius aliquid de his sermo denuntiat: *tunc iusti fulgebunt sicut sol in regno Patris eorum*; sol scilicet *iustitiae timentibus nomen Domini oritur, cuius in pinnis est sanitas*, qui in monte faciem Moysi cum Elea coram apostolis euacuauit, cui dum sancti conpatiuntur simul conglorificabuntur.

2. In eo autem quod prius dixerat: *erunt sicut angeli in caelo*, hoc intuendum est, quod sicut angeli prius per naturam motabiles facti — quod probatum est in his qui ceciderunt — nunc uero inmotabiles, ut peccare non metuant nec possint, per Dei contemplationem effecti sunt, sic homines et ipsi per naturam motabiles, quod in Adam et eius semine exploratum est, creati ergo post resurrectionem conditoris contemplatione inmotabiles effecti nec desiderabunt peccare nec poterunt.

Omnis enim rationabilis creatura, quae Dei contemplatione reficitur, peccare non potest, 3. non quod liberae uoluntatis arbitrium uitio carentes angeli et homines non habeant (omne enim quod uolunt in illa uita hoc faciunt), sed uelle aliquid quod bonum non sit nequaquam possunt. Unde, quia nunquam male uolunt, delictum aliquid omnino non admittunt; 4. sed haec perfecta bona uoluntas per contemplationem superni conditoris perficitur, dum quod creatura per se habere non potuit ipsius largitoris munere donatur; unde perspicue intellegitur quod angeli uel homines qui siue in caelo siue in paradiso peccauerunt Deum non uiderunt, quoniam si illum uidissent, nullo modo postea delinquere possent.

5. Sed haec contra respondens forte aliquis dicat: cur ergo post uisionem gloriae, unde facies Moysi in solitudine rutula-

15. The Life to Come

1. Holy Scripture expounds on the blessedness of the life to come, saying that *eye has not seen, nor ear heard, neither has it entered into the heart of man, what things God has prepared for those who love him.*[202] And the Lord said about them: *they shall be as the angels in heaven.*[203]

And the same most high Lord affirms the following about them: *Then shall the just shine as the sun in the kingdom of their Father;*[204] that is, the sun *of justice shall rise for those who fear the name of the Lord, in whose rays there is health*[205] and He who, on the mountain, made appear as nothing* the countenance of Moses together with Elias in the presence of the apostles, as the saints suffer with Him, so they will be glorified with Him.

2. In what was said above, namely: *they will be as the angels in heaven,*[206] the following must be noted, that just as the angels who were first created changeable by nature — as is evident from those who fell — have now become immutable through the contemplation of God,[207] so that they do not fear to sin, nor can they commit sin,[208] * thus men who were also created changeable by nature — as can be seen in Adam and his descendants — will also, after their resurrection, become immutable through contemplation of the Creator and they will neither desire nor be capable of committing sin.

For every rational creature who is renewed by the contemplation of God is incapable of sinning. 3. Not that sinless angels and men do not have the use of free will, for they do everything they want in that life, but it is entirely impossible for them to will anything that is not good. Thus, since they never will what is evil, they commit absolutely no offence. 4. This perfect good will occurs through contemplation of the supreme Creator, when that which the creature cannot obtain by itself is granted as a gift by the most gracious Lord.* Whence it must be clearly grasped that angels and men who sinned either in heaven or in Paradise had not seen God, for had they seen Him, in no way could they have sinned thereafter.

5. But perhaps someone might object: 'Why then after the vision of Glory, from which the face of Moses was resplendent in solitude, could he give offence

---

202 1 Cor 2:9.
203 Mt 22:30, Mk 12:25.
204 Mt 13:43.
205 Mal 4:2.
206 Mt 22:30, Mk 12:25.
207 Cf. *De ecclesiasticis dogmatibus liber* 61–62 (see, e.g., PL 58:995D–996A or PL83:1240C–1240D).
208 Cf. Isidore, *Differentiae* 2.14.41 (CCSL 111A, 28).

bat, ad aquas contradictionis offendit et Petrus, post unigeniti gloriam in monte cum Moyse et Elea ostensam, in atrio sacerdotum Dominum negauit? Cui praepositione facile responditur quod Moysi per angelum uel per creaturam aliam posteriora gloriae uidit, et Petrus, et ceteri discipuli, per corpus humanum rutulare Christi diuinitatem conspexit; si enim per semetipsos diuinitatem conspexissent, nullo modo in carne postea uiuere possent. 6. Ipse namque Dominus Moysi respondit: *nemo uidebit faciem meam et uiuet.* Sancti ergo post resurrectionem non per figuras et aenigmata Dominum uidebunt, sicut de hoc eodem gentium insignis magister pronuntiat *quia nunc per speculum et aenigmata uidemus, cum autem uenerit quod perfectum est, tunc cognoscam sicut cognitus sum*; quemadmodum adsessor dominici pectoris conuiua potens ait Iohannis: *uidebimus eum sicut est,* quando conplebitur quod ecclesiae per Esaiam prophetatur: *non erit tibi amplius sol ad lucendum per diem neque splendor lunae inluminabit te, sed erit tibi Dominus in lucem sempiternam et Dominus tuus in gloriam tuam.* 7. Ex quo intellegitur quod non per creaturas, sed per Domini ipsius maiestatem ecclesia inluminabitur, cum perpetuae felicitatis serenitate secura consortium angelicae dignitatis subire permittitur, in qua serenitate cuncta prospera sine arguente pressura possedebit, cum neque tenebris lux, neque morte uita, neque dolore salus, neque tristitia gaudium, neque senectute iuuentus, neque amor carorum absentia uel defectione, neque ulla uilitate pulcritudo, neque infirmitate fortitudo, neque iustitia peccato terminabitur, et supra haec etiam fuerunt illa quae nec cogitatus nec ratio ulla hominis adhuc in terra positi adprehendere ualet.

    8. Ex his autem omnibus creaturis, quorum praestrinximus ordinem, quaedam ex aliquo, quaedam ex nihilo conditor fecit. Caelum enim et terram et mare et quae in his sunt facta ex informi materia condidit; ipsam uero informem materiam et angelorum ordines de quibus praediximus et animam humanam ex nihilo fecit: animam etenim neque de semetipso neque ex aliqua qualibet subiacente creaturarum corporalium materia

later on, by the waters of contradiction?[209] And how could Peter, when the glory of the only Son had been revealed to him on the mountain together with Moses and Elias, later deny the Lord in the priests' courtyard?'[210] To this argument it can easily be countered that Moses saw only the back of the glory of the Lord[211] through an angel or through some other creature, and that Peter and the other disciples saw the divinity of Christ shine through his human body. For had they seen the divinity directly, they could in no way go on living in the flesh thereafter. 6. For the Lord himself answered to Moses: *no one will see my face and live.*[212] After the resurrection, the saints will not see the Lord through figures and riddles,[213] * as the celebrated teacher of the gentiles affirmed: *We see now through a glass and through riddles, but when that which is perfect is come, then I shall know even as I am known.*[214] The powerful John, the table companion sitting close to the bosom of the Lord,* says similarly: *we will see Him as He is*[215] when will be fulfilled Isaiah's prophecy pertaining to the Church: *The sun shall be no more your light by day, nor shall the brightness of the moon give you light: but the Lord will be your everlasting light, and your Lord will be in your glory.*[216] 7. Which means that the Church will not be lighted by creatures but by the majesty of the Lord himself, when it is allowed to participate fully in the dignity of the angels with the secure serenity of perpetual bliss. In this serenity it will enjoy all prosperity, entirely free from the oppression of adversity, when light shall not be ended by darkness, nor life by death, nor health by pain, nor happiness by sorrow, nor youth by old-age, nor love by the absence or desertion of the loved ones, nor beauty by any vileness, nor strength by weakness, nor justice by sin.* And there will be things above and beyond this which cannot be grasped by the thought and the reason of any man still in this world.

8. Of all those creatures whose nature we have discussed, God created some from something and some from nothing.[217] For it was from unformed matter that he created heaven and earth and the sea and all that was made in them; but this very unformed matter, and the angelic orders of which we have spoken, and the human soul, these he made from nothing.* And God made the soul, which we do not believe to be a part of God but one of his creatures, neither from himself nor

---

209 Cf. Num 20:12–13.
210 Cf. Mt 26:69–74.
211 Cf. Ex 33:23.
212 Ex 33:20.
213 Cf. Num 12:8.
214 Cf. 1 Cor 13:12 and 13:10.
215 1 Jn 3:2.
216 Cf. Is 60:19.
217 Isidore, *Differentiae* 2.11.31 (CCSL 111A, 23).

fieri Deus instituit, quo non Dei partem, sed Dei creaturam esse credimus. Si enim de semetipso eam Deus fecisset, nequaquam passibilis et motabilis et misera esset; 9. item si ex creaturis corporalibus illam creasset, corporale aliquid in sua natura haberet: aut namque calorem de igne, aut flatum de aere, aut humorem ex aquatica, aut crassitudinem et soliditatem ex terrena haberet materia; sed quia his omnibus caret, incorpoream esse conditam conuenit, et per ipsam incorporalitatem et aeternitatem et motabilitatem et liberi arbitrii potestatem, eandem cum angelis habere substantiam creandique originem dignoscitur. Haec autem Dei imaginem in aeternitate, similitudinem in arbitrio liberae potestatis possedet; de qua imaginis Dei similitudine inpressa propheta conmemorat dicens: *signatum est super nos lumen uultus tui Domine.*

10. Utrum autem singulis corporibus singillatim a Deo mittuntur, an ex Adam uenire et ex parentibus sicut nascentium corpora putandum sit, cum a multis et sapientibus uiris disputatum sit et tamen de hac questione nihil, cui plus fides accommodanda esse poterit, relinquerunt, quid nos de tanta et tam periculosa re aliquid temptare oportet, uel quid nos ad horum ambages, in quibus se inuicem partes uincunt cum proprias expositiones adstruere non ualent, proferre emulamenti confert? 11. Idcirco ne supra nos aliquid appetamus, hanc quaesitionem, quae a multis lectoribus insolubilis esse dicta est, scientiae conditoris reseruemus: quia quaecumque ex carnibus agni pascalis comedentis saturitas consumere non potuit, cura non exigua uorax crastino flamma consumit. Per quod intellegitur quod omnia quae ex scripturae sacrae corpore nostrae inuestigationis scientiam effugiunt, dominicae sapientiae rogo inlustrata et consumpta fiant; 12. sed et illa, quae uelut per exiguam fenestram ex parte aliqua eius gratiae inluminatione adtingimus ad perfectum omnia scire sicut oportet non ualemus: *ex parte enim cognoscimus,* quandiu in hoc saeculo sumus; sed si ad illud Patris luminum inaestimabile lumen perueniamus, *tunc cognoscemus sicut cogniti sumus.*

13. Ecce, uenerabilis pater, de ordine creaturarum tibi proponenti iuxta ingenioli mei modulum compendioso sermo-

from any lower substance of the corporeal creatures. For if God had made it from himself, it could not be in any way passible, changeable and wretched. 9. Again, if God had created it from corporeal creatures, it would contain something corporeal in its nature: either the heat of fire, or the breath of air, or the moisture of water, or the firmness and solidity of earth. But because it lacks all these, it must be that it was created incorporeal,[218] and by this very incorporeality and immortality and mutability, and the power of free choice, it is seen to have been created from the same substance and to share in the same origin as the angels. It bears the image of God in its immortality, and His resemblance in its power of free choice. The Prophet* speaks of this imprinted similarity to the image of God, saying: *The light of your countenance, O Lord, is sealed upon us.*[219]

10. Whether we should think that souls are sent one by one by God to individual bodies, or whether they come from Adam and our parents like the bodies of those who are born, since many learned men have discussed this and yet left behind nothing on this question which is best reconciled with the faith, how can it be fitting for us to attempt anything on such weighty and dangerous matters, and what is to be gained by adding to their ambiguities, in which the parties prevail over one another without being able to sustain their own arguments?[220] * 11. Thus, that we may not seek something beyond our reach, we shall leave to the knowledge of the Creator this question which many experts declare to be insoluble. I pray that, just as the voracious flame thoroughly consumed on the following day that part of the Paschal Lamb which those eating together had been unable to finish,[221] * thus all those things from the body of Holy Scripture beyond the reach of our inquiry will be lit up and consumed by the wisdom of God. 12. But even for those things which we now understand in some part through the illumination of His grace — as though through a narrow window* — we are not worthy to know everything perfectly as they should be known, *for now we know in part*[222] so long as we are in this world. But if we reach that bright inestimable light of the Father, *then we shall know even as we are known.*[223]

13. Thus, Venerable Father, at your prompting and subject to the weakness of my feeble mind, I have written briefly on the ordering of all creation. I ask no more

---

218 Isidore, *Differentiae* 2.25.92 (CCSL 111A, 57) and 2.28.100–02 (CCSL 111A, 63–65).
219 Ps. 4:7.
220 Cf. Isidore, *Differentiae* 2.28.105–08 (CCSL 111A, 66–69), also Augustine, *Gen. litt.* 10 (CSEL 28/1, 326–27).
221 Cf. Ex 12:10 and Ex 34:25.
222 1 Cor 13:9.
223 1 Cor 13:12.

ne summatim respondi; cuius opusculi mercedem orationibus tuis conpensabo, non quod exiguitatis meae obsequium tua ueneratione et auctoritate conferre possit digna, sed oboedientiae conatus et ea quae non ualet adsequi implet omnia. Ecce in gazaphilacio templi pauperis uiduulae aeris exiguum munus multorum diuitum auro copioso praefertur, et in aurato tabernaculo, ubi aurum argentumque et gemmarum pretiosarum, bissi et purpurae et hiacinthi et cocci dona conferuntur, etiam eorum qui pelles caprarum deferunt diligentia non dispicitur.

14. Hanc igitur tu dissimili modo meae paruitatis oboedientiam placido pectoris tui portu recipere non dedignare, et contra transgarrientium instabiles fluctos timore tuae auctoritatis praesentis opusculi nauiculam non te pigeat gubernare.

Ego enim bonis et catholicis lectoribus consentiens, inuidorum non curo querellas qui sine pinnis in terra reptantes uolatu ranarum auium nidos inridunt. Contra quos tuae orationis scutu protectus, et Domini perquam suffragio armatus, ad patriam festinare tutus utroque latere curabo.

Deo enim placere curantes minas hominum penitus non timemus.

than your prayers as reward for this little treatise, not that the obedience of my minuteness can contribute anything worthy to your venerableness and authority, but the effort of obedience fulfils all requests, even those it is not really fit to carry out. See, in the treasure of the temple, the tiny brass coin of the poor widow is placed above the plentiful gold of many wealthy people,[224] and in the gilded tabernacle, where are brought together gold and silver and offerings of precious stones, of linen, of purple, of hyacinth and of scarlet, even the zeal of those who bring but goat skins is not despised.[225]*

14. In a similar way, do not scorn to welcome your insignificant servant in the sheltered harbour of your bosom, and with the prestige of your authority to pilot the frail bark of this modest work through the rough waters of noisy babble.*

As for me, I am in full agreement with good and catholic experts, so that I do not fear the quarrels of jealous detractors who crawl along the ground for lack of wings, and with their froglike flight[226]* mock the nests of soaring birds. Protected from them by the shield of your prayer and fully armed with the approval of the Lord, I am sheltered on both sides, and will strive to hasten toward the true homeland.

For when we endeavour to please God, we have nothing to fear from the threats of men.[227]*

---

224 Mk 12:42–44; cf. Jerome, *Epistula* 53.11 (CSEL 54, 465).
225 Ex 25:3–5; cf. Jerome, *Comment. in Hiezechielem* 12.40 (CCSL 75, 558).
226 Cf. Augustine, *Gen. litt.* 1.20 (CSEL 28/1, 30).
227 Cf. Jerome, Introduction to the Vulgate *Book of Esther*.

Appendix

In his edition of *Liber de ordine creaturarum*, Manuel Díaz y Díaz identified and described twenty-one manuscripts dating from the eighth to the fifteenth century containing at least parts of DOC. While preparing this translation, I identified several additional manuscripts, catalogue entries and citations. The combination of these extant manuscripts, of the entries in medieval catalogues, and of medieval borrowings from the text, shows that the treatise *De ordine creaturarum* was copied repeatedly and spread rapidly soon after it was written. The first surviving manuscripts are from Britain, and extant witnesses to the early stages of transmission range over the areas most in contact with the Irish and Anglo-Saxon missions. The text then spread throughout most of Europe.

The description of the manuscripts provided here relies heavily on the more detailed accounts provided by Díaz y Díaz. For more information, the reader is encouraged to refer to the introduction (in Spanish) to his 1972 edition of DOC.[1] In order to facilitate such consultation, the sigla used in that edition have been retained. I have endeavoured to incorporate the results of more recent scholarship and an updated bibliography into the descriptions below. The three earliest manuscripts are described at greater length here since they are most important for establishing the text's origin; information on the other manuscripts is given in summary form.

B Basle, Universitätsbibliothek, MS F. III. 15b. Manuscript in vellum, made up of two parts of different date and script. The first and oldest part (A, 19 folios) contains DOC on fols 1–19, and is written in two different hands, both in Anglo-Saxon minuscule dating from the first half of the eighth century. This appears to be the earliest extant text of DOC. Folios in Section A measure 270 × 210 mm., with writing area of 225/40 × 165/70 mm. and 26–28 long lines per page.

The manuscript must have come early to the monastery of Fulda, since the item recorded as *liber de creaturarum sancti Esidorum* [*sic*] in the eighth- or ninth-century catalogue of the library of Fulda[2] is almost certainly this very text. Indeed, a tenth-century list of the books at Fulda is written inside the cover of

---

1 Díaz y Díaz (1972), 47–72.
2 On fols 17–18 of Basle, Universitätsbibliothek, MS F. III. 15a, saec. VIII–IX (CLA, vii [Oxford, 1956], no. 842, p. [2]); K. Christ, *Die Bibliothek des Klosters Fulda im 16. Jahrhundert: Die Handschriften-Verzeichnisse*, Beiheft zum Zentralblatt für Bibliothekswesen 64 (Leipzig, 1933; repr. Wiesbaden, 1968), pp. 65, 167–68.

the codex. As is clear from the well-known Fulda shelf-mark — XXIIII or.14 — in a hand of the fifteenth century, the codex remained in Fulda during the Middle Ages.

Two hands occur in section A, of which the first, which wrote fols 1–8^v, is according to Lowe, 'rapid and graceful', perhaps Northumbrian; the second, in contrast, is 'more compressed and stiff.' Lowe believes that the codex was 'written in England', probably 'in the North.' The abbreviations show both typical Insular forms as well as common forms. The initials are typically Insular, in black with red dots. There are many corrections, mostly contemporary. The binding was done at Fulda and is early, according to van Regemorter.

Bibliography: E. A. Lowe, *Codices Latini Antiquiores* (= CLA), VOL. 7 (Oxford, 1956), no. 844, p. [2] (with an ample selection of earlier literature); B. van Regemorter, 'La reliure souple des manuscrits carolingiens de Fulda', *Scriptorium* 11 (1957), 249–57, at p. 256; H. Hoffmann, *Buchkunst und Königtum im ottonischen und frühsalischen Reich*, Schriften der Monumenta Germaniae Historica 30.1 (Stuttgart, 1986), p. 141; K. Gugel, *Welche erhaltenen mittelalterlichen Handschriften dürfen der Bibliothek des Klosters Fulda zugerechnet werden? Teil I: Die Handschriften*, Fuldaer Hochschulschriften 23a (Frankfurt am Main, 1995), p. 31; M. Steinman, *Die Handschriften der Universitätsbibliothek Basel: Register zu den Abteilungen C I–C VI, D-F sowie weiteren mittelalterlichen Handschriften und Fragmenten* (Basle, 1998), p. 36; H. Gneuss, *Handlist of Anglo-Saxon Manuscripts: A List of Manuscripts and Manuscript Fragments Written or Owned in England up to 1100*, Medieval and Renaissance Texts and Studies 241 (Tempe, Ariz., 2001), p. 117, no. 785; H. Gneuss and M. Lapidge, *Anglo-Saxon Manuscripts: A Bibliographical Handlist of Manuscripts and Manuscript Fragments Written or Owned in England up to 1100*, Toronto Anglo-Saxon Series (Toronto, 2014), p. 562, no. 785; additional bibliography on e-*codices*.

P Paris, Bibliothèque Nationale, MS lat. 9561, on vellum, 81 folios, 285 × 220 mm., with a writing area of 245 × 200 mm. The manuscript was written in Anglo-Saxon uncial, in 29–39 long lines per page, definitely during the second half of the eighth century according to Díaz y Díaz, for whom **P** is the earliest extant manuscript of DOC. Bischoff argued for a date in the first half of the eighth century, while Gneuss and Lapidge opt for the first half or the middle of the eighth century. Even with the earliest dating for **P**, it would seem that manuscript **B** is older.

The titles of the chapters were written in red uncials, often faded. On folio 81^v, the colophon FINIT is in black uncials. The chapters often begin with a large capital letter decorated with red dots. Abbreviations and symbols are those which are common in Insular texts. Spelling is frequently incorrect: *miso, minesteria, commonia, cerubhin, longeus, occausu, sponcgeas, sapiti*, etc.; in some cases, the readings in this manuscript make it possible to surmise some features of the codex from which it was copied, perhaps an Irish codex which allows our scribe to put *post est* for *potest, tartatum* for *tantarum*. As Lowe indicated, the script shows both

Anglo-Saxon and continental influences and he deduced that the manuscript was written 'either in England or by an English scribe on the Continent, perhaps at St Bertin.' Dumville has pointed out, however, that St Bertin is not known to have been a centre of Insular culture during the eighth century, so that it is most unlikely that the manuscript was copied there.[3] The scribal note at the end of DOC on fol. 14^v contains two words in Anglo-Saxon minuscule, and there are tenth-century Anglo-Saxon glosses on fols 33^v–42^v.

The manuscript was used during the twelfth century, when the text was transcribed into gothic letters between the lines in DOC 14.1 (fol. 13^v), to facilitate reading or copying. It was certainly at St Bertin during the fourteenth century in view of the note in the lower margin of fol. 1^v: *de libraria sancti Bertini*, and it remained there into the seventeenth century. It contains:

> fols 1–14, *Liber de ordine creaturarum*;
> fols 15–81, *Gregorius regula pastoralis*.

Despite its errors and mistaken spellings, the text is in general correct and was fundamental for establishing the text of the treatise.

Bibliography: L. Delisle, *Inventaire des manuscrits conservés à la Bibliothèque Impériale sous les Nos. 8823–11503 du fonds latin* (Paris, 1863), p. 38 (summary description; the codex is assigned to the seventh century); E. A. Lowe, CLA, VOL. 5 (Oxford, 1950), no. 590, p. [21] (with full bibliography up to that time) and Suppl., p. [54]; E. A. Lowe, *English Uncial* (Oxford, 1960), p. 23 and Plate XXXV (a less detailed account than in the earlier work); B. Bischoff, *Mittelalterliche Studien: Ausgewählte Aufsätze zur Schriftkunde und Literaturgeschichte*, 3 VOLS (Stuttgart, 1966–1999), 2:332–33; N. R. Ker, *Catalogue of Manuscripts Containing Anglo-Saxon* (Oxford, 1957), p. 441, no. 369; see also Bruno Judic, 'Introduction', in *Grégoire le Grand: Règle pastorale*, SC 381 (Paris, 1992), pp. 15–102, at p. 91, n. 6 and p. 109; Gneuss, *Handlist*, p. 137, no. 894; Gneuss and Lapidge, p. 646, no. 894.

M Munich, Bayerische Staatsbibliothek, MS clm 6302, parchment, 69 folios, 255 × 185 mm., writing area *c*. 200 × 145 mm., 24–26 long lines per page, except for fol. 1^r which is in 2 columns with the numbered *capitulatio* in the left column. Lowe set the copying of this manuscript at the end of the eighth century or at the beginning of the ninth; Bischoff inclined towards an earlier dating, arguing that it must have been copied in the scriptorium of bishop Arbeo of Freising (that is, in the period 764–784), or in the surrounding area. Certain details are reminiscent of Peregrinus, the probably Northumbrian monk active at Freising at that time (see also **M2**, below).

Even without taking into account the facts associating this manuscript with the scriptorium of Freising, one can almost immediately suspect Insular origin in

---

3 I thank David Dumville for his comments on this manuscript (private correspondence, 15 April 2000).

view of certain characteristics of the orthography which require a model in Insular minuscule: *anguente* instead of *arguente, pluus, creaturarum* for *creaturam, officiunt* for *officium, item* for *iterum, abstullit, atumno, suffogaret, scaeleris*. The manuscript was preserved in Freising, where it carried the shelfmark 102. On folio 1, a note entered in a hand of the twelfth century, states: *iste liber est sce. marie et sci. corbin. frisingen*. It contains:

> fols 1–29, *De ordine creaturarum*. The title in rustic capitals in the upper margin of the first page reads *De origine* [sic] *creaturarum*; the text is preceded by the incipit/invocation *In nomine domini incipit liber sancti Isidori de ordine creaturarum* (the abbreviations have been expanded) in large capital letters similar to those used for other titles in the collection;[4]
> fols 29–46, *Incipit genelogium ihesu xpisti secundum carnem* (CLH 71; BCLL 770);
> fols 46–49, *Incipit pauca secon* [sic] *Marcum* (excerpts from BCLL 345; CPPM iiA 2366);
> fols 49–64, *Incipit de operibus sex dierum quando creauit Deus caelum et terram* (CLH 38; BCLL 1258);
> fols 64–69ʳ, *Incipit prebiarum de multorium* [sic] *exemplaribus* (CLH 37; BCLL 777);
> fols 69ʳ–69ᵛ, *Incipit clericalis uel monachalis sci. Hieronimi Presbiteri*.[5]

This collection of texts with strong Irish associations confirms the suspicion that this manuscript depends on an Irish model.

Bibliography: E. A. Lowe, CLA, VOL. 9 (Oxford, 1959), no. 1267, p. [62] (with earlier bibliography); see also CLA Suppl., p. [63]. List of contents in CCSL 108B:155 and CCSL 108D: xx–xxii; see also B. Bischoff, 'Wendepunkte in der Geschichte der lateinischen Exegese im Frühmittelalter', *Sacris erudiri* 6 (1954), 189–279, at pp. 221–22, 230–31, 254–55 (repr. *Mittelalterliche Studien*, VOL. 1 (Stuttgart, 1966), pp. 205–73); B. Bischoff, *Die südostdeutschen Schreibschulen und Bibliotheken in der Karolingerzeit*, 2 VOLS, 2nd rev. ed. (Wiesbaden, 1960), 1:61, 63, 81–82, 2:212, no. 18; E. Kessler, *Die Auszeichnungsschriften in den Freisinger Codices von den Anfängen bis zur karolingischen Erneuerung*, Österreichische Akademie der Wissenschaften, Phil.-Hist. Klasse, Denkschriften, 188. Band (Vienna, 1986), pp. 104, 223–24, No. 18, Abb. 102–08; K. Bierbrauer, *Die vorkarolingischen und karolingischen Handschriften der Bayerischen Staatsbibliothek in München*, Katalog der illuminierten Handschriften der Bayerischen Staatsbibliothek in München 1, 2 VOLS (Wiesbaden, 1990), 1:21, no. 16; I. Schäfer, *Buchherstellung im frühen Mittelalter: Die Einbandtechnik in Freising*, Wolfenbütteler Mittelalter-Studien 14 (Wiesbaden, 1999), pp. 283–85; B. Bischoff, *Katalog der festländischen Handschriften des neunten Jahrhunderts (mit Ausnahme der wisigotischen), Teil II: Laon-Paderborn*, Bayerische Akademie der Wissenschaften, Veröffentlichungen der Kommission für die Herausgabe der mittelalterlichen

---

4 This is the *Auszeichnungsschrift* II2 identified by Kessler (see the bibliography for this manuscript), Fig. 102. For other titles in **M**, see Figs 103–08.
5 Glauche (1994).

Bibliothekskataloge Deutschlands und der Schweiz (Wiesbaden, 2004), p. 237, Nr. 3038.

N Paris, Bibliothèque Nationale, MS lat. 3848B, saec. VIII–IX, probably from Burgundy.

> fols 64ᵛ–65ᵛ, Chapter 1 of DOC, with the title *de fide trinitatis Isidori epi.*

The script shows Irish symptoms: thus, for example, our text contains the Insular symbol for *est*, as well as the abbreviations for *-bus* and *-que*.
Bibliography: Described and analyzed, with important bibliographic citations, by E. A. Lowe, CLA, VOL. 5 (Oxford, 1950), no. 555, p. [11], [55]. This collection is number 11, and DOC is text number 263a in the lists compiled in Susan Ann Keefe, 'Creed Commentary Collections in Carolingian Manuscripts', in *Ritual, Text and Law: Studies in Medieval Canon Law and Liturgy Presented to Roger E. Reynolds*, ed. K. G. Cushing and R. F. Gyug, Church, Faith and Culture in the Medieval West (Aldershot, Hampshire, 2004), pp. 185–204.

H Bamberg, Staatsbibliothek, MS B. V.18 (Patr. 102). Bischoff assigned this manuscript to Bavaria, in the first third of the ninth century.

> fols 78–101, *Incipiunt capilae* [sic] in red letters; there follow the titles of the fifteen numbered chapters of DOC; then one can read *Incipit lib. sci. Isydori de ordine creaturarum/de fide trinitatis ratione et unica debet intelle…*/ in red letters.

Bibliography: H. Fischer, *Katalog der Handschriften der Königlichen Bibliothek zu Bamberg*, 3 VOLS (Bamberg, 1887–1912), 1:483–84; K. Hartung, *Ein Traktat zur Apokalypse des Ap. Johannes* (Bamberg, 1904); B. Bischoff, *Katalog der festländischen Handschriften des neunten Jahrhunderts (mit Ausnahme der wisigotischen), Teil I: Aachen-Lambach*, Bayerische Akademie der Wissenschaften, Veröffentlichungen der Kommission für die Herausgabe der mittelalterlichen Bibliothekskataloge Deutschlands und der Schweiz (Wiesbaden, 1998), p. 53, Nr. 237.

K Bern, Burgerbibliothek, MS 178, saec. IX. This manuscript derives from an archetype originating from a centre with obvious grammatical concerns and presents a text which has been extensively corrected, though clearly related to an excellent tradition. The manuscript contains numerous examples of Insular abbreviations in the various texts.

> fols 90–108, acephalous DOC.

Bibliography: H. Hagen, *Anecdota Helvetica* (Leipzig, 1870), pp. cxvii–cxix; H. Hagen, *Catalogus Codicum Bernensium* (Bern, 1875), pp. 238–39; M. L. Uhlfelder, *De proprietate sermonum uel rerum*, Papers and Monographs of the American Academy of Rome 15 (Rome, 1954), p. 36; M. Mostert, *The Library of Fleury: A Provisional List of Manuscripts*, Middeleeuwse Studies en Bronnen/

Medieval Studies and Sources 3 (Hilversum, 1989), BF099, p. 61; B. Bischoff, *Katalog der festländischen Handschriften, Teil I: Aachen-Lambach*, p. 115, Nr. 547.

U Paris, Bibliothèque Nationale, MS lat. 2183, saec. X*ex*. This manuscript seems to be associated with Angers, though a connection with an area more to the east should not be excluded. Its content depends on a manuscript which is either Insular or strongly influenced by an Insular milieu.

fols 49–63, DOC with no introductory rubric.

The chapters have no titles. The copyist seems to have recognized that the treatise was not complete, and ended it with several dots followed by a blank space. A contemporary hand placed a summary index of the contents of the manuscript at the beginning, on folio 1ᵛ. This refers to DOC as *libellus quidam pulcer et utilis*. In many places (DOC 6.2, 9.9, 13.10, 14.11) a hand (or hands) of the eleventh century draws attention to these passages.

Bibliography: *Catalogus codicum manuscriptorum Bibliothecae Regiae*, 4 VOLS (Paris, 1739–1744), 3:251; *Bibliothèque Nationale: Catalogue général des manuscrits latins*, 7 VOLS (Paris, 1939–1988), 2:357; M.-Th. Vernet, 'Notes de Dom André Wilmart† sur quelques manuscrits latins anciens de la Bibliothèque Nationale de Paris', *Bulletin d'Information de l'Institut de Recherche et d'Histoire des Textes* 6 (1957), 16–17.

F Florence, Biblioteca Medicea Laurenziana, MS Gaddianus lat. 89. Sup.31, saec. XII*ex*.

fols 1–15, DOC (incomplete) with heading *Incipit liber Isidori de ordine creaturarum*.

According to Bischoff, the manuscript was probably written in France, perhaps in the South. This conjecture, based on palaeographical criteria, is corroborated by the observation that the text, despite numerous gaps, corrections and emendations, is closely related to that in manuscripts **T** and **E**, below. Though the end of the text is missing in **F**, Arévalo used it as the control manuscript for the second edition by d'Achery (1665) and the third edition by Martène and Baluze (1723) when producing his 1797 edition of DOC. The last text in this manuscript is *De duodecim abusiuis saeculi* (BCLL 339).

Bibliography: A. M. Bandini, *Catalogus codicum latinorum Bibliothecae Mediceae Laurentianae*, 5 VOLS (Florence, 1774–1778), 3:299–302; F. Arévalo, PL81:130.

O Oxford, Bodleian Library, MS Bodl. 633 (olim Miscellaneous 1966 and 654), assembled in Worcester. Section D (fols 127–65), saec. XII.

fols 127–56, DOC, bearing neither the title nor the name of the author.

The title and table of contents of DOC would probably have been on an initial folio which has been lost.

Bibliography: F. Madan and H. H. E. Craster, *A Summary Catalogue of Western Manuscripts in the Bodleian Library at Oxford*, 7 vols (Oxford, 1895–1953), 2:1, pp. 136–37; see also Ph. Delhaye and C. H. Talbot, *Florilegium Morale Oxoniense: Ms. Bodl. 633*, Analecta Mediaevalia Namurcensia 5–6 (Louvain, 1955–1956); F. Chatillon, 'Sur quelques citations de Fulgence le mythographe, de Boèce et de Maximien dans le florilège d'Oxford (Bodl. 633)', *Revue du Moyen Age Latin* 12 (1956), 5–26; Birger Munk Olsen, 'Les florilèges d'auteurs classiques', (originally published in 1982), in *La réception de la littérature classique au Moyen Age (IXe–XIIe siècle)* (Copenhagen, 1995), pp. 257–58.

C Troyes, Médiathèque de l'Agglomération Troyenne, MS 423. Copied in the twelfth century, probably at Clairvaux since the red and blue initials, though small, are very characteristic.

fols 74–91, *Lib. Ysidori epi. de ordine creaturarum*.

The manuscript written with great accuracy and skill contains a text of DOC which is correct, and close to that in manuscripts **T** and **E**.

Bibliography: *Catalogue général des manuscrits des bibliothèques publiques des départements*, Quarto series, 7 vols (Paris, 1849–1885), 2:190–91; A. Vernet, J. P. Bouhot and J.-E. Genest, *La bibliothèque de l'abbaye de Clairvaux du XIIe au XVIIIe siècle*, 2 vols (Paris-Turnhout, 1997), 2:344–45.

T Burgo de Osma, Archivo Biblioteca de la Santa Iglesia Catedral, MS 101. Though Rojo Orcajo assigned it to the thirteenth century, it was probably copied at the end of the twelfth century, according to Díaz y Díaz (who cites a private communication from M. Mundó). Possibly this manuscript originated from Fitero, a foundation of monks from Scala Dei (Escaledieu, Tarbes, South of France).

fols 93–108, *Incipit liber sancti Ysidori de ordine creaturarum*.

Bibliography: T. Rojo Orcajo, *Catálogo descriptivo de los códices que se conservan en la Santa Iglesia Catedral de Burgo de Osma* (Madrid, 1929), pp. 183–84; P. O. Kristeller, *Iter italicum*, vol. 4 (London, 1989), pp. 496–97.

E El Escorial, Real Biblioteca de San Lorenzo, MS e.IV.13, written at the end of the twelfth century. At the end of the thirteenth century the codex, together with manuscript **T**, was at Burgo de Osma, and is cited in the old catalogue of that library: *item otro de ordine creaturarum qui incipit Universitatis*.

fols 1–38^v and 53^v, *Incipit liber sci ysidori spalensis de ordine creaturarum*, with the table of contents.

Bibliography: G. Antolín, *Catálogo de los Códices Latinos de la Real Biblioteca del Escorial*, 5 vols (Madrid, 1910–1923), 2:100–02 and 5:72.

R2 Paris, Bibliothèque Mazarine, MS 625 (911). In the thirteenth-century section of this manuscript:

fols 145–61, *Incipit liber sancti ysidori de ordine creaturarum.*

The manuscript comes from the Abbey of Chaalis (old diocese of Senlis, Beauvais), as shown by the note in the lower margin of fol. 145: *liber beate marie karoliloci.*[6]

Bibliography: A. Molinier, *Catalogue général des manuscrits des bibliothèques publiques de France: Catalogue des manuscrits de la Bibliothèque Mazarine*, 4 VOLS (Paris, 1885–1898), 1: 273–74; see also the notes of E. A. Anspach preserved in the Archivo Historico Diocesano of León.[7]

I Worcester, Cathedral and Chapter Library, MS F 57, saec. XIIImed. The manuscript was most likely written at Worcester itself.

fols 306^v–11^v, DOC with the heading: *Ysodorus* [*sic*] *de ordine creaturarum.*

De duodecim abusiuis saeculi and Augustinus Hibernicus, *De mirabilibus Divinae Scripturae* are among the forty-two separate items in this manuscript.

Bibliography: E. Bernard, *Catalogi librorum manuscriptorum Angliae et Hiberniae in unum collecti cum indice alphabetico*, 2 VOLS in one (Oxford, 1697), 2:17, no. 732 (57); H. Schenkl, *Bibliotheca Patrum Latinorum Britannica*, 3 VOLS (Vienna, 1891–1908; repr. Hildesheim, 1969), 3(2):49–51, no. 4308; J. K. Floyer and S. G. Hamilton, *Catalogue of Manuscripts Preserved in the Chapter Library of Worcester Cathedral* (Oxford, 1906), pp. 25–28; *Catalogus librorum manuscriptorum Bibliothecae Wigorniensis*, made in 1622–1623 by Patrick Young, Librarian to King James I, ed. with an Introduction by W. Atkins and N. R. Ker (Cambridge, 1944), p. 36; R. M. Thomson and M. Gullick, *A Descriptive Catalogue of the Medieval Manuscripts in Worcester Cathedral Library* (Cambridge & Woodbridge, 2001), pp. 34–35.

L London, British Library, MS Additional 15407, saec. XIIIex. This manuscript once belonged to the Abbey of Sainte Marie de Cambron (Tournai), in Belgium.

---

6 It is not, however, described in the catalogue preserved in Paris, Bibliothèque de l'Arsenal, 351, fols 123^v–27; see *Catalogue général des manuscrits des bibliothèques publiques de France: Catalogue des manuscrits de la Bibliothèque de l'Arsenal*, ed. H. Martin, 9 VOLS (Paris, 1885–1892), 8:439–46.

7 Observations by Díaz y Díaz on the Fondo Anspach in the *Archivo Historico Diocesano de León*: 'Though some of Anspach's notes, especially the collations, are practically unusable, many other notes can be consulted with great profit, among them the summary descriptions of Isidorian or pseudo-Isidorian codices, and of those by the other writers in whom he was interested. See the publications of J. M. Fernández Catón: 'Catálogo de los materiales codicológicos y bibliográficos del legado scientifico del Prof. Anspach' and 'Las Etimologias en la tradición manuscrita medieval', *Archives Leoneses* 129 (1965), 29–120 and 121–384.'

fols 192–202, DOC with the heading: *Incipit liber Ysidori episcopi sancti de ordine creaturarum ad Braulium episcopum urbis Rome.*

This manuscript corresponds closely to the lost manuscript of Rheims which was the basis for the first edition by d'Achery;[8] not only does it have the same heading, but most of the characteristic readings coincide.

Bibliography: *Catalogue of Additions to the Manuscripts in the British Museum in the years MDCCCXLI–MDCCCXLV* (London, 1850), list of additions in 1845, pp. 2–3.

S Sankt Florian, Stiftsbibliothek, MS XI. 346, saec. XIV, Sankt Florian?

fols 210^v–15^v: *Incipit Ysidorus de ordine creaturarum*, followed by the index of chapters.

Bibliography: Albin Czerny, *Die Handschriften der Stiftsbibliothek St Florian* (Linz, 1871), pp. 140–41.

Q Zwettl, Stiftsbibliothek, MS 76, Teil II, dated to 1321, from Zwettl.

fols 258^v–92^r, DOC with the title: *Tractatus Ysidori de ordine creaturarum* and preceded by the capitula on fol. 258^v.

Bibliography: S. Rossler, 'Verzeichnis der Handschriften der Bibliothek des Stiftes Zwettl', in *Xenia Bernardina, II: Die Handschriften-Verzeichnisse der Cistercienser Stifte*, 2 vols (Vienna, 1891), 1:329–30; Charlotte Ziegler, *Zisterzienserstift Zwettl: Katalog der Handschriften des Mittelalters: Teil I, Codex 1–100*, Scriptorium ordinis cisterciensium (Vienna-Munich, 1992), pp. 144–46.

Z Zwettl, Stiftsbibliothek, MS 148, Teil II, dated to the first half of saec. XIV, from Zwettl.

fols 188–99^v, *tractatus Isidori de ordine creaturarum*.

Bibliography: Summarily described by S. Rossler, 'Verzeichnis der Handschriften der Bibliothek des Stiftes Zwettl', in *Xenia Bernardina, II*: 1:353; Charlotte Ziegler, *Zisterzienserstift Zwettl: Katalog der Handschriften des Mittelalters: Teil II, Codex 101–200*, Scriptorium ordinis cisterciensium (Vienna-Munich, 1985), pp. 132–34.

W Vienna, Österreichische Nationalbibliothek, MS lat. 1039, saec. XIV, origin?

fols 65–79, *Isidorus de ordine creaturarum*, with index of the chapter headings on fol. 65.

Bibliography: *Tabulae codicum manuscriptorum praeter Graecos et Orientales in Bibliotheca Palatina Vindobonensi asservatorum*, 11 vols (Vienna, 1864–1912), 1:180–81.

---

8 See manuscript **A**, below.

D Durham, Cathedral Library, MS B.II.20, saec. XIV, perhaps saec. XIV*in.*, Durham.

This appears to be the only manuscript with noteworthy decoration. Its miniatures have been described briefly by Rud.

fols 81–91^v, *De ordine creaturarum*.

Bibliography: E. Bernard, *Catalogi librorum manuscriptorum Angliae et Hiberniae*, 2:7, no. 152 (87); H. Schenkl, *Bibliotheca Patrum Latinorum Britannica*, 3(2):80–81, no. 4404; Thomas Rud and James Raine, *Codicum manuscriptorum ecclesiae Cathedralis Dunelmensis catalogus classicus descriptus a Thoma Rud* (Durham, 1825), p. 125.

G Graz, Universitätsbibliothek, MS 348, fols 1–48, saec. XIV*ex.* and fols 49–243, saec. XV*in.* Provenance: Zisterzienserstift Neuberg.

fols 49–62^v, *Incipit Ysidorus de ordine creaturarum*.

Bibliography: Anton Kern, *Die Handschriften der Universitätsbibliothek Graz*, Verzeichnis der Handschriften im Deutschen Reich 2, 3 VOLS (Leipzig & Vienna, 1942–1967), 1:204–06.

R1 Paris, Bibliothèque Mazarine, MS 755 (320), saec. XV*in.* Provenance: Collège de Navarre (?).

fols 231^v–233, a much abbreviated text of DOC, with many haplographies.

Bibliography: A. Molinier, *Catalogue général*, 1:360–61.

X Cambridge, Peterhouse, MS 193. Though Schenkl assigns the codex to the fourteenth century, James is probably more correct to set it in the first half of the fifteenth.

fols 197–206, DOC with the title *Incipit liber de disposicione uniuersi*.

In the margin, a later hand wrote in cursive: *secundum quosdam Ysidorus de ordine creaturarum*. The text is very close to that copied in **D** and the manuscript may originate from the neighbourhood of Durham.

Bibliography: E. Bernard, *Catalogi librorum manuscriptorum Angliae et Hiberniae*, 1(3):152, no. 1838; H. Schenkl, *Bibliotheca Patrum Latinorum Britannica*, 2(2):72–73; M. R. James, *A Descriptive Catalogue of the Manuscripts in the Library of Peterhouse* (Cambridge, 1899), pp. 224–26; Ch. Duggan, 'Primitive Decretal Collections in the British Museum', *Studies in Church History* 1 (1964), 132–44, at p. 143.

J Prague, Knihovna Metropolitní Kapituly, MS B. XXXIII (334), dated 1455, origin?

fols 219–37, DOC.

Among numerous other items, the manuscript also contains *De duodecim abusiuis saeculi*.

Bibliography: A. Patera and A. Podlaha, *Soupis rukopisů Knihovny Metropolitní kapitoly pražské*, VOL. 1 (Prague, 1910), pp. 202–03.

V Vienna, Österreichische Nationalbibliothek, MS lat. 4576, saec. XV*med*. Both origin and provenance are unknown.

fols 230–38, DOC without title, though preceded by a list of the chapter headings.

Bibliography: *Tabulae codicum manuscriptorum ... in Bibliotheca Palatina Vindobonensi asservatorum*, 3:317–19.

Four further manuscript witnesses do not alter the overall pattern for the transmission of the text of DOC (sigla are assigned by me):

M2 Munich, Bayerische Staatsbibliothek, MS clm 6433, written in Freising by the Anglo-Saxon Peregrinus during the second half of the eighth century.

The first work (fols 1–24ᵛ) in this collection is a florilegium known as the *Florilegium Frisingense* (Clm 6433) which contains DOC 1.2–4 on fols 1ᵛ–2ʳ, within the section devoted to the Trinity with the title *Fides senodi Cartaginiensium*. Given the practice in this florilegium of carefully naming the authors of all citations, it is curious that Isidore is not mentioned as the author of this selection since **M** (clm 6302) — which clearly attributes DOC to Isidore — would probably have been available at Freising at that time (see above).

Bibliography: E. A. Lowe, CLA, VOL. 9 (Oxford, 1959), no. 1283, p. [15] (with earlier bibliography). See also CLA Suppl., p. [63]; *Florilegia*, ed. A. Lehner, CCSL 108D; B. Bischoff, *Die südostdeutschen Schreibschulen*, no. 8, 1:75, 2:212; K. Bierbrauer, *Die Ornamentik frühkarolingischer Handschriften aus Bayern*, Bayerische Akademie der Wissenschaften, Phil.-Hist. Klasse, Abhandlungen, N. F. Heft 84 (Munich, 1979), p. 125, Taf. 3:4 & 6, Taf. 4:3, Taf. 5:2–6; E. Kessler, *Die Auszeichnungsschriften in den Freisinger Codices*, pp. 64–77, 169–73, no. 8, Abb. 35–41; K. Bierbrauer, *Die vorkarolingischen und karolingischen Handschriften*, 1:19, no. 10; I. Schäfer, *Buchherstellung im frühen Mittelalter*, pp. 373–75.

N2 Paris, Bibliothèque Nationale, MS lat. 3802, saec. XI.

fols 136ᵛ–137, excerpts from DOC 1 with the title *Dicta sancti Ysidori de sancta trinitate et quod amplius nihil est quam creator et creatura*, in the section *Florilegium patristicum et biblicum de Trinitate et Symbola Fidei* (fols 127–41).

Bibliography: See the electronic BnF catalogue description at https://archivesetmanuscrits.bnf.fr/ark:/12148/cc61765j

O2 Oxford, Bodleian Library, MS Laud. misc. 345, saec. XIII or saec. XIV, Durham.

fols 45ʳ–60ᵛ, DOC with the title *Augustini liber de ordine creaturarum*.

Bibliography: The entry of H. O. Coxe, *Catalogi codicum manuscriptorum bibliothecae Bodleianae. Partis secundae fasciculus primus* (Oxford, 1858), is reprinted in H. O. Coxe, *Bodleian Library Quarto Catalogues. II: Laudian Manuscripts*, Oxford, 1973, col. 260–63; F. Madan and H. H. E. Craster, *A Summary Catalogue of Western Manuscripts in the Bodleian Library at Oxford*, 7 VOLS (Oxford, 1895–1953), 2(1):55; Franz Römer, *Die handschriftliche Überlieferung der Werke des heiligen Augustinus*, VOL. II/2: *Grossbritannien und Irland: Verzeichnis nach Bibliotheken*, Österreichische Akademie der Wissenschaften, Phil.-Hist. Klasse, Sitzungsberichte, 276. Band (Vienna, 1972), p. 277.

Y Ottobeuren (Bavaria), Bibliothek der Benediktinerabtei, MS O.22 (II.353), dated to *c.* 1465, Ottobeuren (?). This manuscript was owned by Ulrich Ellenbog.

fols 13ʳ–26ʳ, DOC with the title *Liber de fide trinitatis et natura creaturarum*.

Bibliography: Hermann Hauke, *Die mittelalterlichen Handschriften in der Abtei Ottobeuren: Kurzverzeichnis* (Wiesbaden, 1974), pp. 34–37; Friedrich Zoepfl, 'Kloster Ottobeuren und der Humanismus', in *Ottobeuren: Festschrift zur 1200-Jahrfeier der Abtei*, ed. Aegidius Kolb & Hermann Tüchle (Augsburg, 1964), pp. 187–267, at 223–24.

In addition to the codices reviewed above, we are aware of others that are now lost, the earliest of which seems to be
A (siglum assigned by Díaz y Díaz), a now lost Rheims manuscript, on which d'Achery based his first (1655) edition.

D'Achery left no definite information on this manuscript. We may conjecture that it was written in the eighth/ninth century, if we can trust his statement that it was copied *non procul ab auctoris aeuo*; it was at St Remy in Rheims in the middle of the seventeenth century, and probably contained other treatises besides DOC. We also know that the title probably read: *liber Isidori episcopi de ordine creaturarum ad Braulium episcopum Vrbis Romae*. Since d'Achery knew no other manuscript of the work, we can assume that he preserved the text of this manuscript accurately, apart from obvious editorial corrections.

Entries in Medieval Library Catalogues:

We have seen that DOC (probably in manuscript **B**) was almost certainly mentioned already in the ninth-century catalogue of the library at Fulda. Lorsch, another Anglo-Saxon foundation, also owned a copy of the text during the ninth century, in a manuscript containing both DOC and Adomnán's *De locis sanctis*

(BCLL 304).[9] It is likely that this same copy of the text is mentioned as the separate item *Isidori de origine creaturarum in quaternione* in the somewhat later Lorsch catalogue on fol. 1 of Vatican City, Biblioteca Apostolica Vaticana, MS Palat. lat. 57.[10] Confusion with Isidore's *De natura rerum* would explain the curious entry 74 in the sixteenth-century catalogue of Fulda, reading: *liber Isidori de ordine creaturarum id est rotarum*.[11] During the tenth century there was also a copy of DOC at Bobbio, a monastery with well-known Irish connections.[12] The Cistercian abbey of Pontigny owned a copy in the twelfth century,[13] and manuscripts of the text could be found later in a number of medieval libraries in Britain.[14]

---

9   Gustav Becker, *Catalogi bibliothecarum antiqui* (Bonn, 1885), p. 115, no. 553: *descriptio Arculphi de situ Hierusalem et locorum sanctorum in circuitu eius et Isidori de ordine creaturarum in uno codice.*
10 Becker, *Catalogi*, pp. 106–07, under the number 336. Bischoff emphasized that the listing by Becker is misleading in that it combines the entries in the catalogues in Vat. Pal. lat. 1877 with the derived data in Vat. Pal. lat. 57; see Bernhard Bischoff, *Die Abtei Lorsch im Spiegel ihrer Handschriften*, 2nd edn (Lorsch, 1989), pp. 18–28, at 27–28; Sigrid Krämer, *Handschriftenerbe des deutschen Mittelalters. Teil 2: Köln-Zyfflich*, Mittelalterliche Bibliothekskataloge Deutschlands und der Schweiz, Ergänzungsband 1 (Munich, 1989), pp. 499–501. In manuscript **M**, the title in rustic capitals in the upper margin of fol. 1 reads: *De origine* [sic] *creaturarum*, showing that DOC was also known under that name.
11 M. Manitius, *Handschriften antiker Autoren in mittelalterlichen Bibliothekskatalogen* (Leipzig, 1935), p. 341. Karl Christ, *Die Bibliothek des Klosters Fulda*, pp. 167–69, noted that in the group of manuscripts from the collection of Remigius Faesch now at the University Library in Basle, Isidore's *De natura rerum* appears more than once with the title *De ordine creaturarum id est rotarum* (see F III 15a and F III 15f).
12 Becker, *Catalogi*, p. 66, number 175: *librum de ordine creaturarum.* DOC might also be listed in the catalogue of Resbach (c. 1200) by the entry *unus sancti Hisidori de omnibus creaturis*; see Becker, *Catalogi*, p. 275, number 5.
13 See Item [77] in Monique Peyrafort-Huin, *La bibliothèque médiévale de l'abbaye de Pontigny (XII–XIXe siècles): Histoire, inventaires anciens, manuscrits*, Documents, Études et Répertoires IRHT (Paris, 2001), p. 260.
14 In addition to manuscripts of English origin mentioned above, the very useful *List of Identifications* provided by the *British Medieval Library Catalogues* project — https://www.history.ox.ac.uk/british-medieval-library-catalogues#tab-266421 — makes it clear that at least three Benedictine libraries in Britain had manuscripts of the work before the end of the thirteenth century and that many other monastic houses owned a copy later in the Middle Ages. See Introduction, n. 77, above.

Notes

Chapter 1

1.1. Depending on the context, *creaturae* has been translated variously as *the created, created natures, created world, creation, creations,* and, when possible, *creatures*. The title *Liber de ordine creaturarum* was difficult to translate since speaking of *the order of creatures* sounds odd in English, and I therefore opted for *creation*. However, *the order of creation* evokes the seven-day sequence of Genesis, which is not the topic of DOC. Translating *ordo* as *ordering* solved that problem and moreover it is a reminder of the temporal dimension assumed in the treatise.

1.2. In his sermon *De Fide*, Columbanus similarly asserted that Christians should believe in *Deum unum ac trinum, unum substantia, trinum subsistentia*; see *Instructio* 1.2 (SLH 2, 60). For other examples of the early use of *subsistentia*, see Smyth (2003–2004), 28.

1.2. These formulations overlap and systematize expressions occurring in Rufinus, *Expositio Symboli* 4 (see CCSL 20, 137–39); in Ps.-Rufinus, *Liber de Fide* 1 (PL 21:1125); in the *Quicunque uult* (see Pelikan and Hotchkiss (2003), 1:673–77); and in *De ecclesiasticis dogmatibus liber* 4 (PL 83:1229C).

1.2. Not surprisingly, the author nonetheless follows the convention of assigning the grammatical masculine gender to God, as is clear from the inflection of adjectives referring to the divinity.

1.2. The translation assumes the common Insular spelling *mot-* for *mut-* and its compounds.

1.2. St Augustine formulated his influential teaching on the nature of evil, or rather on its lack of independent existence, in the context of the anti-Manichean controversy. See for example, *De natura boni* 1–18, in particular statements such as: *prius quaerendum est quid sit malum; quod nihil aliud est quam corruptio uel modi uel speciei uel ordinis naturalis. Mala itaque natura dicitur quae corrupta est* (CSEL 25/2, 857); *Enchiridion* 3.11 (CCSL 46, 53): *Quid est autem aliud quod malum dicitur, nisi priuatio boni? ... non enim ulla substantia, sed carnalis substantiae uitium est uulnus aut morbus; De ciuitate Dei* 11.22 (CCSL 48, 341): *cum omnino natura nulla sit malum nomenque hoc non sit nisi priuationis boni.*

1.2. Once more, we see the influence of St Augustine on such formulations; e.g., *De Trinitate* 5.1 (CCSL 50, 207): *ut sic intellegamus deum si possumus, quantum possumus, sine qualitate bonum, sine quantitate magnum, sine indigentia creatorem, sine situ praesentem, sine habitu omnia continentem, sine loco ubique totum, sine tempore sempiternum, sine ulla sui mutatione mutabilia facientem nihilque patientem.*

1.3. As noted by Díaz y Díaz, Aeneas, bishop of Paris in the ninth century, quoted DOC 1.3–5 in *Liber aduersus Graecos* 94 (PL 121:721B–C), though it is not clear why Aeneas chose this formulation of the Creed which is in no way exceptional according to Kattenbusch (1894–1900), 2:854, n. 79 (see also 2:432, n. 105).

1.3. See Smyth (2003–2004), 24–28, disproving the claim that such statements are derived from the Creed of Toledo XI.

1.4. This is an early formulation of the doctrine at the root of the Filioque controversy. See the survey in Siecienski (2010), especially Chapter 3: The Latin West (pp. 51–72); see also Bischoff and Lapidge (1994), 143–46. This particular statement encapsulating the general opinion in the western Church at that time could have been drawn from the credal statement introducing the decrees of the Fourth Council of Toledo, a major council held in 633 at which Isidore of Seville presided over sixty-two bishops from Spain and from Gaul: *Spiritum uero sanctum, nec creatum, nec genitum, sed procedentem ex Patre et Filio profitemur*; see Mansi (1901–1927), 10:615.

1.6. For similar formulations, some from Ireland, see Smyth (2003–2004), 27–28.

Chapter 2

2.1. Much of the content of this chapter is derived from Gregory the Great's *Homily 34 on the Gospels* (CCSL 141, 299–319). For information on the various types of angels, see Davidson (1967), Guiley (2004) or Klein (2018).

2.2. It is difficult to translate *promeruit*, though the author might well have meant that Isaiah 'merited' to have his mouth cleansed. See the notes to Chapter 12, concerning the at least semi-Pelagian tendencies in Ireland at that time.

2.2. Ez. 10:14, speaking of the four wheels, says that each one had four faces: a cherubim, a man, a lion and an eagle. These came to be the standard symbolic representations of the four evangelists, as in Gregory, *Homily 4 on Ezekiel* (CCSL 142, 47–49). The wheels of the chariot therefore prefigure the four Gospels, creating a link (*coniungit*) between the two Testaments (*scripturae utriusque Testamenti*). Jerome, *Epistula 53 in Hiezechielem* had referred to the four evangelists as *quadriga domini et uerum cherubin, quod interpretatur 'scientiae multitudo'* (CSEL 54, 462). Isidore, *Quaestiones in Vetus Testamentum: In Exod.* 46.2 (PL 83, 312A), speaking of the two golden Cherubim by the propitiatory in the temple (Ex 37:7–9) rather than the vision of Ezechiel, mentions several possible interpretations, among them the 'spiritual' interpretation that they represent the two Testaments and face one another to show how well these agree with one another. The association of the evangelists with Ezekiel (mentioned by name) and the four animals (though with no mention of Cherubim or of wheels) can be found in the Irish *Excerpta in Euangeliae* 17 (PLS 4:1616).

2.2. This metaphor derives ultimately from the common practice in the classical world of gathering selections from literary texts. While the Greek word *anthologion* (a bunch of flowers) came into use only during the second century AD as a name for such collections, several Greek garlands (Gk. *stephanos*) had already been assembled. Ivan Illich pointed out that the Latin word '"*legere*" connotes "picking", "bundling", "harvesting", or "collecting"'; see Illich (1999), 58. Hence it is not surprising to find St Jerome, *Epist.* 65 (CCSL 54, 618), *Epist.* 122 (CCSL 56, 69), and *Epist.* 130 (CCSL 56, 188), referring several times to gathering flowers in the meadows of Scripture. Caesarius of Arles (*c.* 470–542), whose sermons seem to have been known in seventh-century Ireland, provided an interesting bovine analogy, encouraging priests to feed on the grasses and flowers in the meadows of Scripture to better produce milk for the faithful; see *Sermo* 4, 4 (CCSL 103, 24). References to the meadows of sacred literature were common in the Insular world of the early Middle Ages. Aldhelm (d. 709 or 710) refers several times to flowers in the meadows of the Scriptures, e.g. *De virginitate* (prose) 19 (CCSL 124A, 225); Lapidge and Herren (1979), 76: *purpureos pudicitiae flores ex sacrorum uoluminum prato decerpens* — 'plucking crimson flowers of purity from the meadow of holy books' or *De uirginitate* (verse), v. 2773–76 (MGH AA 15, 465); Lapidge and Rosier (1985), 164: *Sic lector libri solers et gnarus amator/Nititur electos scripturae carpere fructus/Ut pecus agrestes ex prato uellicat herbas/Nocturnis recubans quas rursus ruminat horis* — 'Thus the skilled reader and expert lover of the Book strives to pluck the chosen fruits of Scripture, as from the meadow a cow munches the wild grass, which she chews over and over again when she reclines during the night.' Bede, *In cantica canticorum* 1.2.5 (CCSL 119B, 215; Holder (2011), 70) refers the flowers and apples in the *Song of Songs* (Song 2:5) 'to the deeds or sayings that we gather as if from the meadows and groves of the writings of the fathers who preceded us' — *de scripturarum quasi pratis ac nemoribus*.

2.4. Gregory drew the meaning of the Hebrew names of the various angels from the work of Jerome, who provided these translations in his *Interpretation of Hebrew Names* (CCSL 72, 57–161) and his *Commentary on Daniel* (CCSL 75A), repeating this information in his other works. For seraphim, see Jerome, *Liber interpretationis hebraicorum nominum* at CCSL 72, 121–22: *seraphim ardentes uel incendentes*.

2.5. For cherubim see Jerome, *Liber interpretationis hebraicorum nominum* at CCSL 72, 74.20–21, and also CCSL 72, 80.16–17: *cherubin scientiae multitudo aut scientia et intellectus*.

2.6. The earliest extant manuscript **B** (Basle, Universitätsbibliothek, MS F.III.15b) reads *in reuelatione angelus Iohanni loquitur*. This corresponds to the account in Apoc 7:15, except that it was not an angel, but one of the ancients who was speaking to John. In view of the unusual version of the immediately following statement from Apoc 7:15, it is likely that the author of DOC is misremembering the biblical text.

2.6. The second part of this citation does not agree with Apoc 7:15 in the Vulgate, which reads *habitabit super illos* instead of *defendet eos*; an earlier version has *inhabitauit in eis*. See *Apocalypsis Johannis* at Gryson (2000), 353. In his *Homily 34 on the Gospels*, the source for this part of DOC, Gregory cites Ps. 9:5, but not Apoc 7:15; see *Homily 34.10* (CCSL 141, 308). I have not been able to trace this unusual version of Apoc 7:15.

2.13–14. The names of all three archangels are also discussed in Jerome, *Comment. in Danielem* 2.16 (CCSL 75A, 857–58).

2.15. It is difficult to translate *reficio* (restore, renew, rebuild). Like Gregory in *Homily 34 on the Gospels*, 14 (see CCSL 141, 313–14), the author is emphasizing that all members of the different orders of angels somehow all share their qualities.

2.15. In this case *motatione* should be taken at face value, because the reasoning seems to be that since God is everywhere, the angels have no need for any additional effort to see him at all times while going about their various duties. The early manuscript **B** reads *sine sui commotatione*, which could translate as 'without his moving about with them [the angels]'.

2.16. Dan 8:16 reads *Gabrihel fac intellegere istum uisionem* in the Vulgate. I have not been able to trace the reading in DOC, which may be the result of a scribal error, or perhaps of quoting the Bible from memory. This is not the example given by Gregory in his *Homily 34*, 13 (see CCSL 141, 312–13).

Chapter 3

3.1. Since *tuae propositionis continentia* could mean either 'the content of your plan' or 'the moderation of your plan', we cannot dismiss the possibility that the author is punning. He has, after all, been asked to describe everything that exists!

3.1. Note the very similar turn of phrase in Augustinus Hibernicus, *De mirabilibus* 1.6: *in his magistrorum quid intentio potuit excogitare indifferenti sermone proferamus* (PL 35:2156med).

3.1. In *De Genesi ad litteram* (see, e.g., 2.8.16), Augustine developed a theory which was to become something of a commonplace during the Middle Ages: When God said: 'Let there be light!' at the very beginning of the Genesis account of Creation, 'light' should not be understood in the usual sense, but was rather referring to the angels and possibly also to the souls of men, that is, to the spiritual creatures he created before the corporeal universe. See Smyth (1996), 40.

3.5. Augustinus Hibernicus, *De mirabilibus* 1.6–7 (PL 35:2157med.–2158in), elaborated on this explanation which seems to be implied in the biblical account of the deluge. See Smyth (1996), 97–103, especially 100–01.

3.5. As Díaz y Díaz indicated, the term *hemisp(h)erium* normally refers to each one of the two halves of a sphere surrounding the earth: one is above it, the other is below; see Isidore, *De natura rerum* 12.3 (Fontaine (1960), 219). However, comparison with Aug. Hib., *De mirabilibus* 1.7 (PL 35:2158) suggests that this term refers here rather to the various meteorological phenomena, perhaps specifically to the various precipitations; see Smyth (1996), 188–89, and the note to 6.2, below. According to the scheme in DOC, clouds and precipitations share the lower layer of the air with the flying birds; see below DOC 6.2 and Smyth (1996), 188–225.

3.5. Adopting the reading *et aurae* from the earliest manuscript **B** (fol. 3ᵛ) or from **U** (fol. 50ᵛ), instead of *ex aere* in the Díaz y Díaz (1972) edition (see **P** (fol. 3ʳ): *exere*). There clearly was some confusion: **M** (fol. 5ᵛ) reads *et aerae* and **H** (fol. 82ʳ) has *et terrae*.

3.5. As noted by Díaz y Díaz, this entire passage is derived from the exposition in Aug. Hib., *De mirabilibus* 1.6–7 (PL 35:2157–58). The last biblical citation — *et caeli dabunt imbrem et terra dabit fructum suum* — is taken verbatim from the Irish Augustine who uses the very same conflation of two phrases of which one evokes Jer 14:22 and the other Ps 66:7. In the Vulgate, Jer 14:22 reads *aut caeli possunt dare imbres*; the rest seems to be a cross between Ps 66:7: *terra dedit fructum suum* and Ps 84:13: *terra nostra dabit fructum suum*. Note: While the 1969 (2nd edn 1975) edition of the Vulgate reads *germen* instead of *fructum* in both cases, the 1906 edition and essentially all early versions of the text read *fructum* (see the *Vetus Latina* database).

3.5. DOC gives an unusual variation on a commonplace theme in hexaemeral literature; see Smyth (1996), 96–98.

Chapter 4

4.1. The disc theory is borrowed from Augustine, *Gen. litt.* 2.9 (CSEL 28/1, 45–46), while the notion of the cosmic egg of the orphic tradition was probably transmitted to Ireland through some grammatical work; see Smyth (1996), 106–09, 276; Carey (1985), 35.

4.2. The previous section is a summary of *De Genesi ad litteram* 2.9 (CSEL 28/1, 45–47), where the discussion of the shape of the material heaven begins: *quid enim ad me pertinet, utrum caelum sicut sphaera undique concludat terram in media mundi mole libratam, an eam ex una parte desuper uelut discus operiat?* and Augustine refuses to endorse any merely human theory on the shape of the world.

4.4. It could be misleading here to translate *inanis* as void or empty. The stars and the luminaries are located in the firmament (Gen 1:14; see DOC 4.7 and 5.2, below), so that it is anything but empty.

4.5. For a discussion of the theory of the four elements as understood by Augustinus Hibernicus and by the author of DOC, see Smyth (1996), 47–87. Since DOC affirms that water, air and fire are located above the earth, it makes no sense to say that the element earth cannot bear up the other elements, as would be implied by *sufferre* in the edition by Díaz y Díaz, who tends to follow **P**, which he believes to be the earliest extant manuscript. See Díaz y Díaz (1972), 108 and **P** (fol. 3ᵛ) (Paris, Bibliothèque Nationale, lat. 9561, fol. 3ᵛ; available on the Gallica site). The reading *sufferri*, however, occurs in other early manuscripts (**B** and **M**, for instance), as well as in Bede, *De natura rerum* 4.2–5 [CCSL 123A, 195], and is much preferable; see Smyth (2011), 146. The 1655 and 1665 (p. 276) and 1723 (p. 227) editions of DOC all read *sufferri*, but Arévalo opted for *sufferre*, as recorded in Díaz y Díaz (1972), 75.

4.5. Manuscripts **B** (fol. 4ʳ) and **M** (fol. 6ᵛ) read *ui* instead of *uim* in the Díaz y Díaz edition (see **P**, fol. 3ᵛ). The author of DOC is giving a summary description of the experiment consisting of immersing an upturned vessel into water, to which Augustine alludes in *De Genesi ad litteram* 2.2 (CSEL 28/1, 35).

4.6. See Augustine, *De Genesi ad litteram* 2.3 (CSEL 28/1, 36), Augustinus Hibernicus, *De mirabilibus* 2.31 (PL 35:2190) and Smyth (1996), 47–56, on the ancient theory of the proper places of the elements, which was generally adopted by early Christian scholars.

4.7. This is a drastic summary of Augustine, *De Genesi ad litteram* 2.3–5 (CSEL 28/1, 36–39).

4.8. See the Vulgate version of Job 37:18: *Tu forsitan cum eo fabricatus es caelos, qui solidissimi quasi aere fusi sunt*, which is cited in Gregory, *Moralia* 27.39.65 (CCSL 143B, 1383) and in Lathcen, *Egloga de moralibus Iob* 27.39.65 (CCSL 145, 300; see Introduction, note 101, at p. 30, above).

4.8. This is very similar to the attitude of Augustinus HIbernicus when confronted with plausible rational arguments which did not contradict Scripture; see e.g., *De mirabilibus* 6–7, where he will not side with any of several theories regarding the origin of the water that caused the Flood (PL 35:2156–59). For more information on the perception of the firmament in seventh-century Irish scholarly circles, see Smyth (1996), 104–24.

Chapter 5

5.1. See Augustine, *De Genesi ad litteram* 4.33–35 (CSEL 28/1, 131–36). The common belief in the instantaneity of all creation was derived from Sir 18:1: *qui uiuit in aeternum creauit omnia simul*. Augustine (followed by Augustinus Hibernicus, *De mirabilibus* 1.1 (PL 35: 2152)) reconciled that statement with the seven-day creation account by explaining that the latter was merely a device to better explain this complex event. See Smyth (1996), 39.

5.3. The question of the animation of the stars was by no means resolved among Christians in Late Antiquity. When Ambrose, *In Hexaemeron* 4.8.31 (CSEL 32/1, 137), spoke of the moon toiling and groaning and travailing, he seems to mean exactly what he is saying and he is not merely quoting Scripture. While Augustine, in *Ad Orosium contra Priscillianistas* 8 (PL 42:674), rejects Origen's view that the souls of sinners are punished by being imprisoned in the celestial bodies (see also *De civitate Dei* 11.23 (CCSL 48, 342)), in *Enchiridion* 15.58 (CCSL 46, 81), he admits that he does not know whether the sun, the moon and the stars belong in the company of angels, and he similarly cannot decide in *De Genesi ad litteram* 2.18 (CSEL 28/1, 62) whether the luminaries are merely corporeal, or whether they each have a spirit, and if so, whether this spirit is within them (as Plato said) or without (Aristotle's opinion). Jerome in *Commentarius in Ecclesiasten* (CCSL 72, 255), seems to be saying that the sun and the moon are indeed animate. Indeed, Jerome's *Commentarius in Esaiam* 9.30.26 (CCSL 73, 395) is an important source for this passage of DOC, and the phrase *Licet ea quidam organa lucis intellegentes, insensibilia esse contendant* is echoed in DOC 5.11: *Haec uero lucis organa nonnulli insensibiles creaturas opinantur*; see Smyth (1996), 173–75.

5.3. The Vulgate reads *ingemescit et parturit*, but DOC is citing from one of the early Latin versions with *dolet* or *condolet* instead of *parturit* (see the Vetus Latina database).

5.4. See Chapter 8.5–6, below, for an explanation of this restoration of man to a more perfect state than that which he held before sin.

5.5. In the Vulgate, Jerome mentions several 'new heavens' in his translation of Is 65:17, but in many of his other works he simply speaks of 'a new heaven' in this context. This is consistent with the **X** group identified by Gryson (1987–1997), 1593. Note, however, that DOC 11.4, below, gives the normal Vulgate reading for this passage.

5.6. Noting that Habakkuk used the past tense to refer to the future, as is usual for prophets, our author has inserted verbs in the future tense into a biblical citation different from the Vulgate text but close to Itala versions.

5.6. This understanding of the status of the sun and of the moon in the world to come was influential throughout the Middle Ages, mainly because of the false attribution of DOC to Isidore. Duly attributed to Isidore, the idea occurs, among others, in the *Glossa ordinaria* and in the *Sentences* of Peter Lombard. See pp. 26-28, above.

5.8. For the meaning of this passage, which refers to the observed changing relative positions of the sun and of the moon, see Smyth (1996), 157–59 and (2013), 81–82. Augustine, *De Genesi ad litteram* 2.15 (CSEL 28/1, 57), described this same phenomenon in terms of the time of day or night at which the moon first appears; see also *Enarr. in Ps. 10.3* (CCSL 38, 76).

5.8–9. For a discussion of these section, see Smyth (1996), 157–62. As noted there, 'the use of the term *rota* in the second alternative, apparently contrasting with *spera* in the first, is frankly puzzling' since Augustine believed the moon was a sphere in both alternatives … whether it was bright on one side and dark on the other, or whether it was illuminated by the sun. On the other hand, terms involving roundness could be ambiguous.

5.9. When the moon appears merely as a crescent.

5.9. As noted by Díaz y Díaz, this explanation depends ultimately on Augustine, *In ps.* 10.3 (CCSL 38, 75–76).

5.10. This is the period when the church in Ireland was striving towards uniformity in the method for calculating the date of Easter, so that one cannot assume that all his readers held the same views; see, e.g., Warntjes (2015). Moreover, just because readers of DOC might have expertise in these matters, it does not follow that all scholars did since it is reasonable to assume that, then as now, different scholars had different areas of competence. Indeed, for a discussion of what the author probably meant by 'the courses of the sun and of the moon', see Smyth (1996), 162–71, where the explanation of the 28-year 'solar cycle' on p. 163 is incorrect and should be replaced by 'the 28 years it takes to move the leap-year days through each of the days of the week', as formulated by Wallis (1999), 326.

5.11. See the note to DOC 5.3, above. The author of DOC assumes that the sun and the moon are animate because he understands Scripture (specifically his version of Rom 8:22) to affirm that they are suffering (*dolet, non sine suo dolore*) together with man, though through no fault of their own. They are also said to be ministering to the needs of man, again presumably a conscious activity.

5.11. The author is spelling out his guidelines for dealing with conflicting reasonable views. See, e.g., the last sentence of DOC 4.8, above.

Chapter 6

6.2. DOC 7.5 will explain that rain drops are formed when the wind forces minute drops of water to coalesce into drops too heavy to remain suspended in the air.

The characteristics of the layer of air described in 6.2 correspond to those itemized by Augustine in *De Genesi ad litteram* 3.10 (CSEL 28/1, 73–74).

6.2. The meaning of the phrase *diuersorum hemisperiorum perturbationes* is unclear. The qualifier *diuersorum* is inappropriate should the classical meaning of *hemisphaera* — half a sphere — be intended, unless the author were very sophisticated indeed and not only believed in a spherical universe but also realized that these hemispheres would be different for people in different locations. Díaz y Díaz assigns the plurality of 'hemispheres' in DOC to the various concentric layers which he envisages surrounding the Earth, but this is problematic since we are told elsewhere that 'disturbances' are only associated with one of those layers (Chapter 7) — quite apart from the fact that it is by no means obvious that the author believes in a spherical universe; see DOC 4.1–3, above, and Smyth (1996), 106–09. The use of the term in Aug. Hib., *De mirabilibus* 1.7 (PL 35:2158) and in the heading assigned to Chapter 7 of DOC already by the early eighth century (see p. 30, above), suggests that it refers to the various precipitations. Since the author of DOC has just finished itemizing various meteorological phenomena associated with the lower zone of air, his reference to the 'disturbances of the various hemispheres' could simply summarize the preceding list, or be meant to include any items he had not mentioned explicitly. See Smyth (1996), 188–89 and 272–74, and the note to DOC 3.5, above.

6.3. As noted by Díaz y Díaz, the lore of the calm atmosphere at the top of Mount Olympus has a long history in classical literature. The version given by DOC is close to that which occurs in Augustine, *De Genesi contra Manichaeos* 1.15.24 (PL 34:184). The abbreviated version in *De Genesi ad litteram* 3.2 (CSEL

28/1, 64–65) makes no reference to the messages in the sand or to the sponges. The detail that the sponges were soaked in vinegar seems to be a new embellishment, probably an echo of Mt 27:48, Mk 15:36 or Jn 19:29. See Smyth (1996), 183–84, and (2015), 404.

6.4. Díaz y Díaz suggested that *aut arbustorum* was a gloss for *olerum*.

6.4. Strictly speaking, their life 'cannot be set in motion.'

6.6. As Díaz y Díaz observed, this same conflation of 1 Jn 3:8 and Jn 8:44 occurs in Aug. Hib., *De mirabilibus* 1.2 (PL 35:2153 med).

6.6. Díaz y Díaz adopted the reading *fuisses* from the earliest manuscript **B**, in contrast to *fuisti* in **M**(fol. 10ʳ), in the Vulgate and other early versions (see the Vetus Latina database). **P**(fol. 5ʳ) reads *fuisse*.

6.8. Though the Vulgate has *uidebam*, one finds *uidi*, among others, in Aug. Hib, *De mirabilibus* 1.2 (PL 35:2153); in Columbanus, *Regula Monachorum* 5 (SLH 2, 128); in Jerome, *Comment. in Ez.* 9 (CCSL 75, 388); and in Ps.-Bede, *De sex dierum creatione* (PL 93:214B).

6.8. As Díaz y Díaz noted, this last explanation does not seem to belong here, or at least there is no obvious connection with the development of the theme of the devil. This statement seems to come from a commentary on the *Epistle of Paul to the Ephesians* and should be omitted.

6.9. See Smyth (1998), 508–09.

6.10. The *locus amoenus* theme had long since been applied to the Paradise where good Christians went to enjoy eternal happiness immediately after death. See Stuiber (1957), 193–96; Delumeau (1992), 41–57; Grimm (1977), 18–19 and 54. The author of DOC must have thought these trees and the spring were somehow spiritual; see Smyth (1998), 508–09.

6.11. The Díaz y Díaz edition reads *putationem* instead of *putationum*. This is probably simply a typographical error since early manuscripts read *putationum*: see **B** (fol. 7ʳ), **P** (fol. 5ᵛ), **M** (fol. 10ᵛ) and **U** (fol. 54ʳ), though **H** (fol. 86ʳ) reads *putationes* (as noted in Díaz y Díaz (1972), 126).

Chapter 7

7.4. *Limpaticum spiramentum*, 'aquatic breath'; see also Aug. Hib., *De mirabilibus* 1.7 (PL 35:2157): *lymphaticos imbres*, 'moist showers.' Both Irish authors seem unaware of the classical meanings of *lymphaticus*, which refer to a state of mind associated with having 'water' in the brain. This neologism is an adjective derived from the Latin noun *lympha*, 'water', following the pattern of formations ending in *-aticus* identified by Michael W. Herren in *The Hisperica Famina*: see Herren (1974), 205.

7.4. See DOC 6.1–2, above. For an account of the four-element theory as accepted in scholarly circles in seventh-century Ireland, see Smyth (1996), 47–87, summarized in (2013), 74–75.

7.4. For a discussion of the treatment of meteorological phenomena in this text, see Smyth (1996), 192–225.

7.4. The reading *ui*, replacing *uim*, from **P** (fol. 6ʳ), in the 1972 edition, makes better grammatical sense. It occurs it **B** (fol. 7ᵛ), **M** (fol. 11ᵛ), **H** (fol. 87ʳ) and associated manuscripts.

7.5–6. See Augustine, *Gen. litt.* 2.4 (CSEL 28/1:37), and *Gen. litt.* 3.10 (CSEL 28/1:73).

7.8. See the Introduction, above, at p. 12 and DOC 9.2–3, below.

7.8. As noted by Díaz y Díaz, this passage must have been confusing in the early manuscripts, and he adopted the reading *et uentus* from **P** (fol. 6ʳ), which he considered the earliest extant manuscript. However, **B** (fol. 8₅), **M** (fol. 12ʳ) and **H** (fol. 87ᵛ), for instance, read *uentos et*, which is consistent with the passage of Augustine's *De Genesi ad litteram* from which the language is borrowed: *aer ... qui commotus uentos et uehementiore concitatus etiam ignes ac tonitrua ... facit* (CSEL 28/1, 73). I therefore have modified the Latin text for this passage, where the 1972 edition, p. 132, reads: *Commotatione uero aeris et uentus uehementiore, ignes etiam ac tonitrua ... conditor facit*. Note that the word *concitatione*, which occurs even in manuscript **P**, is missing in the 1972 edition.

The neo-platonic tendencies of Augustine and many Christian writers required an intermediary between the divine and the material world, a role traditionally assigned to the angels. For a discussion of thunder and lightning in this text, see Smyth (1996), 217–22.

7.9. For a discussion of the following statements, which appear to be the result of personal observation rather than influenced by earlier secular works, see Smyth (1996), 219–22.

7.9. *Caumaliter*, adverb derived from Late Latin *cauma*, 'heat' (see Job 30:30: *prae caumate*).

7.10. Checking the readings in the early manuscripts shows that *prodit* is incorrect in the 1972 edition and should be replaced by *perdit*, which makes much better sense (see **B** (fol. 8ʳ), **P** (fol. 6ᵛ) and **M** (fol. 12ᵛ)).

Chapter 8

8.2. *daemones timent et contremescunt*. The Vulgate reads *credunt* instead of *timent*, and so do earlier versions of the text. However, a search in the Vetus Latina database revealed that an eleventh- or twelfth-century manuscript (Wolfenbüttel, Herzog August Bibliothek, 18.4 Aug 20) of *Liber promissionum et praedictorum Dei* by Quodvultdeus reads *tremunt et contremescunt* for Jas 2:19 (see CCSL 60, 156 and xi). This same reading must have been present in the manuscript of *De accedentibus ad gratiam sermones* by the same author which was transcribed in the 1852 edition by Angelo Mai (see CCSL 60, 450). It is likely that the author of DOC had access to a manuscript containing a reading of this type.

8.2. The Vulgate does not mention *ante tempus*, though it occurs in several manuscripts of the Itala type. The phrase occurs, for instance, in Isidore, *Sententiae* 1.14.11 (CCSL 111, 49), but it is unlikely that the first book of the *Sententiae* had reached Ireland when DOC was written; see Smyth (2016), 122–23.

8.4. The use of *mereri* may surprise since the orthodox doctrine spelled out by St Augustine affirms that salvation is always a free gift of God, and the Council of Orange in 529 should have settled the semi-Pelagian threat. Nonetheless, things are not so simple. Isidore, *Differentiae* 2.15.45 (CCSL 111A, 32) had said that the devil and other spirits *nec poscunt ueniam, nec merentur* because their heart is so hardened that they cannot repent. It is not clear, however, what is meant by *mereri*: in this passage of DOC it seems to have more to do with external circumstances making it impossible for the devil to be saved, rather than some internal merit on his part which would allow him to be saved.

8.5. See the previous note on *mereri*, and Isidore, *Differentiae* 2.15.44 (CCSL 111A, 31).

8.6. As noted by Díaz y Díaz, the entire passage DOC 8.4–6 elaborates on the lengthy discussion in Aug. Hib., *De mirabilibus* 1.2 (PL 35:2153–54) on the different nature of the sin of angels and of man. Some sentences, especially in DOC 8.5–6, are literal transcriptions from *De mirabilibus*; see the parallel passages presented in the Introduction, at pages 13-14, above. The underlying idea that man will be restored to a higher condition than that from which he fell may have been derived from passages such as Augustine, *Gen. litt.* 6.20 (CSEL 28/1, 194). Isidore, *Differentiae* 2.15.44 (CCSL 111A, 31), and *Sententiae* 1.10.11 (CCSL 111, 32), gave a simpler explanation for the difference in the possibility of salvation, namely that the devils are unable to repent. Damian Bracken examined the applications in early medieval Ireland of this awareness of the difference between the Fall of devils and of men; see Bracken (2002), 150–56 and also 169 for the relevant section in the *Reference Bible* (CLH 101).

8.7. This passage again borrows closely from Aug. Hib., *De mirabilibus* 1.2 (PL 35:2153).

8.7. The Vulgate reads *discedite a me maledicti in ignem aeternum*. Earlier Latin versions alternate between *discedite* and *ite* (Vetus Latina database). The rendition of Mt 25:41 in DOC 8.7 must be influenced by the variations on *mittere in gehennam ignis* in passages such as Mt 5:29, Mt 18:9, Mk 9:44, 46, and Lk 12:5.

8.8. Cited verbatim from Aug. Hib., *De mirabilibus* 1.2 (PL 35:2153 med).

8.8. Referring to the devil as 'the fugitive slave' — an idea derived from Jerome, *In Matthaeum* 1.8.29 (CCSL 77, 53) — was common practice in the early Irish Church. See note 49, pp. 21-22, in the introductory section, above.

8.10. I am assuming a misprint in the 1972 edition, though the early manuscript **P**, which Díaz y Díaz tends to follow and where word separation is not at all clear, probably reads *in uita* at fol. 7ʳ. On the other hand, **B** (fol. 9ʳ), **H** (fol. 89ʳ), **U** (fol. 56ʳ) and the 1723 edition clearly have *inuita*, which makes good sense in the context.

8.10. The idolatry of Achab is recounted in 1 Kgs 16:31–33; the persecutions to which he and his wife Jezabel submitted the prophets and Elias are mentioned in 1 Kgs 18:4, 1 Kgs 19.1–2, 1 Kgs 22: 26–27 (see also 2 Chr 18:25–26).

8.10. Díaz y Díaz noted that the explanation given by the author of DOC is closely reminiscent of the discussion on the same topic, introducing the same biblical passage, in Gregory, *Moralia* 2.20.38 (CCSL 143, 82–83).

8.16. Isidore, *Differentiae* 2.14.42 (CCSL 111A, 29–30), clearly influenced this passage. The DOC text has omitted some elements, including the reference to the rationality of the demons which is lacking in many manuscripts of Isidore's text — though it occurs, e.g., in the PL83 version (following Arevalo; see the apparatus at CCSL 111A, 29).

8.17. The contrast *impassibiliter/passibiliter* refers to the absolute constancy of the good angels, as opposed to the capacity for change (including suffering) of the demons.

Chapter 9

9.1. The Latin is ambiguous. The plural *terris* suggests that the author is simply thinking of water flowing through the regions of the Earth. On the other hand, since he will soon mention the effects of filtering salt water through the air and *per humum* (DOC 9.3, below), he might be referring to the classical notion that salt water filtered through the soil — in this case through various soils — rises as sweet water in the rivers and lakes. In the *Cosmography of Aethicus Ister*, Ps. Jerome (d. *c.* 740; see Herren (2011), lxxiii–lxxviii) gave this ancient theory an interesting twist, comparing the earth to a sponge which allows the water of the sea to travel through the holes in the sponge and thus be exposed to the moisture of the earth and become sweet; see Herren (2011), 214–15, § 112. For a discussion of the nature of water as described in *De mirabilibus* and DOC, see Smyth (1996), 227–36.

9.3. In view of their high salt content, the ashes of plants were often used to create a brine for the preservation of food, and sea-weed would have been especially suitable for that purpose. Soaking water in ashes had other purposes in early medieval Ireland, witness the episode in the *Lex diei* section of the *Hisperica famina* (A292–4 and, more explicitly, B87–90) when the tired students wish to wash their hair to 'sharpen their wits' and ask their hostess 'make the draughts of water salty by means of ashes' — was this done by stamping the feet (*tripudiauerit*)? See Herren (1974), 86–87, and Jenkinson (1908), 26, though Herren interprets this episode to mean that the hostess douses the fire with salt water. For more details, see the Appendix: *Sea-weed ashes and salt water* in Smyth (1996), 263–65.

9.3. As noted in the Introduction (pp. 12-13, above), this passage is clearly dependent on Aug. Hib., *De mirabilibus* 1.22 (PL 35: 2168).

9.4. This is the topos of the utility of the sea, a commonplace in classical and late classical treatises dealing with this subject matter.

9.4. As noted below, while this appeal to observation is generally appropriate in the passage that follows, it cannot apply in all cases. Díaz y Díaz drew attention to the fact that Pierre Duhem [in Duhem (1913–1959), 3:15–16] had shown that this whole theory depends on Aug. Hib., *De mirabilibus* 1.7 (PL 35:2159). See pp. 9-11 of the Introduction, above, and Smyth (1996), 241–62.

9.4. It should be noted that in DOC the term *ledo* does not refer to the tides themselves, but rather to the period during which less intense tides occur, that is, several days before and after the neap tide. Smyth (1996), 252, notes that (provided of course the sky is clear) a half moon is visible in the sky a little before the neap tides, which are described by experts as those tides for which the high-water mark reaches minimal level, so that there is strictly speaking only one neap tide for each quadrature.

9.4. In DOC, the term *malina* does not refer to the spring tides themselves, but rather to the period around the new moon and the full moon when the high-water mark is higher than the average (for a spring tide, the high-water mark is of course maximal). Bede will use the term with the same meaning, though in *De temporum ratione* 29 (CCSL 1977, 369) he points out that local circumstances affect the duration of the alternating *ledo* and *malina* stages; see Wallis (1999), 308–10. As noted in Smyth (1996), 254–55, the unusual terms *ledo* and *malina* occur not only in *De mirabilibus*, but also in the *Hisperica Famina*. The French equivalent, *les malines*, can be found with the meaning of a very high tide in the description of salt-pans along the Atlantic coast of France in the eighteenth-century *Encyclopédie* of Diderot. See also Smyth (2003–2004), 8, n. 43.

9.5. The *Commentary on Job* by Philippus Presbyter was known in Ireland by the mid-seventh century. Jane Stevenson (1999), 351–52, observed that it was used 'no less that seventeen times' in the alphabetic *Altus prosator*. Augustinus Hibernicus knew this commentary, as did Bede (see Smyth (1996), 16–17, 246–48).

9.5. Jacopo Bisagni correctly points out that DOC says nothing about the duration of the *ledo* period. He is preparing a study in which he shows how one later (possibly eighth-century) computist secured agreement between the pattern of the tides and the lunar month of 29 ½ days required by early medieval science at least from the early eighth century onwards (Private communication, June 2022). Augustinus Hibernicus had assigned 7 days to each of the two *malina* periods in each month, with the *ledones* occurring 'in the same way in the entervening periods', which would suggest a lunar month of 28 days; see Smyth (1996), 252. The author of DOC may have seen that this did not agree with the lunar month of the computists and attempted to rectify the situation by increasing the duration of the *malina* period and leaving the duration of the *ledo* period unspecified, or perhaps tacitly retaining the seven-day duration of the *ledo* period as indicated by Augustinus Hibernicus.

At another level, Díaz y Díaz ((1972), 149–50, n. 6) already noted that 'observation' would contradict the statement that the new moon is born in the middle of the *malina* period, since there is a time lag between the cosmic phenomenon and its repercussion on the tides. This 'age of the tide' varies by location on the globe, and is generally one or two days (Garrett and Munk (1971); Cartwright (1999), 8, 194, 274).

9.6. It remains puzzling what the author of DOC meant when he stated that the *malina* is *rursus tenebrosa* after the full moon. We recall that for Augustinus Hibernicus (*De mirabilibus* 1.7; PL 35.2159) and DOC 9.4–6, *malina* refers to the periods of some seven days straddling the new moon and straddling the full moon when the tides are more intense than average, although the Irish authors only talk of the duration of each tide: the flow of a *malina* tide lasts 5 hours and the ebb lasts 7 hours (Smyth (1996), 252–58). Since the moon is still almost full for several days after full moon, it is difficult to associate the phrase *rursus tenebrosa* with the decreasing brightness of the moon just past the full-moon stage (see Díaz y Díaz (1972), 151, n. 1, referring to DOC 5.8 though the author of DOC does not in any way commit to either of the possible explanations given there for the changing phases of the moon). The author of DOC, moreover, ascribes the condition of *tenebrosa* to the malina and not to the moon, and there is nothing in the early manuscripts to suggest the text is corrupt. It is not clear from DOC what a 'dark' *malina* tide might be, and why the tide occurring after the full moon — as well the tides in the next few days — should be '*rursus tenebrosa* — dark again' (see Bisagni (2017), 32–33 and (2019), 262). In earlier work, I connected *tenebrosa* with the assumption in the *Hisperica Famina* that the *malina* tides are accompanied by rough weather (Smyth (1996), 255 and (2011), 189, n. 117), thereby suggesting that in DOC 9.6, *tenebrosa* might mean 'stormy' or 'destructive'. On checking for possible meanings of *tenebrosus* in the Insular world at that time, the Brepols Cross-Database reveals that Bede used the term in his commentaries on Matthew and on Mark, reflecting on Jesus sleeping in the boat crossing the Sea of Galilee during a storm. Bede equates the stormy sea with the *tenebrosus amarusque praesentis saeculis aestus*, which I would translate in that context as 'the stormy and bitter swell of this present life.' This usage of *tenebrosus* by Bede would support the above association of *malina* tides with stormy weather. It should be noted, however, that the *Hisperica Famina* assumption is not justified, since rough weather is not necessarily associated with tides around either the full moon or the new moon.

I have noted elsewhere that both Augustinus Hibernicus and the author of DOC claim that 'observation' supports what are, in fact, incorrect statements about the tides (e.g., Smyth (1996), 256, (2011), 188–89, and also the last comment in note 9.5, above, as well as note 9.7, below). In earlier work, I was intent on stressing that in these Hiberno-Latin texts, *malina* tides and *ledo* tides are not just the spring tides (maximal intensity) and the neap tides (minimum intensity), but that the terms were intended to refer to tides of greater and lesser magnitude, respectively, occurring over several days. I did not then point out the incongruity of the posited jump occurring four times in every lunar month: suddenly, presumably from one tide to the next, the duration of ebb and flow would have changed by a full hour! The overall impression created by these seventh-century sources is that some vague and incorrect lore about the tides was circulating in Irish scholarly circles, as scholars strove to describe a phenomenon which they did not comprehend. And yet, it should be stressed that both the authors of *De mirabilibus* and of DOC have a good basic grasp of the relationship between the tides and the phases of the moon — knowledge which was acquired from observation, independently of earlier scientific work (Smyth (1996), 260–62). Their mistake was to impose order, symmetry and precision on a much more fluid phenomenon. Given the presence of tidal mills in Ireland at that time (Smyth (2019), 75–76), there must have been people familiar with the actual behaviour of tides in their own locality, not to mention how tides are affected by factors such as the wind. The authors of *De mirabilibus* and of DOC may have consulted these experts, but they did not fully understand them.

Recent work on the influence of Irish scholarship in early medieval Brittany further complicates matters. Jacopo Bisagni ((2017), 32–33) spotted *the only other known use* of the phrase *malina tenebrosa* on folio 12^r of the tenth-century Breton manuscript Angers, Bibliothèque municipale, 476 (which can be consulted at https://bvmm.irht.cnrs.fr). The phrase occurs in a discussion of the tides following the section on the divisions of time common in computistical material. It becomes clear on folio 12^v that the author distinguished between the *malina tenebrosa* which occurs around the new moon and the *malina lucida* around the full moon — a natural distinction given the difference in brightness between nights around new-moon and nights around full-moon. The question now becomes: is this the work of an enlightened computist trying to make sense of the DOC phrase *malina tenebrosa* (see Bisagni (2017), 33), or is the text repeating earlier Irish terminology distinguishing between the two *malina* periods, terminology which the author of DOC had misused?

9.6. It appears that for the author of DOC, attention to the phases of the moon was the only way of forecasting the changing pattern of the tides. In Smyth (1996), 252–55, I suggested that practical realities account for such emphasis on a convenient way to determine when greater or lesser tides are about to occur. In that 1996 work I conjectured that the maintenance of salt pans required such advance notice. That may well be so, though the experts say that salt is not known to have been produced in that way in Ireland at that time; see Smyth (2019), 87, n. 92. A much simpler explanation for the need to predict the pattern of tides is provided by the archaeological discovery at the end of the twentieth century of seventh-century tidal mills along the Irish coast; see Smyth (2019), 87 and 75–76. It is curious, though, that the author of DOC never mentions that the main characteristic of *malina* tides and *ledo* tides is that they involve higher and lower high-tide levels, respectively. Should we understand that the author of DOC took it for granted that his readers knew this? Perhaps, but this is not obvious, since 'observation' cannot have been at the root of his statement that the *malina* tides at both the solstice and the equinox are 'stronger' than usual (see note 9.7, below).

9.6. Common years and embolismic years: these technical terms from the science of computus, refer, respectively, to a lunar year of twelve lunar months and to a lunar year of thirteen lunar months, where the lunar months oscillate between 29 and 30 days in a well-defined pattern.

9.7. Mistake of the Irish Augustine copied in DOC; see p. 11, above, Duhem (1913–1959), 3:16, Smyth (1996), 260, Wallis (1999), 310. and Cartwright (1999), 8–9. In regions experiencing semidiurnal tides, spring tides around the equinoxes are greater than spring tides around the solstices; see, e.g., Cartwright (1999), 8.

9.7. The rising tide was called *adsissa* in medieval Ireland. See DMLCS 1:17.

9.7. DOC does not subscribe to the possibility that rising tides are due to the water in the sea somehow increasing in volume, an option mentioned by Augustinus Hibernicus. He has a more 'mechanical' view of tides, which implies that the sea is swinging to and fro — whether from the abyss or from distant shores is not clear. See Smyth (1996), 246–50 and (2013), 84–86.

9.7. See Aug. Hib., *De mirabilibus* 1.7 (PL 35:2159 med & fin), in particular: At *uero rationabilis huius perseuerantiae inundatio, quo recedit, mentibus nostris occultata est* and *Maris inundantis tumores considerare permittimur, sed recedentis illius intelligentia priuamur.*

9.9. Belief that birds and fishes were created from water was a commonplace of early Christian exegesis (see Gen 1:20). It was also common to explain the significance of any number mentioned in the Bible. This particular interpretation of Jn 21:11 is clearly derived from Jerome who, when talking about the miraculous catch by the apostles claims that 'the philosophers who speak of the nature of things' affirm that there are 153 species of fishes (Jerome, *Comment. in Hiezechielem* 14.47.6–12 (CCSL 75, 717)). Despite claims to the contrary in the secondary literature, there is no mention of 153 types of fishes or of birds in *De mirabilibus*. This topic does, however, occur in at least one text which has been associated with Ireland and its culture, namely, the *Reference Bible* (CLH 101). The long version of the section on the Pentateuch asserts that there are 153 *reptilium genera in aquis*, and the short version attributes this information to Plinius secundus; see *Pauca problesmata de enigmatibus ex tomis canonicis. Praefatio. De Pentateucho Moysi* (CCCM 173, 55 and also 234). The exegesis of the 153 fishes in the *Commentary on John* (see CCSL 108C, 130) is of a different type, stressing the religious symbolism associated with the number 153. See Bischoff (1954), 209, 229 and 265 or (1966–1981), 1:220, 235, 262–63.

9.10. This lengthy discussion on the origin of the various types of birds is unexpected in this treatise; for a possible explanation, see Smyth (2014B), 72–73 and (1995), 36–40. An accurate summary of this passage is included in the *Commentary on Genesis* recorded in the upper script of the palimpsest Sankt Gallen, Stiftsbibliothek 908 (Northern Italy, specifically the area of Milan, or possibly Switzerland, saec. VIII/IX) listed as no. 4 in Bischoff's *Wendepunkte* survey (1954 and 1966–1981); see also CLH 40 and BCLL 1260 (among the *dubia*). The summary is introduced by *Isidorus interrogat*, so that is likely that the author of the Sankt Gallen commentary had access to a text of DOC attributing the treatise to Isidore.

9.11. The author of the *Commentary on Genesis* in the upper script of the palimpsest Sankt Gallen, Stiftsbibliothek 908 (see previous note) apparently felt the need to explain *constillatio arborum* in DOC 9.11, by affirming that 'in the beginning, when they were newly created, stones, trees, plants and all things were oozing water' — *in ipso principio novellae creaturae sudabantur petrae, arbores, erbae, omnes res* (see pp. 20–21 of the manuscript, available electronically on the *e-Codices* site).

The word *constillatio* is problematic; see TLL and DMLCS 1:184. It is derived from *stilla* (drop) and is probably equivalent to *stillatio* (falling down in drops, dripping), though it could also refer to drops pooling together. In the Vulgate, *stilla* is used for drops of rain or dew (Job 36:27; Job 38:28; Jer. 3:3). Michael Herren (private communication, 5 March 2021) has drawn my attention to an entry for the letter G in the Epinal-Erfurt Glossary: *geneissis: constillatio* (CGL 5: 363,53; available since March 2021 on the *Epinal-Erfurt Glossary Project* site). The archetype of that glossary can be set in the 680s, possibly the late 670s, probably in Canterbury. This use of *constillatio* to explain another word suggests it was a familiar term in Insular circles at that time. Moreover, it was somehow associated with Creation, as in the Sankt Gallen commentary.

It is very difficult to know what *constillatio arborum* means in DOC. Since the author is talking about the origin of birds, he may well be referring to the water 'oozing out' of the newly created trees of Sankt Gallen 908. More prosaically, he could be thinking of sap oozing out when a tree is cut, or dripping from the bark (as resin for some trees, or due to bacterial wetwood, a disease affecting many varieties). Or is it 'honeydew' (produced by insects gorging on the sap) deposited on the leaves in small drops that eventually gather into bigger sticky drops falling to the ground? Or is the author simply thinking of raindrops gathering in hollows (whether on the bark or the leaves) and showering to the ground at a gust of the wind? Or is it yet something else?

Chapter 10

10.1. This is almost certainly more than a figure of speech since Augustinus Hibernicus, *De mirabilibus* 1.29 (PL 35:2171) held that the Earth was an animate being, with a 'life' — however insensible — which allowed it to open its mouth and swallow up the opponents of Moses (Num. 16:32): *uitam enim insensibilem terra habere indubitanter dignoscitur*. The author of DOC goes a step further in assuming that the Earth is sensible and suffering like the sun and the moon; see Smyth (1996), 292.

10.1. As noted by Díaz y Díaz, *beneuolentium* evokes the phrase *homines bonae uoluntatis* (Lk 2:14).

10.2. Throughout this text the meaning of words associated with *mereor* is tricky. See the notes to DOC 2.2, 8.4, 8.6, above, and to DOC 12.1, 12.2, below.

10.2. In this section, there is conscious play on terms involving many aspects of primacy; see Smyth (1996), 268–70.

10.3. Given the natural downward flow of water, the presence of this spring 'irrigating the entire surface of the earth' would argue for Grimm's claim that the garden of Paradise was believed to be located on a high mountain; see Grimm (1977), 83–84. It is not at all clear, however, that this was the assumption in DOC, where the author seems to be speaking metaphorically about the location of the garden of Paradise; see Smyth (1998), 509–13.

10.6. As noted by Díaz y Díaz, the sequence *historia, tropologia, allegoria* occurs in Isidore, *Sententiae* 1.18.12 (CCSL 111, 64). While Aldhelm talks about four ways of interpreting Scripture, they actually amount to the three ways mentioned in DOC; see Herren (2005), 71–73. In his commentary on the Book of Proverbs, Bede refers to the threefold way of interpreting Scripture and uses *tripertitus* in the same way as DOC: *non incongrue tripertitus intellectus sacrae scripturae potest intellegi* (PL 91:1053B).

10.6. It is tempting to translate *sequens Adam* as 'the second Adam' since reference to *secundus Adam* was not unusual in Christian texts. However, it is my understanding that *sequens* with the meaning 'second' might connote inferiority and would therefore be an unlikely option.

10.8. That is, in Paradise.

10.8. Note the play on words between *subiectio* and *subiaceret*, with a recurrence of the theme of primacy.

10.8. For the common Christian theme that initial creation was perfectly good, which could be interpreted to mean that thorns, for example, did not hurt before the Fall, see Smyth (1996), 38, note 6. This is different, however, as the author of DOC apparently assumes that Paradise was a special place within the world which was otherwise created from the beginning as it is now. He had stated in DOC 1.2 that 'nothing has been created evil by nature' and so he must have believed that the natural properties of thorns and fierce lions, for instance, were fundamentally good. Augustine certainly held that view. See Smyth (1998), 507; Augustine, *Gen. litt.* 3.15–18 (CCSL 28/1, 80–84).

10.9. Thomas O'Loughlin reminds me that the tradition of interpreting Genesis — of which DOC is a part — is broader than our extant *corpus* of sources. This tradition, utilising Rom 5:12 with its statement that human death is an outcome of Adam's sin, tended to locate the origin and cause for all human ills in Adam's action (private communication, September 2022). Augustine elaborated the doctrine that when Adam was first created his body had both the potential to be immortal and to die: *posse mori* and *posse non mori*; see *Gen. litt.* 6.25 (CCSL 28/1, 197). Citing Rom 8:10–11, he affirmed that Adam would not have died if he had not sinned; see *Gen. litt.* 6.22 (CCSL 28/1, 195). See Bracken (1995),

170–78, for an overview of the influences on early Christian Irish scholars of Augustine's ideas on immortality.

10.10. While Díaz y Díaz adopted the reading *fastiditate* 'with much hesitation', the author of DOC might simply be saying that Adam was full of energy and would want to explore the world, that he might indeed have been bored if he remained idle, and boredom was incompatible with his original state of felicity. Moreover, it should be remembered that God had assigned non-trivial tasks to Adam: he must cultivate and guard Paradise (Gen 2:15) — St Augustine elaborated on this in *Gen. litt.* 8.8–9 (CSEL 28/1, 242–44) — as well as rule over the entire world (Gen 1:28).

10.12. Curiously, the manuscripts tend to read *uoluntatis* instead of the usual *uoluptatis*.

E.g., **B** (fol. 13^v), **P** (fol. 10^r), **M** (fol. 19^v).

10.13. The author of DOC is clearly suggesting that Adam and Eve ate from the fruit of a fig-tree. The same identification, with the reference to Jesus cursing the fig-tree, can be found in the *First Commentary on the Pentateuch* from the Canterbury school; see PenI 36, in Bischoff and Lapidge (1994), 310.

10.16. Such speculation on the condition of man doomed to live eternally on earth, should Adam and his descendants somehow succeed in removing the punishment of death though not all other aspects of the divine punishment, conjures up scenes from *Gulliver's Travels*, specifically the visit to the island of Luggnagg. DOC 12.2, below, lists the three wounds inflicted upon man after the original sin: suffering, old age and death.

10.16. *Culpa* suggests not only the offence itself, but the condition, the responsibility, of the person who has offended.

10.16. As noted in the Introduction (see p. 24, above), emphasis on 'the call' (*uocatio*) of the elect at the Last Judgement is a recurring theme in early Irish Christianity.

Chapter 11

11.2. As noted by Díaz y Díaz, this explanation of the names of the cardinal directions occurs in other early Hiberno-Latin texts such as in Ps.-Jerome, *Expositio quattuor euangeliorum* (see PL 30:533B) and the *Commentary on Genesis* in Sankt Gallen, Stiftsbibliothek 908 (see p. 22 of that manuscript on e-CODICES site) and also in the *Liber de numeris* (see McNally (1957), 72–73). In DOC, as in its likely source, Augustine, *In Iohannis euangelium tractatus* 10.12 (CCSL 36, 108), the Greek names refer to the four parts of the inhabited world corresponding to the four cardinal directions.

11.2. The Latin sequence in DOC does not correspond to the Greek order which is 'east, west, north, south', the normal Latin translation being *Oriens, Occidens, Aquilo, Meridies* as in Augustine's *Commentary on St John* cited above. See Smyth (1996), 281–83, where it is noted that the arrangement OAAO of the initial letters of the Latin list in DOC (*Oriens, Aquilo, Auster, Occidens*) suggests a mnemonic device which may correspond to the usual order when naming the cardinal directions in early Ireland; see Hamp (1974), 253.

11.3. It was commonly assumed in the early Middle Ages that Creation took place at the vernal equinox. The *Prologue to the Easter Cycle* of Victorius of Aquitaine was one likely route for transmission of this belief to Ireland; see MGH,AA 9:683; PLS 3:385. For evidence of this belief in seventh-century Ireland, see Smyth (2014A), 121. In particular, *Pauca de Genesi* (CHL 44) asserts that Easter should not be celebrated *ante aequinoctium, id est ante principium mundi* (Clm 17739, fol. 9^v), 'before the equinox, that is, before the beginning of the world.' See Ó Cróinín (2001), 260–61.

11.3. A similar version occurs in Isidore, *Etym.* 5.35.3–6.

11.4. This is the Vulgate reading, but like Jerome, the author of DOC often simply speaks of 'a new heaven'; see DOC 5.5, above, with the relevant note, and also DOC 11.6, below.

11.5. See **P** (fol. 10^v). However, the various readings in the early extant manuscripts suggest utter confusion with this passage. Both d'Achery's editions from the lost Rheims manuscript **A** reads *corruptilibus* instead of *immortalibus* (see p. 296; PL 83:0943B). **K** (saec. IX) and **U** (saec. X) have *mutabilibus*.

11.7. Díaz y Díaz aptly referred to this passage as a 'biblical mosaic.'

Chapter 12

12.1. Pelagius devoted the beginning quarter of his *Letter to Demetrias* to his understanding of *bonum naturale*, that natural goodness which is part of man's created nature and which the patriarchs of the Old Testament were able to maintain; see *To Demetrias* 2.1–8, in Rees (1991), 36–45. Commenting on Rom 2:14: *cum enim gentes quae legem non habent naturaliter quae legis sunt faciunt*, Pelagius offers the following interpretation: 'Either: He means those who were by nature righteous in the period before the law. Or: Those who even now do some good'; see de Bruyn (1993), 73. To Pelagius, this meant that man has a natural ability to be righteous, simply because he was created good, so that even pagans have *naturale bonum*. After the Fall, man got into the habit of sinning, which made it harder and harder to be righteous. Pelagius developed this idea in *To Demetrias* 8.3 (see Rees (1991), 44): 'Nor is there any reason why it is made so difficult for us to do good other than that long habit of doing wrong which has infected us from childhood ... so that it seems somehow to have acquired the force of nature.' As noted by Kelly ((1978), 108), Pelagius's *Commentary to the Pauline Epistles* was cited by seventh-century Irish exegetes such as the Anonymous commentator on the Catholic Epistles and Ps. Hilary. The *Letter to Demetrias*, on the other hand, was certainly available to Aldhelm and to Bede, and may well have been available in seventh-century Ireland; see Herren and Brown (2002), 97–98. It seems to me that DOC can be added to the dossier of evidence gathered by Herren and Brown (pp. 87–97) for the presence of Pelagian ideas in seventh-century Ireland.

12.2. The mention of sin would have evoked the well-known triad of 'thought, word and deed' which frequently occurs in this context in the Christian tradition, more especially in the Celtic world; see Sims-Williams (1978). On the other hand, the text which Michael Gorman defines as the core text (α) of the seventh-century *Commentary on the Pentateuch* once attributed to Bede but which he assigns to Visigothic Spain, contains an account of original sin fitting the threefold assumption in DOC: *Tribus autem modis peccatum admittitur: delectatione, suggestione, consensu. Per serpentem, suggestionem accipimus; per mulierem, animalem corporis sensum; per uirum, rationem. Serpens suadet, delectatio obtemperat, ratio consentit*; see Gorman (1996b), 297. This is clearly modelled on St Augustine's *De sermone domini in monte* 1.12.34 (CCSL 35, 37). See also Bracken (2002), 158–60.

12.2. This must have been a standard triad in seventh-century Ireland, as the author of DOC cites it four times, almost as a refrain: DOC 10.10, 10.16, 12.2 and 12.3.

12.2 This emphasis on the need for the gift of divine grace, combined with the concept of 'natural goodness', is the position of those fifth- and sixth-century Christians who protested both Pelagius's insistence that salvation was possible through free will alone and St Augustine's perceived pre-destinarianism. They held that turning towards God is an act of free will, but after baptism divine grace intervenes, making it possible to lead a good life. This view, later named 'semi-Pelagianism', was condemned in 529 by the group of bishops attending what is known as the Council of Orange: 'Canon 5: If anyone says that not only the increase of faith but also its beginning and the very desire for faith, by which we believe in him who justifies the ungodly and come to the regeneration of holy baptism — if anyone says that this belongs to us by nature and not by a gift of grace ... it is proof that he is opposed to the teaching of the apostles' (Pelikan and Hotchkiss (2003), 1:693). Not that this settled the question: a young Thomas Aquinas, for instance, was 'willing to allow the initiation into the state of grace to be determined by human action: One will receive habitual justifying grace after preparing oneself through naturally good action for this grace'; see Wawrykow (1995), 270.

12.2. As Díaz y Díaz noted, *propter iniquam mammonam* alludes to the parable of the crafty steward (Lk 16:11). The 'wicked mammon' thus represents worldly goods, which may be obtained dishonestly. The author of DOC is saying that unlike material goods, spiritual goods are not transmissible to the next generation, in spite of their greater value.

12.3. See Isidore, *Differentiae* 2.14.43 (CCSL 111A, 30–31): *de praeteritis nudi, de praesentibus exigui, de futuris incerti*.

12.4. This is not necessarily an endorsement of Augustine's doctrine of the transmission of original sin. The author could simply be saying that all men are suffering the consequences of the first sin.

12.4. There is strong evidence from early medieval Ireland for belief in the salvation of virtuous pagans following 'the law of nature' before 'the law of Scripture' became known to them. They were put on equal footing with the patriarchs of the Old Testament, who were after all in a similar position and will nonetheless be in 'the Kingdom of God' (e.g., Lk 13:28). The pivotal study on the concept of natural law in early medieval Ireland remains John Carey (1990), where it is made clear that *recht aicnid*, 'the law of nature', referred to the law of the patriarchs, that is, to the pre-Mosaic law. See also Carey (1994), and (2000), 143. The two episodes in late-seventh-century hagiographical texts involving pagans who were baptized after having 'preserved natural goodness throughout [their] whole life' can be interpreted as evidence for the perceived need to spread the doctrine that baptism is essential for salvation, presumably to counter the opposite view; see Herren and Brown (2002), 95.

Chapter 13

13.1. The notion of the fourfold division of mankind described in Chapters 13 and 14 is already present in Gregory, *Moralia* 26.27.50–51 (CCSL 143B, 1304–6), and was common in the British Isles during the early Middle Ages. See Biggs (1989/90) and Smyth (2003).

13.2. As noted above at DOC 12.2, the concept of 'meriting' the gift of faith is an essential element for a 'semi-Pelagian' position on the relationship between grace and free will.

13.4. References to St John as the Apostle who sat close to Christ at the Last Supper are common in texts associated with Ireland. The apostle was often called *Eoin Bruinne* in Irish, that is, 'John of the Breast.' See p. 21, above; also Herbert & McNamara (1989), 180–81 and Smyth (2003–2004), 36–37.

13.5. The allusion is to Mt 25:42–45, where *in metallis* does not occur in any version of which I am aware, nor indeed is there mention of 'being shackled', in prison or elsewhere. While we cannot eliminate the possibility that some manuscript had found its way to Ireland with an unusual reading of this section of Matthew's Gospel, I have not been able to trace a scriptural source for the additional mention of prisoners *in metallis*. It is clear from a search in the Brepols *Cross Database Searchtool*, that several Christian authors — Cyprian, Athanasius, Jerome and Augustine, among others — had listed among the many trials of martyrs, not only being sent to *carceres*, but also to *metalla*. There is no evidence, however, that any of the particular works raised by the database search had found their way to Ireland by the mid-seventh century. On the other hand, Gregory did mention *damnatis in metallo* in the *Moralia*, a work which was known in Ireland at that time; see *Moralia* 2.15.25 (CCSL 143, 75).

There is no doubt that the word *carcer* was understood to mean at place of long-term — if not permanent — confinement and punishment, since it was used by both the Irish Augustine and the author of DOC to refer to the eternal fire to which the devil is condemned; see DOC 8, 8. Is it possible, however, that the word *carcer* did not correspond to a physical structure in the seventh-century Irish context? Was *alligatis in metallis* added to provide a more relevant equivalent, meant to convey the general meaning of a person enduring hardship and loss of freedom? The word *metallum* can be translated either as 'mine' or 'quarry', and perhaps both meanings are intended here. We know from the early medieval laws — already beginning to be recorded in the seventh century — that there were slaves of both sexes in Ireland. The hard labour they were expected to do might include mining for ore — likely a surface occupation at that time, since it appears to have mostly involved digging for layers of iron ore in bogs; see Dolan (2012). There would also have been digging gravel pits to 'metal' roads (Smyth (2019), 90–91), not to mention the quarrying and carving of millstones. I have therefore opted for the more general translation 'shackled in forced labour' — without knowing exactly how such slaves would have been shackled.

13.6. This same idea that good deeds are essential for salvation occurs in the seventh-century Hiberno-Latin moral treatise *De XII abusiuis saeculi* and in the alphabetical hymn *Apparebit repentina* which I believe was composed in Ireland at that time; see Smyth (2003), 98–101.

13.8. The PL edition of Philippus Presbyter, *Commentary on Job* 26.5 (*ecce gigantes gemunt sub aquis*) contains the statement *in inferioribus terrae, ubi inferi esse perhibentur, unde et ipsi inferi nominati sunt*, with no mention of *in profundo aquarum*; see PL 26:688B. In the 1527 Sichardus edition of the *Commentary on Job*, however, the section on the *gigantes* contains an additional phrase which corresponds to the DOC location of hell, though oddly in reverse order: '*Sicut ergo inferi in profundo terrarum sunt, ita terrae in profundo aquarum*'; see p. 102 of the Sichardus edition. This location of hell is consistent with the author's layered view of the universe.

13.8. For another understanding of Apoc 5:3 in seventh-century Ireland, see Smyth (1998), 521–22.

13.9. St Augustine had wrestled with the problem the nature of the fire of hell in *Gen. litt.* 12.32 (CSEL 28/1, 426–27) and in *Civ. Dei* 21.2–10 (CCSL 48, 759–76). See also Gregory, *Moralia in Iob* 15.29.35 (CCSL 143A, 769–70).

13.10. Jerome, *Comment. in Esaiam* 8.24 (CCSL 73, 323) comments on the statement *et post multos dies uisitabuntur* and seizes the opportunity to swipe at those who believe that this means that the devils will eventually be given the chance to repent. In early medieval Ireland, the phrase must have evoked apocryphal accounts of those visits to hell by saintly people which resulted in temporary reprieves for the damned. The *Visio sancti Pauli* was almost certainly known in Ireland during the first half of the seventh century; see Smyth (2003), 113. In that account of St Paul's visit to heaven and to hell, he is so distressed at the suffering of the damned that, together with St Michael, he successfully pleads with Christ to have mercy on them, and they are granted a reprieve from their suffering every Sunday forever. For evidence that the *Visio* was well known in Anglo-Saxon England by 675, see diPaolo Healey, 'Apocalypse of Paul', in Biggs

(2007), 67–70, at 68. Another similar account may have been provided by the apocryphal traditions associated with the death of the Virgin Mary: after her death, she was shown the torments of hell and won the damned a three-hour reprieve — three hours every Sunday in some versions. A version of *De assumptione Sancte Marie* edited from a thirteenth century manuscript can be found in Wenger (1955), 258–59; see Clayton, 'Apocalypse of the Virgin', in Biggs (2007), 66–67; see also Herbert and McNamara (1989), and McNamara (1975).

Chapter 14

14.2. The call of the elect which will take place after the Last Judgement. The author of DOC is not talking here about a promise of something to be hoped for, but about an immediate reality, already in this life.

14.6. The concept of Purgatory had not yet reached Ireland, but that transitory period of punishment after the death of lesser sinners would soon be understood to take place in some upper region of hell. In contrast, the cleansing by fire under discussion in DOC will take place at the Last Judgement. See Smyth (2003), 95–99.

The proto-version of the *Canones Hibernenses*, composed in Ireland between 669 and 700, uses *De ecclesiasticis officiis* extensively, so that this reference to Isidore's text is less surprising than previously thought; see Smyth (2016), 123–25.

14.11. As noted by Díaz y Díaz, many elements in this series agree with Caesarius of Arles's list in *Sermo* 179.3 (CCSL 104, 725). In *Dialogues* 4.41.4 (SC 265, 148–49), Gregory mentions only continuous garrulity, immoderate laughter, excessive care for property, and redeemable errors or ignorance in matters not pertaining to the faith.

14.11. This may refer to participation in the communal liturgy of the hours.

14.11. *inordinatum habitum habere* could refer either to disorderly appearance or to disorderly behaviour. I do not know which is intended here.

Chapter 15

15.1. This refers to the splendour of the transfigured Christ, far outshining his companions Moses and Elias. See Augustinus Hibernicus, *De mirabilibus* 3.11 (PL 35:2198), discussed in Smyth (2008), 539–40.

15.2. See Isidore, *Differentiae* 2.14.41 (CCSL 111A, 28), where angels are said to be *natura mutabiles conditi, sed contemplatione dei inmutabiles facti*. Gregory formulated the same idea in Moralia 5.38.68 (CCSL 143, 267–68).

15.4. Man may have natural goodness, but only the gift of direct contemplation of God makes it possible to completely overcome the habit of sin.

15.6. See Num 12:8: *per enigmata et figuras*.

15.6. Since John was 'the disciple whom Jesus loved', it was reasonable to assume that he would have great intercessory powers with Christ, which would make him 'powerful.' Because of this closeness to Christ, especially at the Last Supper (Jn 13:23-25), the apostle John was very important in the Irish Church; witness the appeal to his authority by Colman when justifying the Irish point of view at the Council of Whitby (Bede, *Hist. Eccles.* 3.25), as well as the attribute commonly assigned to him in Irish: *Eoin Bruinne* (John of the Breast). See DOC 13.4, and Introduction, p. 21, above.

15.7. As Díaz y Díaz noted, this formulation is strongly reminiscent of the enumeration of the seven things which are not found in this world: *uita sine morte, iuuentus sine senectute, lux sine tenebris, gaudium sine tristitia, pax sine discordia, uoluntas sine iniuria, regnum sine conmutatione*; see Ps.-Bede, *Collectanea* 177 (SLH 14, 142 and 239-40, n. 177). Similar lists occur in other texts with strong Irish connections, such as the *Liber de numeris* (see McNally (1957), 116) or the *Florilegium frisingense* (CLM 6433) (CCSL 108D, 35-36), both from the end of the eighth century. In the Pseudo-Bede text, the list is followed by the comment: *Septem uero haec inueniuntur in regno coelorum*, which corresponds to the sentiment expressed here, though the DOC list is somewhat different and has been extended from seven to nine items.

15.8. For a discussion of creation from unformed matter (*materia informis* in the Old Latin translation of Wis 11:18 from the Septuagint) as it was understood in early medieval Irish circles, see Smyth (2014A), 135-37. Whereas Augustinus Hibernicus held that the unformed matter God created out of nothing was the substratum of all creation — spiritual and material — the author of DOC believed that only the material world was formed from unformed matter. For information on the patristic background of such ideas, see Smyth (1996), 41-43.

15.9. Unless the author of DOC thinks of the author of the psalms as a prophet, he must be misremembering the origin of the biblical citation Ps 4:7.

15.10. Chapter 10 of *De Genesi ad litteram* is devoted to St Augustine's discussion of the origin of individual human souls. After reviewing a number of opinions, he eventually acknowledged that it is difficult to argue one way or the other, whether from reason or from Scripture. However, on account of the practice of infant baptism, he weighed in on the side of those who believe that the soul is generated by the parents; see *Gen. litt.* 10.23 (CSEL 28/1, 326-27). This position will later harden in the context of the Pelagian controversy, but it would be reasonable for a reader of Augustine's early works to assume that the question was still open.

15.11. According to Ex 12:10 and Ex 34:25, the left-over paschal lamb should not be kept until the following day, but must be consumed by fire.

15.12. The idea behind St Paul's *per speculum et aenigmata* (cited in DOC 15.6, above) is rendered here as *uelut per exiguam fenestram*, perhaps to avoid repetition, but perhaps also to clarify what was meant by the scriptural text. This raises the question of what the word *fenestra* meant to readers in Ireland at the time DOC was written. The word for 'window' in Old-Irish, *senester*, is first documented in the mid-ninth century *Saint Gall Priscian Glosses*, explaining *catarecta* [*sic*]. The Greek καταρράκτης was used in the Septuagint account of the Flood (Gen 7:11), with the meaning 'trap door.' Among Christian authors, *cataractae caeli* became the standard phrase, and this was understood to refer to the *fenestrae caeli*, by Bede among others (see *Hexaemeron*, Bk 2, Ch. 7, line 1576; CCSL 118A, 117).

Even though we cannot assume that he had access to all books of the Bible, a seventh-century scholar would know from Scripture, if not from life, that a *fenestra* was an opening, usually in the side of a building, through which one could see outside and through which one could fall or be lowered in a basket (see e.g., Gen 6:16, 8:6, 26:8; Jds 5:28; 2 Sam 6:16; 1 Chr 15:29; Act 20:9; 2 Cor 11:33, in the Vulgate and often in earlier versions. More especially, *fenestrae* are mentioned several times in Ez 40, the vision on which Jerome is commenting in Book 12 of his *Comment. in Hiezechielem* — see note to 15.13, below). However, the round houses usual in Ireland at that time would not easily allow lateral openings other than the entrance. This would be true of post-and-wattle structures with insulating materials packed between two walls as in the conjectured reconstruction based on the remains at Deer Park Farms (see O'Sullivan, O'Neill, and Reilly (2017), 81–84). It would be similarly difficult to have side openings in the occasional sod church, and if there were *clocháin* — stone bee-hive huts — in seventh-century Ireland, they would not yet have benefitted from the know-how needed to reinforce windows in stone structures.

Aidan O'Sullivan explains that we have no material evidence above ground for early medieval Irish structures (private communications, March 2021). We do however know from Cogitosus, writing in the seventh century, that the term *fenestra* did correspond to a physical reality in Ireland at that time. In his *Vita Sanctae Brigitae* 32:3 (see Connolly and Picard (1987), 26), he states that the great church at Kildare — a wooden rectangular structure, as were almost all churches built in Ireland at that time (Smyth (2019), 71–72; Ó Carragáin (2013), 15–47) — had *multas fenestras*. We can safely assume therefore that in Ireland in the seventh century, *fenestra* meant at the very least an opening in a church wall, presumably to let in light. Such church windows may have been provided with wooden shutters as protection from the weather, but they certainly were not glazed at this early period.

15.13. After following Jerome (*Epistula* 53, 11 (CSEL 54, 465)), in appealing to the great value of the widow's minute gift — as related in Mk 12:41–44 — the author of DOC applies to his own treatise the apology coined by Jerome for the imperfection of his interpretation of the elements of Ezekiel's complex vision in Ez 40 (CCSL 75, 558). It seems likely that when Jerome compared his contribution to the modest gift to the temple of *pelles caprarum pilosque* — rather than the normal Vulgate reading of Ex 25:4–5: *pilos caprarum et pelles arietum rubricatas* (see Smyth (1996), 306, n. 26) — he was thinking metaphorically of the parchment on which the commentary was written. In the Mediterranean area at that time, parchment was commonly made from goat skin (the alternative being sheep skin). It is tempting to surmise that when borrowing the phrase *pelles caprarum*, the author of DOC might also be thinking of the parchment of his own treatise. As already noted in Smyth (1996), 306, it is generally believed, however, that Irish parchment was made from calf skin only. There were goats in Ireland from early times, but Kelly notes in his book on early Irish farming that goats were not even mentioned in the early eighth-century law text *Críth Gablach* and appeared to have had little value as livestock (Kelly (1997), 78). It is just possible, however, that DOC was first written on imported goat parchment, since we know that there was foreign trade along the Irish coast (Smyth (2019), 88). Moreover, Jiří Vnouček has shown that goat-skin parchment was used for many bifolia of the early eighth-century Codex Amiatinus written in Northumbria, and he argued convincingly that this parchment was imported from the Continent, probably from Italy or Southern Gaul (Vnouček (2019), 29–30/34; see also his authoritative study of various types of parchment in Vnouček (2021); I thank Jiří Vnouček for several very helpful and enlightening private communications in March 2022). Could something similar have already been happening in Ireland toward the end of the seventh century? Given the very special nature of the production of the luxurious Codex Amiatinus, that is most unlikely.

15.14. I agree with Michael Herren's suggestion that *trans-* was originally a gloss to *contra* and should therefore be ignored. The text should then read *contra garrientium instabiles fluctos*, literally: 'against the changeable waves of chatterers.'

15.14. Díaz y Díaz observed that whereas modern editions of *De Genesi ad litteram* 1.20.40 read *uolaturarum auium nidos* (CSEL 28/1, 30), *uolatu ranarum auium nidos* is the reading given by the Auerbach edition (Cologne, 1506) and that of the Maurists (Paris, 1689), as well as some codices related to Paris, Bibliothèque Nationale, lat. 1804, saec. IX, where it is the best reading. See more recently, Michael Gorman (1996); repr. in Gorman (2001).

15.14. The last phrase is borrowed from Jerome's introduction to his translation of the Book of Esther from the Hebrew; see *Biblia sacra iuxta Vulgatam versionem*, ed. R. Weber et al. (1975 or 1983), 1.712, lines 12–13; Smyth (1996), 19–20.

Bibliography

Abbreviations

ACW = *Ancient Christian Writers: The Works of the Fathers in Translation*, New York, NY.
BCLL = Lapidge, M. and R. Sharpe (1985) *A Bibliography of Celtic-Latin Literature, 400–1200* [Royal Irish Academy Dictionary of Medieval Latin from Celtic Sources: Ancillary Publications 1], Dublin.
CGL = Goetz, G. et al., eds (1888–1923) *Corpus glossarium latinorum* [7 VOLS], Leipzig.
CLH = Ó Corráin, D. (2017) *Clavis litterarum hibernensium: Medieval Irish Books & Texts (c. 400-c. 1600)* [3 VOLS], Turnhout.
CPL = Dekkers, E. and A. Gaar (1995) *Clavis patrum latinorum: Editio tertia aucta et emendata*, Steenbrugge [available online as part of *Clavis clavium* (Brepolis)].
CPPM = Machielsen, J. (1990–2004) *Clavis patristica pseudepigraphorum medii aevi* [5 VOLS], Turnhout.
DMLCS = Harvey, A. and J. Power, eds (2005) *The non-Classical Lexicon of Celtic Latinity*, VOL. 1: *Letters A-H* [Royal Irish Academy Dictionary of Medieval Latin from Celtic Sources: Constituent Publications 1], Turnhout.
MGH, AA = *Monumenta Germaniae historica. Auctores antiquissimi*, Munich [available online].
PL = *Patrologia latina*, Migne, J.-P., ed. (1841–1855), Paris [available online].
PLS = Patrologiae latinae supplementum, Hamman, A., ed. (1958–1974) [5 VOLS], Paris [available online].
SC = *Sources chrétiennes*, Lyon [available online].
SLH = *Scriptores latini Hiberniae*, Dublin Institute for Advanced Studies, Dublin.
TLL = *Thesaurus linguae latinae*, Leipzig and Munich, 1900– [letters A-M, N–*nemo*, O-P, R-*repressio* as of 2022; the already printed material is available online]
TU = *Texte und Untersuchungen*, Berlin.

Previous Editions

Dom Luc d'Achery, *Liber Isidorii episcopi de ordine creaturarum ad Braulium episcopum Vrbis Romae*, in *Veterum aliquot scriptorum qui in Galliae Bibliothecis, maxime Benedictorum, supersunt Spicilegium, Tomus primus*, Paris, 1655, 268-307 [from the now lost Rheims manuscript **A**]; 2nd edn, Paris, 1665, 268-307.

Martène, Edmond et Etienne Baluze, *S Isidori Hispalensis episcopi, ad Braulium episcopum urbis Romae Liber de ordine creaturarum* in *Spicilegium sive collectio veterum scriptorum qui in Galliae Bibliothecis delituerant*. Tomus primus, Paris, 1723, 1:225–37.

Arévalo, Faustino, *S. Isidori Hispalensis episcopi Liber de ordine creaturarum* in *S. Isidori Hispalensis episcopi Hispaniarum doctoris opera omnia denvo correcta et avcta recensente Favstino Arevalo* [7 VOLS], Rome, 1797–1803, VI:582–620.

Isidori Hispalensis De ordine creaturarum liber, PL 83: 913–54 [copied from the Arévalo edition].

Díaz y Díaz, Manuel (1972) *Liber de ordine creaturarum: un anónimo irlandés del siglo VII* [Monografías de la Universidad de Santiago de Compostela 10], Santiago de Compostela [with Spanish translation; a very slightly modified version of this edition is used in the present volume].

Ancient and Medieval Authors

Aldhelm, *De Virginitate* (prose) (S. Gwara, *Aldhelmi Malmesbiriensis prosa De virginitate, cum glosa latina atque anglosaxonica*, 2001, CCSL 124A; transl. M. Lapidge and M. Herren, *Aldhelm: The Prose Works*, 1979, Cambridge).

— *De uirginitate* (verse) (R. Ehwald, 1919, MGH AA 15; trans. J. L. Rosier in *Aldhelm: The Poetic Works*, ed. M. Lapidge and J. L. Rosier, 1985, Cambridge).

Aeneas, bishop of Paris, *Liber aduersus Graecos* (PL 121:683–762).

Aethicus Ister, *Cosmography* (M. Herren, 2011, *The Cosmography of Aethicus Ister: Edition, Translation, and Commentary* [Publications of the Journal of Medieval Latin 8], Turnhout).

Ambrose, *In Hexaemeron* (K. Schenkl, 1897, CSEL 32/1, 1–261) [CPL 123].

Anonymous, *Altus Prosator* (Clemens Blume in 'Hymnodia Hiberno-celtica', *Analecta Hymnica Medii Aevi* 51 (1908), 257–365 at 271–83) [CLH 267; CPL 1131]. See also D. Howlett (1997).

— *B Glosses to Bede's De temporum ratione* (PL 90:297–518, 685–98 and 699–702 at the bottom of the columns).

— *Catechesis Celtica* (A. Wilmart, 1933, in *Analecta Reginensia: extraits des manuscrits latins de la reine Christine conservés au Vatican* [Studi e Testi 59], Vatican, 29–112, incomplete) [CLH 192; BCLL 974].

— *Collectanea Pseudo-Bedae* (M. Bayless and M. Lapidge, *Collectanea Ps-Bedae*, 1998, SLH 14) [CLH 33, CPL 1129, BCLL 1257].

— *Commemoratorium* (R. Gryson, *Commentaria minora in Apocalypsin Johannis*, 2003, CCSL 107, 192–229) [CLH 98].

— *Commentarius in Iohannem* (J. F. Kelly, *Scriptores Hiberniae minores II*, 1974, CCSL 108C, 105–31) [CLH 86].

— *Commentarius in Lucam* (J. F. Kelly, *Scriptores Hiberniae minores II*, 1974, CCSL 108C, 1–101) [CLH 84].

— *Commentary on Genesis*, Sankt Gallen, Stiftsbibliothek 908, pp. 1–27 [electronic images are available on the *e-Codices* site] [CLH 40 and CLH 381].

— *Críth gablach* (D. A. Binchy, *Críth gablach*, Mediaeval and Modern Irish Series XI, Dublin, 1941, repr. Dublin, 1979) [CLH 668 (esp. p. 868) and CLH 683].
— *De duodecim abusiuis saeculi* (S. Hellmann, *Ps-Cyprianus De XII abusiuis Saeculi*, 1909, TU 34) [CLH 576].
— *De ecclesiasticis dogmaticis liber* (PL 58:979-1054; see also PL83:1227-44) [CCPM iiA 174; CCPM iiA 766; CCPM iiA 1085].
— *Excerpta in Euangeliae* (R. E. McNally, in *Patrologiae Latinae Supplementum*, ed. A. Hamman, 1958-1974, 5 VOLS, Paris, 4:1614-1618).
— *Florilegium frisingense (clm 6433)* (A. Lehner, *Florilegia*, 1987, CCSL 108D, 1-39).
— *Hisperica famina* (M. W. Herren, 1974, *The Hisperica Famina: I. The A-Text: A New Critical Edition with English Translation and Philological Commentary* [Studies and Texts 31], Toronto; also, F. Jenkinson, 1908, *The Hisperica famina*, Cambridge) [CLH 570].
— *Irish Penitentials* (L. Bieler, 1963, *The Irish Penitentials*, Dublin, SLH 5) [CLH 579-84].
— *Liber de numeris* (PL 83:1293-02; for extensive extracts, see R. E. McNally (1957)) [CLH 577; BCLL 778].
— *Liber questionum in evangeliis* (J. Rittmueller, 2003, CCSL 108F) [CLH 69, CPL 1168, BCLL 764, 1267].
— *Pauca de Genesi* (D. Ó Cróinín, 2001, 'A New Seventh-century Irish Commentary on Genesis', *Sacris erudiri* 40, 231-65 [excerpts from Munich clm 17739]) [CLH 44].
— *Pauca problesmata de enigmatibus ex tomis canonicis. Praefatio. De Pentateucho Moysi* (G. MacGinty, 2000, CCCM 173) [CLH 101].
— *Quicunque uult* (J. Pelikan & V. Hotchkiss, 2003, *Creeds and Confessions of Faith in the Christian Tradition*, New Haven & London, 1:673-77).
— *Saltair na rann* (for editions, see CLH 103; for translation of strophes I-III see J. Carey, 1998, *King of Mysteries: Early Irish Religious Writings*, Dublin, 97-124) [CLH 103].
— *St Gall Priscian Glosses*, Sankt Gallen, Stiftsbibliothek 904 [electronic images are available on the *e-Codices* site] [CLH 805].
— *Stavelot commentary* (A. E. Burn, 1896, *The Athanasian Creed and its Early Commentaries* [Texts and Studies, Contributions to Biblical and Patristic Literature 4/1], Cambridge, 11-20).
— *Würzburg glosses to Matthew*, Würzburg Universitätsbibliothek, M. p. th. f. 61 [see CLH 394; BCLL 768].
Augustine of Hippo, *Ad Orosium contra Priscillianistas et Origenistas* (PL 42:669-78; Kl. Daur, 1985, CCSL 49, 168-78, 180) [CPL 327].
— *De civitate Dei. Libri XI–XXII* (B. Dombart & A. Kalb, 1955, CCSL 48) [CPL 313].
— *De Genesi ad litteram* (J. Zycha, 1894, CSEL 28/1, 1-435; J. H. Taylor (transl.), 1982, ACW 41-42; see also P. Agaësse & A. Solignac, 1972, Bibliothèque augustinienne 48-49, Paris) [CPL 266].
— *De Genesi contra Manichaeos* (PL 34:173-220) [CPL 265].
— *De natura boni* (J. Zycha, 1892, CSEL 25/2, 853-89) [CPL 323].
— *De ordine* (W. M. Green, 1970, CCSL 29, 87-137) [CPL255].
— *De sermone domini in monte* (A. Mutzenbecher, 1967, CCSL 35) [CPL 274].
— *De Trinitate libri I–XII* (W. J. Mountain & F. Glorie, 1968, CCSL 50) [CPL 329].

— *Enarrationes in psalmos I–L* (E. Dekkers & J. Fraipont, 1956, 2nd edn 1990, CCSL 38) [CPL 283].

— *Enchiridion* (M. Evans, 1969, CCSL 46, 49–114) [CPL295].

— *In Iohannis euangelium tractatus CXXIV* (R. Willems, 1954, 2nd edn 1990, CCSL 36) [CPL 278].

Augustinus Hibernicus (= the Irish Augustine) *De mirabilibus sacrae Scripturae* (PL 35:2149–00; for an edition of both the long and the short versions, see F. P. MacGinty, 1971, 'The Treatise *De Mirabilibus Sacrae Scripturae*' [Ph.D. diss., University College Dublin]) [CLH 574; CPL 1123].

Bede, *In cantica canticorum* (D. Hurst, 1983, CCSL 119B, 165–375; A. Holder (transl.), *The Venerable Bede: On the Song of Songs and Selected Writings*, 2011, New York) [CPL 1353].

— *In proverbia Salomonis* (D. Hurst, 1983, CCSL 119B, 21–163; PL 91:1051–66) [CPL 1352].

— *In Lucae euangelium expositio* (D. Hurst, 1960, CCSL 120, 1–425) [CPL 1356].

— *In Marci euangelium expositio* (D. Hurst, 1960, CCSL 120, 427–648) [CPL 1355].

— *De natura rerum* (Ch.W. Jones and F. Lipp, 1975, CCSL 123A, 173–234; C. B. Kendall and F. Wallis (transl.), *Bede: On the Nature of Things and On Times* [Translated Texts for Historians 56], 2010, Liverpool) [CPL 1343].

— *De temporum ratione* (Ch.W. Jones, 1977, CCSL 123B) [CPL 2320].

— *Historia Ecclesiastica Gentis Anglorum* (B. Colgrave and R. A. B. Mynors, *Bede's Ecclesiastical History of the English People* [Oxford Medieval Texts], 1969, Oxford) [CPL 1375].

Biblia Latina cum glossa ordinaria. Facsimile reprint of the editio princeps Adolph Rusch of Strassburg 1480/81 [4 VOLS], 1992, Turnhout.

Biblia sacra iuxta Vulgatam versionem, ed. Weber et al., 1975 [2nd rev. edn], Stuttgart [3rd edn 1983].

Caesarius of Arles, *Sermones* (G. Morin, 1953, CCSL 103–04) [CPL 1008].

Cogitosus, *Vita Brigitae* (J. Colgan, *Trias thaumaturga*, 1647, Louvain [repr. 1997, Dublin], 518–26; translated in S. Connolly and J.-M. Picard (1987), 'Cogitosus's *Life of Brigit*: Content and Value', *Journal of the Royal Society of Antiquaries of Ireland* 117, 5–27) [CLH 228; CPL 2147].

Columbanus, *Instructio I: De fide* (G. S. M. Walker, 1957, Dublin, SLH 2, 60–66) [CLH 329; CPL 1107].

— *Regula Monachorum* (G. S. M. Walker, 1957, Dublin, SLH 2, 122–43; also, Ivo auf der Maur, *Columban von Luxeuil. Mönchsregeln*, 2007, St Ottilien) [CLH 330; CPL 1108].

Defensor of Ligugé, *Liber scintillarum* (H. M. Rochais, 1957, CCSL 117, vii–307; also, H. M. Rochais, *Defensor de Ligugé: Livre d'étincelles*, 1961–1962, SC 77 & 86) [CPL 1302].

Gregory the Great, *Dialogues* (A. de Vogüé & P. Antin, 1978–1980, *Grégoire le Grand: Dialogues*, SC 251, 260 & 265) [CPL 1713].

— *Homilia 34 in euangelia* (R. Étaix, 1999, CCSL 141, 299–319; D. Hurst (transl.), *Gregory the Great: Forty Gospel Homilies*, 1990 [Cistercian Studies Series 123], 280–300) [CPL 1711].

— *Moralia in Iob* (M. Adriaen, 1979 and 1985, CCSL 143–143B) [CPL 1708].
— *Homilia 4 in Hiezechielem prophetam* (M. Adriaen, 1971, CCSL 142, 47–56) [CPL 1710].
Haimo of Auxerre, *Commentary on Isaiah* (PL 116:713–1086D).
Isidore, *De ecclesiasticis officiis* (C. M. Lawson, 1989, CCSL 113) [CPL 1207].
— *De natura rerum* (J. Fontaine, *Isidore de Séville. Traité de la nature*, 1960, Bordeaux) [CPL 1188].
— *Liber differentiarum (II)* (M. A. Andrés Sanz, 2006, CCSL 111A) [CPL 1202].
— *Quaestiones in Vetus Testamentum* (PL 83:207–424) [CPL 1195, CPPM iiA 2655].
— *Sententiae* (P. Cazier, 1998, CCSL 111) [CPL 1199].
Jerome, *Commentariorum in Danielem libri III* (F. Glorie, 1964, CCSL 75A) [CPL 588].
— *Commentarius in Ecclesiasten* (M. Adriaen, 1959, CCSL 72, 247–361) [CPL 583].
— *Commentariorum in Hiezechielem libri XIV* (F. Glorie, 1964, CCSL 75) [CPL 587].
— *Commentariorum in Esaiam libri XVIII* (M. Adriaen, 1963, CCSL 73–73A) [CPL 584].
— *Commentariorum in Matthaeum libri IV* (D. Hurst & M. Adriaen, 1969, CCSL 77) [CPL 590].
— *Epistula 51* (I. Hilberg, 1910, CSEL 54, 395–412).
— *Epistula 53* (I. Hilberg, 1910, CSEL 54, 442–65).
— *Epistula 65* (I. Hilberg, 1910, CSEL 54, 616–47).
— *Liber interpretationis hebraicorum nominum* (P. de Lagarde, 1959, CCSL 72, 57–161) [CPL 581].
Lathcen mac Baith, *Egloga quam scripsit Lathcen filius Baith de Moralibus Iob quas Gregorius fecit* (M. Adriaen, 1969, CCSL 145) [CLH 566; CPL 1716].
Martin of León, *Sermo secundus in adventu Domini* (PL 208:37–64).
— *Sermo vicesimus quintus de resurrectione Domini* (PL 208:925–32).
Pelagius, *Commentary on St Paul's Epistle to the Romans* (Th. de Bruyn (transl.), 1993, *Pelagius's Commentary on St Paul's Epistle to the Romans. Translated with Introduction and Notes* [Oxford Early Christian Studies], Oxford) [CLH 215; CPL 728; BCLL 2].
— *To Demetrias* (PL 33:1099–1120; B. R. Rees (transl.), 1991, *The Letters of Pelagius and his Followers*, Woodbridge, 29–70) [BCLL 7; CPL 737].
Peter Lombard, *Sententiae* (3rd edn, 1971–1981, *Magistri Petri Lombardi Parisiensis episcopi Sententiae in IV libris distinctae* [Spicilegium Bonaventurianum 4–5], Grottaferrata).
Philippus Presbyter, *Commentary on Job* (Sichardus, 1527, *Philippi presbyteri uiri longe eruditissimi in historiam Iob commentariorum libri tres*, Basle; see also the abbreviated version (*Commentarii in librum Job*) in PL 26:619–802) [CPL 643].
Pseudo-Bede, *Collectanea* (M. Bayless and M. Lapidge, 1998, *Collectanea Pseudo-Bedae*, SLH 14) [CLH 33; CPL 1129].
— *De sex dierum creatione liber sententiarum ex patribus collectarum* (PL 93:207–34) [CPPM iiA 2036 = Ps. Ambrosius, CPPM iiA 1819b; see CPMM iiA 4b/3].
Pseudo-Gennadius, *Libri ecclesiasticorum dogmatum* (PL 58: 979–1054) [CPL 958a; CPMM iiA 766].
Pseudo-Jerome, *Expositio quattuor euangeliorum* (PL 30:547–608; PL 114:861–916) [CLH 65 and CLH 381; CPL 631; CPPM iiA 2364a-d (pp. 545–47)].
Pseudo-Rufinus, *Liber de fide* (PL 21:1123–1154) [CPL 199; CPPM iiA 1530–35].

Quodvultdeus, Liber promissionum et praedictorum Dei (R. Braun, 1976, CCSL 60, 1–189; also, R. Braun, 1964, SC 101–02) [CPL 413].
— *De accedentibus ad gratiam sermones* (R. Braun, 1976, CCSL 60, *Sermo I*: 439–58 [CPL 408]; *Sermo II*: 459–70 [CPL 409]).
Rufinus, *Expositio Symboli* (M. Simonetti, 1961, CCSL 20, 125–82) [CPL 196].
Victorius of Aquitaine, *Cursus Paschalis* (B. Krusch, 1938, in 'Studien zur christlich-mittelalterlichen Chronologie II', *Abhandlungen der Preussischen Akademie der Wissenschaften; Philosophisch-historisch Klasse* (1937), 1–85, at 16–51; reprinted in *Patrologiae Latinae Supplementum*, A. Hamman (ed.), 1958–1974 [5 VOLS], Paris, 3:380–426) [CPL 2282].

Modern Authors

Bayless, M. and M. Lapidge, eds and transl. (1998) *Collectanea Ps-Bedae* [Scriptores Latini Hiberniae 14], Dublin.
Becker, G. (1885) *Catalogi bibliothecarum antiqui*, Bonn.
Bieler, L., ed. and transl. (1963) *The Irish Penitentials* [Scriptores Latini Hiberniae 5], Dublin.
Biggs, F. (1989–1990) 'The Fourfold Division of Souls: The Old-English "Christ III" and the Insular Homiletic Tradition', *Traditio* 45, 35–51.
— ed. (2007) *Sources of Anglo-Saxon Literary Culture: The Apocrypha* [Instrumenta anglistica mediaevalia 1], Kalamazoo.
Bisagni, J. (2017) 'The Newly Discovered Irish and Breton Computistica in Città del Vaticano, BAV, MS Reg. Lat. 123', *Peritia* 28, 13–34.
— (2019) 'La littérature computistique irlandaise dans la Bretagne du haut Moyen Âge: nouvelles découvertes et nouvelles perspectives', *Britannia monastica*, 241–85.
Bischoff, B. (1954) 'Wendepunkte in der Geschichte der lateinischen Exegese im Frühmittelalter', *Sacris Eruditi* 6, 189–281; repr. (with revisions) in B. Bischoff (1966–1981) *Mittelalterliche Studien: Ausgewählte Aufsätze zur Schriftkunde und Literaturgeschichte* [3 VOLS], Stuttgart, 1:205–73; transl. O'Grady, C. (1976) 'Turning-points in the History of Latin Exegesis in the Early Middle Ages', in M. McNamara (ed.) *Biblical Studies: The Medieval Irish Contribution* [Proceedings of the Irish Biblical Association 1], Dublin, 73–160.
— (1989) *Die Abtei Lorsch im Spiegel ihrer Handschriften,* 2nd edn, Lorsch.
— and M. Lapidge (1994) *Biblical Commentaries from the Canterbury School of Theodore and Hadrian* [Cambridge Studies in Anglo-Saxon England 10], Cambridge.
Blume, Cl. (1908) 'Hymnodia Hiberno-celtica', *Analecta Hymnica Medii Aevi* 51, 257–365.
Bracken, D. (1995) 'Immortality and Capital Punishment: Patristic Concepts in Irish Law', *Peritia* 9, 167–86.
— (2002) 'The Fall and the Law in Early Ireland', in P. Ní Chatháin & M. Richter (eds) *Ireland and Europe in the Early Middle Ages: Texts and Transmission = Irland und Europa im früheren Mittelalter: Texte und Überlieferung*, Dublin, 147–69.

Breen, A. (2002) '*De XII abusiuis*: Text and Transmission', in P. Ní Chatháin & M. Richter (eds) *Ireland and Europe in the Early Middle Ages: Texts and Transmission = Irland und Europa im früheren Mittelalter: Texte und Überlieferung*, Dublin, 78–94.

British Medieval Library Catalogues project: *List of Identifications* available at https://www.history.ox.ac.uk/british-medieval-library-catalogues#tab-266421

Burn, A. E., ed. (1896) *The Athanasian Creed and its Early Commentaries* [Texts and Studies, Contributions to Biblical and Patristic Literature 4/1], Cambridge.

Carey, J. (1985) 'Cosmology in *Saltair na rann*', *Celtica* 17, 33–52.

— (1986) 'A Tract on Creation', *Éigse* 21, 1–9.

— (1987) 'Angelology in *Saltair na Rann*', *Celtica* 19, 1–8.

— (1990) 'The Two Laws in Dubtach's Judgment', *Cambridge Medieval Celtic Studies* 19, 1–10.

— (1994) 'An Edition of the Pseudo-historical Prologue to the *Senchas Már*', *Ériu* 45, 1–32; translated in J. Carey (2000), *King of Mysteries: Early Irish Religious Writings*, Dublin, 139–44.

Cartwright, D. E. (1999) *Tides: A Scientific History*, Cambridge.

Christ, K. (1933; repr. 1968) *Die Bibliothek des Klosters Fulda im 16. Jahrhundert: Die Handschriften-Verzeichnisse* [Beiheft zum Zentralblatt für Bibliothekswesen 64], Leipzig; repr. Wiesbaden.

Clayton, M. (2007) 'Apocalypse of the Virgin', in F. Biggs (ed.) *Sources of Anglo-Saxon Literary Culture: The Apocrypha* [Instrumenta anglistica mediaevalia 1], Kalamazoo, 66–67.

Colgrave, B. and R. A. B. Mynors (1969) *Bede's Ecclesiastical History of the English People* [Oxford medieval texts], Oxford.

Connolly, S. and J.-M. Picard (1987) 'Cogitosus's *Life of Brigit*: Content and Value', *Journal of the Royal Society of Antiquaries of Ireland* 117, 5–27.

Contreni, J. J. (2005) 'Bede's Scientific Works in the Carolingian age', in S. Lebecq, M. Perrin, O. Szerwiniack (eds) *Bède le Vénérable entre tradition et postérité – The Venerable Bede: Tradition and Posterity* [Histoire de l'Europe du Nord-Ouest 34], 247–59.

— (2011–2012) '"Old Orthodoxies Die Hard": Herwagen's *Bridferti Ramesiensis Glossae*', *Peritia* 22–23, 15–52.

Cross, J. E. (1972) '*De ordine creaturarum liber* in Old English Prose', *Anglia* 90, 132–40.

— (1981) 'The Influence of Irish Texts and Traditions on the *Old English Martyrology*', *Proceedings of the Royal Irish Academy* 81C, 173–92.

— (1985) 'On the Library of the Old English Martyrologist', in M. Lapidge & H. Gneuss (eds) *Learning and Literature in Anglo-Saxon England: Studies Presented to Peter Clemoes on the Occasion of his Sixty-fifth Birthday*, Cambridge, 227–49.

d'Achery, Dom Luc (1655) *Veterum aliquot scriptorum qui in Galliae Bibliothecis, maxime Benedictinorum, supersunt Spicilegium*, Paris.

Davidson, Gustav (1967) *A Dictionary of Angels, Including the Fallen Angels*, New York.

de Bruyn, Th., ed. and transl. (1993) *Pelagius's Commentary on St Paul's Epistle to the Romans. Translated with Introduction and Notes* [Oxford Early Christian Studies], Oxford.

Delumeau, J. (1992) *Une histoire du paradis: Le jardin des délices,* Paris.
Díaz y Díaz, M. C. (1953) 'Isidoriana I. Sobre el "Liber de ordine creaturarum"', *Sacris erudiri* 5, 147–66.
— (1958) Review of the CCSL 117 edition of Defensor of Ligugé, *Liber scintillarum, Hispania Sacra* 11:2, 3–4.
— (1972) *Liber de ordine creaturarum: un anónimo irlandés del siglo VII* [Monografias de la Universidad de Santiago de Compostela 10], Santiago de Compostela [with Spanish translation; a very slightly modified version of this edition is used in the present volume].
diPaolo Healey, A. (2007) 'Apocalypse of Paul', in Frederick Biggs (ed.) *Sources of Anglo-Saxon Literary Culture: The Apocrypha* [Instrumenta anglistica mediaevalia 1] Kalamazoo, 67–70,
Dolan, B. (2012) 'The Social and Technological Context of Iron Production in Iron Age and Early Medieval Ireland c. 600BC–AD900', Ph.D., University College Dublin [pdf file available in *Research Repository UCD*].
Duhem, P. (1913–1959) *Le système du monde: Histoire des doctrines cosmologiques de Platon à Copernic* [10 vols], Paris.
Esposito, M. (1919) 'On the Pseudo-Augustinian Treatise *De Mirabilibus Sacrae Scripturae* Written in Ireland in the Year 655', *Proceedings of the Royal Irish Academy* 35C, 189–207.
Fernández Catón, J. M. (1965a) 'Catálogo de los materiales codicológicos y bibliográficos del legado scientifico del Prof. Anspach', *Archives Leoneses* 129, 29–120.
— (1965b) 'Las Etimologias en la tradición manuscrita medieval', *Archives Leoneses* 129, 121–384.
Fontaine, J., ed. and transl. (1960) *Isidore de Séville. Traité de la nature,* Bordeaux.
Garrett, C. J. R. and W. H. Munk (1971) 'The Age of the Tide and the "Q" of the Oceans', *Deep-Sea Research* 18, 493–503.
Glauche, G. (1994) 'Incipit clericalis vel monachalis sancti Hieronymi presbyteri', in *Karl Dachs zum 65. Geburtstag = Bibliotheksforum Bayern* 22, 141–47.
Gorman, M. M. (1996a) 'The Glosses of Bede's *De temporum ratione* Attributed to Byrhtferth of Ramsey', *Anglo-Saxon England* 25, 209–32.
— (1996b) 'The Commentary on the Pentateuch Attributed to Bede in PL 91.189–394; Second Part', *Revue bénédictine* 106, 255–307.
— (1996c) 'Augustine Manuscripts from the Library of Louis the Pious: Berlin Phillips 1651 and Munich, clm 3824', *Scriptorium* 50, 98–105.
— (2001) *The Manuscript Traditions of the Works of St Augustine* [Millennio medievale 27], Florence.
Grimm, R. R. (1977) *Paradisus coelestis, paradisus terrestris: Zur Auslegungsgeschichte des Paradieses im Abendland bis um 1200* [Medium Aevum 33], Munich.
Grosjean, P. (1955) 'Sur quelques exégètes irlandais du VIIe siècle', *Sacris erudiri* 7, 67–98.
Gryson, R., ed. (1987–1997) *Vetus latina: Die Reste der altlateinischen Bibel,* vol. 12: *Esaias,* Freiburg.
— (2000) *Vetus latina: Die Reste der altlateinischen Bibel,* vol. 26/2: *Apocalypsis Johannis,* Freiburg.

Guiley, R. E. (2004) *The Encyclopedia of Angels*, 2nd edn, New York.
Hamman, A., ed. (1958–1974) *Patrologiae Latinae Supplementum* [5 vols], Paris.
Hamp, E. P. (1974) 'On the Fundamental IE Orientation', *Ériu* 25, 253–61.
Herbert, M. & M. McNamara (1989) *Irish Biblical Apocrypha: Selected Texts in Translation*, Edinburgh.
Herren, M. W., ed. and transl. (1974) *The Hisperica Famina: I. The A-Text: A New Critical Edition with English Translation and Philological Commentary* [Studies and Texts 31], Toronto.
— (1982) 'Sprachliche Eigentümlichkeiten in den hibernolateinischen Texten des 7. und 8. Jahrhunderts', in H. Löwe (ed.) *Die Iren und Europa im früheren Mittelalter* [2 vols], Stuttgart, 1:425–33.
— ed. (1987) *The Hisperica famina. II. Related Poems: A Critical Edition with English Translation and Philological Commentary* [Studies and Texts 85], Toronto.
— (1998) 'Irish Biblical Commentaries before 800', in J. Hamesse (ed.) *Roma, magistra mundi: itineraria culturae medievalis. Mélanges offerts au père L. E. Boyle à l'occasion de son 75e anniversaire* [Textes et études du moyen âge 10, 3 vols], Louvain-la-Neuve, 1:391–407.
— (2005) 'Aldhelm the Theologian', in K. O'Brien O'Keeffe and A. Orchard (eds) *Latin Learning and English Lore: Studies in Anglo-Saxon Literature for Michael Lapidge* [Toronto Old English series 14, 2 vols], Toronto, 1: 68–89.
— ed. and transl. (2011) *The Cosmography of Aethicus Ister: Edition, Translation, and Commentary* [Publications of the Journal of Medieval Latin 8], Turnhout.
Herren, M. W. and Sh.A. Brown (2002) *Christ in Celtic Christianity: Britain and Ireland from the Fifth to the Tenth Century* [Studies in Celtic History 20], Woodbridge.
Holder, A., transl. (2011) *The Venerable Bede: On the Song of Songs and Selected Writings*, New York.
Howlett, D. (1997) 'Insular Latin Writers' Rhythms', *Peritia* 11, 53–116.
— ed. and transl. (2015) 'The "Altus Prosator" of Virgilius Maro Grammaticus', in E. Purcell, P. MacCotter, J. Nyhan and J. G. Sheehan (eds) *Clerics, Kings and Vikings: Essays on Medieval Ireland in Honour of Donnchadh Ó Corráin*, Dublin, 363–88.
Illich, I. (1993) *In the Vineyard of the Text: A Commentary to Hugh's 'Didascalion'*, Chicago.
Iogna-Prat, D. (1991) 'L'oeuvre d'Haymon d'Auxerre: État de la question', in D. Iogna-Prat, C. Jeudy and G. Lobrichon (eds) *L'école carolingienne d'Auxerre: de Murethach à Remi, 830–908* [Entretiens d'Auxerre 1989] Paris, 157–79.
Jones, C. W. (1939) *Bedae Pseudepigrapha: Scientific Writings Falsely Attributed to Bede*, Ithaca.
Kattenbusch, F. (1894–1900) *Das Apostolische Symbol* [2 vols], Leipzig (repr. Hildesheim, 1962).
Kavanagh, A. K. (1999) 'The Ps.-Jerome's *Expositio IV euangeliorum*', in Th. O'Loughlin (ed.) *The Scriptures and Early Medieval Ireland* [Instrumenta patristica 31], Turnhout, 125–31.
Kelly, F. (1997) *Early Irish Farming* [Early Irish Law Series 4], Dublin [repr. 2016].
Kelly, J. F. (1978) 'Pelagius, Pelagianism and the Early Christian Irish', *Mediaevalia* 4, 99–124.

Klein, Elizabeth (2018) *Augustine's Theology of Angels*, Cambridge.

Krämer, S. (1989) *Handschriftenerbe des deutschen Mittelalters. Teil 2: Köln-Zyfflich* [Mittelalterliche Bibliothekskataloge Deutschlands und der Schweiz, Ergänzungsband 1], Munich.

Lapidge, M., ed. (2009) *Byrhtferth of Ramsey: The lives of St Oswald and St Ecgwine*, [Oxford Medieval Texts], Oxford.

—— and M. Herren, eds and transl. (1979) *Aldhelm: The Prose Works*, Cambridge.

—— and J. L. Rosier, eds and transl. (1985) *Aldhelm: The Poetic Works*, Cambridge.

Lowe, E. A. (1934–1966) *Codices latini antiquiores* [11 vols and Supplements, Oxford; see now elmss.nuigalway.ie].

Löfstedt, B. (1965) *Der hibernolateinische Grammatiker Malsachanus* [Acta Universitatis Upsaliensis. Studia Latina Upsaliensia 4], Uppsala.

MacGinty, F. P. (= MacGinty, Gerard), ed. and transl. (1971) 'The Treatise *De Mirabilibus Sacrae Scripturae*' [Ph.D. diss., University College Dublin].

Madoz, J. (1938) *Le symbole du XIe concile de Tolède: ses sources, sa date, sa valeur* [Spicilegium sacrum lovaniense: études et documents 19], Louvain.

Manitius, M. (1935) *Handschriften antiker Autoren in mittelalterlichen Bibliothekskatalogen*, Leipzig.

Mansi, J. D., ed. (1901–1927) *Sacrorum conciliorum nova et amplissima collectio* [58 vols], Paris.

McNally, R. E., ed. (1957) *Der irische Liber de Numeris* [Doctoral Dissertation, Munich].

McNamara, M. (1975) *The Apocrypha in the Irish Church*, Dublin.

Martène, Ed. and E. Baluze (1723) *Spicilegium sive collectio veterum scriptorum qui in Galliae Bibliothecis delituerant*, Paris.

Martin, H., ed. (1885–1892) *Catalogue général des manuscrits des bibliothèques publiques de France. Catalogue des manuscrits de la Bibliothèque de l'Arsenal*, 9 vols, Paris.

Meyer, H. and R. Suntrup (1987) *Lexikon der mittelalterlichen Zahlenbedeutungen* [Münstersche Mittelalter-Schriften 56], Munich.

Ó Carragáin, T. (2013) *Churches in Early Medieval Ireland: Architecture, Ritual and Memory*, New Haven.

Ó Cróinín, D. (1983) 'The Irish Provenance of Bede's Computus', *Peritia* 2, 229–47.

— (2000) 'Bischoff's *Wendepunkte* Fifty Years On', *Revue Bénédictine* 110, 204–37.

— (2001) 'A New Seventh-century Commentary on Genesis', *Sacris erudiri* 20, 231–65.

O'Loughlin, Th. (1992) '*Aquae super caelos* (Gen 1:6–7): The First Faith-Science Debate', *Milltown Studies* 29, 92–114.

— (1995) 'The Waters Above the Heavens: Isidore and the Latin Tradition', *Milltown Studies* 36, 104–17.

Orchard, A. P. McD. (1987–1988) 'Some Aspects of Seventh-Century Hiberno-Latin Syntax: A Statistical Approach', *Peritia* 6–7, 158–201.

O'Sullivan, A., O'Neill, B., and E. Reilly (2017) 'Early Medieval Houses in Ireland: Some Perspectives from Archaeology, Early Irish History, and Experimental Archaeology', *Eolas: Journal of the American Society for Irish Medieval Studies*, 10, 77–88.

Pelikan, J. and V. Hotchkiss (2003) *Creeds and Confessions of Faith in the Christian Tradition* [4 vols], New Haven & London.

Peyrafort-Huin, M. (2001) *La bibliothèque médiévale de l'abbaye de Pontigny (XII–XIXe siècles): Histoire, inventaires anciens, manuscrits* [Documents, Études et Répertoires IRHT], Paris.

Picard, J.-M. (2005) 'Bède et ses sources irlandaises', in S. Lebecq, M. Perrin, O. Szerwiniack (eds) *Bède le Vénérable entre tradition et postérité – The Venerable Bede: Tradition and Posterity* [Histoire de l'Europe du Nord-Ouest 34], 43–61.

Rees, B. R., ed. (1991), *The Letters of Pelagius and his Followers*, Woodbridge.

Rittmueller, J. (1983) 'The Gospel Commentary of Máel Brigte ua Máeluanaig and its Hiberno-Latin Background', *Peritia* 2, 185–214.

— (1984) 'Postscript to the Gospels of Máel Brigte', *Peritia* 3, 215–18.

Savigni, R. (2005) 'Il commentario a Isaia de Aimone d'Auxerre e le sue fonti', in Cl. Leonardi and G. Orlandi (eds) *Biblical Studies in the Early Middle Ages* [Millennio medievale 52], Florence, 215–38.

Shimahara, S. (2007) *Études d'exégèse carolingienne: Autour d'Haymon d'Auxerre* [Collection Haut Moyen Age 4], Turnhout.

Siecienski, E. A. (2010) *The Filioque: History of a Doctrinal Controversy*, Oxford.

Sims-Williams, P. (1978) 'Thought, Word and Deed: An Irish Triad', *Ériu* 29, 78–111.

Smyth, M. (1995) 'The Earliest Written Evidence for an Irish View of the World', in D. Edel (ed.) *Cultural Identity and Cultural Integration; Ireland and Europe in the Early Middle Ages*, Dublin, 23-44.

— (1996) *Understanding the Universe in Seventh-Century Ireland* [Studies in Celtic History 15], Woodbridge.

— (1998) 'Perceptions of Physical and Spiritual Space in Early Christian Ireland', in J. A. Aertsen & A. Speer (eds) *Raum und Raumvorstellungen im Mittelalter* [Miscellanea Mediaevalia 25] Berlin, 505–24.

— (2003) 'The Origins of Purgatory through the Lens of Seventh-Century Irish Eschatology', *Traditio* 58, 91–132.

— (2003–2004) 'The Date and Origin of *Liber de ordine creaturarum*', *Peritia* 17–18, 1–39.

— (2008) 'The Body, Death and Resurrection: Perspectives of an Early Irish Theologian', *Speculum* 83, 531–71.

— (2011) 'The Seventh-Century Hiberno-Latin Treatise *Liber de ordine creaturarum*. A Translation', *Journal of Medieval Latin* 21, 137–222. [Note: The present publication is based on that work.]

— (2013) 'From Observation to Scientific Speculation in Seventh-Century Ireland', in M. Kelly and Ch. Doherty (eds) *Music and the Stars: Mathematics in Medieval Ireland* [Royal Society of Antiquaries of Ireland, First International Conference on the History of Science in Medieval Ireland], Dublin, 73–98.

— (2014a) 'The Word of God and Early Medieval Irish Cosmology: Scripture and the Creating Word', in J. Borsje, A. Dooley, S. Mac Mathúna and G. Toner (eds) *Celtic Cosmology: Perspectives from Ireland and Scotland* [Papers in Mediaeval Studies 26], Toronto, 112–43.

— (2014b) 'Zoologists in Seventh-Century Ireland?' in A. Handy and B. Ó Conchubhair (eds) *The Language of Gender, Power and Agency in Celtic Studies* [Conference of the Celtic Studies Association of North America: *Saints, Sinners, and Scribes in the Celtic World*], Dublin, 59–74.

— (2015) 'The Irish Hybrid Lists of the Seven Heavens', in E. Purcell, P. MacCotter, J. Nyhan and J. G. Sheehan (eds) *Clerics, Kings and Vikings: Essays on Medieval Ireland in Honour of Donnchadh Ó Corráin*, Dublin, 399–410.

— (2016) 'Isidorian texts in seventh-century Ireland', in A. Fear and J. Wood (eds) *Isidore of Seville and his Reception in the Early Middle Ages. Transmitting and Transforming Knowledge* [Late Antique and Early Medieval Iberia], Amsterdam, 111–30.

— (2019) 'Monastic Culture in Seventh-Century Ireland' [2018 Farrell Lecture], *Eolas: Journal of the American Society for Irish Medieval Studies*, 64–101.

Stegmüller, F. (1951) *Repertorium biblicum medii aevi*, Tomus III: *Commentaria*, Auctores H-M, Madrid.

Stevenson, J. (1999) '*Altus Prosator*', *Celtica* 23, 326–69.

Stotz, P. (1996) *Handbuch zur lateinischen Sprache des Mittelalters. Dritter Band: Lautlehre*, Munich.

Stuiber, A. (1957) *Refrigerium interim: Die Vorstellungen vom Zwischenzustand und die frühchristliche Grabekunst* [Theophaneia 11], Bonn.

Thurneysen, R. (1975) *A Grammar of Old Irish* [D. A. Binchy and O. Bergin (transl.)], Dublin.

Vnouček, J. (2019) 'The Parchment of the Codex Amiatinus in the Context of Manuscript Production in Northumbria Around the End of the Seventh Century: Identification of the Animal Species and Methods of Manufacture of the Parchment as Clues to the Old Narrative?', *Journal of Paper Conservation*, 20, 179–204.

— (2021) 'Not All that Shines Like Vellum in Necessarily So', in M. J. Driscoll (ed.) *Care and Conservation of Manuscripts 17* [Proceedings of the Seventeenth International Seminar Held at the University of Copenhagen 11th–13th April 2018], Charlottenlund, 27–59.

Walker, G. S. M., ed. (1957) *Sancti Columbani opera* [Scriptores Latini Hiberniae 2], Dublin.

Wallis, F., transl. (1999) *Bede: The Reckoning of Time* [Translated Texts for Historians 29], Liverpool.

Warntjes, I. (2010) *The Munich Computus: Text and Translation. Irish Computistics Between Isidore of Seville and the Venerable Bede and its Reception in Carolingian Times* [Sudhoffs Archiv Beihefte 59], Stuttgart.

— (2015) 'Victorius vs Dionysius: The Irish Easter Controversy of AD 689', in P. Moran and I. Warntjes (eds) *Early Medieval Ireland and Europe: Chronology, Contacts, Scholarship; A Festchrift for Dáibhí Ó Cróinín* [Studia Traditionis Theologiae 14], Turnhout, 33–97.

Wawrykow, J. P. (1995) *God's Grace & Human Action: 'Merit' in the Theology of Thomas Aquinas*, Notre Dame.

Wenger, A. (1955) *L'assomption de la T. S. Vierge dans la tradition byzantine du VIe au Xe siècle* [Archives de l'Orient chrétien 5], Paris.

Wieland, G. (1994 for 1991) 'Anglo-Saxon Culture in Bavaria, 739–850', *Mediaevalia* 17, 177–200.

Wilmart. A. (1926) 'Un ancien manuscript de Saint-Bertin en lettres onciales', *Bulletin de la Société des antiquaires de la Morinie* 14, no. 270, 353–60.

Winterbottom, M. (1977) 'Aldhelm's Prose Style and its Origins', *Anglo-Saxon England* 6, 39–76.

Wright, Ch.D. (1987) 'Apocryphal Lore and Insular Tradition in St Gall, Stiftsbibliothek MS 908', in P. Ní Catháin & M. Richter (eds) *Irland und die Christenheit: Bibelstudien und Mission = Ireland and Christendom: The Bible and the Missions*, Stuttgart, 124–45.

— (1989) 'The Irish Enumerative Style in Old English Homiletic Literature, Especially Vercelli Homily IX', *Cambridge Medieval Celtic Studies* 18, 27–74.

— (1993) *The Irish Tradition in Old English Literature* [Cambridge Studies in Anglo-Saxon England 8], Cambridge.

— (2000) 'Bischoff's Theory of Irish Exegesis and the Genesis Commentary in Munich clm 6302: A Critique of a Critique', *Journal of Medieval Latin* 10, 115–75.

Index of Biblical References

Genesis
    1:10 83
    Cf. 1:9-10 83
    1:14 55, *cf. 141*
    Cf. 1:14-18 55
    Cf. 1:20 85, *cf. 152*
    1:28 91, 93, *cf. 155*
    2:6 91
    2:8 89
    Cf. 2:15 *cf. 155*
    2:16 89
    3:2 91
    Cf. 3:7 93
    3:17-19 63
    3:19 *14*
    Cf. 3:22-24 95
    3:23 93
    3:24 20, 93
    Cf. 3:24 95
    Cf. 6:16 *cf. 162*
    7:11-12 49, *cf. 141*
    Cf. 8:6 *cf. 162*
    Cf. 26:8 *cf. 162*

Exodus
    Cf. 9:24-25 71
    Cf. 12:10 119, *cf. 161*
    15:23-25 12, *18*
    Cf. 25:3-5 121, *cf. 162*
    Cf. 25:16-20 39
    33:20 117
    Cf. 33:23 117
    Cf. 34:25 119, *cf. 161*
    Cf. 37:6-9 39
    Cf. 37:7-9 *cf. 138*

Numbers
    Cf. 12:8 117, *cf. 160*
    Cf. 16:32 *cf. 153*
    Cf. 20:12-13 117

Judges
    Cf. 5:28 *cf. 162*

II Kings (= 2 Sam)
    Cf. 6:16 *cf. 162*
    Cf. 22:12 20

III Kings (= 1 Kgs)
    Cf. 6:23-35 39
    Cf. 7:29 39
    Cf. 16:31-33 77, *cf. 148*
    Cf. 18:4 77, *cf. 148*
    Cf. 19:1-2 77, *cf. 148*
    Cf. 22:22 77
    Cf. 22:26-27 77, *cf. 148*

I Paralipomenon (= 1 Chr)
    15:29 *cf. 162*

II Paralipomenon (= 2 Chr)
    Cf. 18:21 77
    Cf. 18:25-26 77, *cf. 148*

Tobias
    Cf. 3:25 43

Job
    1:10 79
    1:12 79
    1:21 79
    26:5 *cf. 159*

180 INDEX OF BIBLICAL REFERENCES

26:8   12, 69
Cf. 36:27   cf. 153
Cf. 37:18   53, cf. 142
Cf. 38:28   cf. 153

Psalms
1:5   103
4:7   119
9:5   41, cf. 140
Cf. 10:3   57
36:27   105
66:7   49, cf. 141
77:24   49
79:2-3   43
84:13   49, cf. 141
Cf. 85:13   107
Cf. 87:13   107
103:2   51
103:4   43
103:5-6   97
147:16-17   69
147:18   69
148:4   47
148:7   47
148:7-8   67
148:9   67

Wisdom
Cf. 11:18   cf. 161
11:21   85
Cf. 16:19-22   71

Ecclesiasticus (= Sir)
18:1   75, 75
Cf. 48:27   99, cf. 156

Isaias
1:16-17   105
Cf. 6:2-7   39
Cf. 14:11   105
24:22   107
Cf. 25:8   99, cf. 156
30:25-26   27, 55
Cf. 35:10   99(2), cf. 156

Cf. 60:19   117
Cf. 60:19-20   27, 28
Cf. 61:3   99, cf. 156
Cf. 65:17   55
65:17-18   97
Cf. 65:18   99, cf. 156

Jeremias
Cf. 3:3   cf. 153
Cf. 11:20   113
14:22   49, cf. 141
Cf. 15:16   99, cf. 156
Cf. 17:10   113
Cf. 20:11   99, cf. 156
Cf. 20:12   113

Ezechiel
Cf. 10:1-22   39
Cf. 10:14   cf. 138
18:22   113
28:12-13   63
28:13   41
33:12   113
Cf. 40:16-36   cf. 162

Daniel
7:10   45
8:16   45, cf. 140

Habacuc
Cf. 3:11   27, 28, 57

Malachias
4:2   57, 115

Matthew
3:10   111
3:11   111
3:12   111
5:3   109
5:10   109
5:22   111
Cf. 5:29   cf. 147
6:10   73

INDEX OF BIBLICAL REFERENCES

8:28-32   21
8:31   77
13:43   115
Cf. 13:43   99, cf. 156
Cf. 17:2-5   115, cf. 160
Cf. 18:9   cf. 147
18:18   109
21:19   93
22:30   14, 75, 107, 115, 115
24:29   27
25:30   105
25:34   24, 95, 109, 111
Cf. 25:34-46   23
25:41   73, 75, 105, cf. 147
Cf. 25:41   73
Cf. 25:42-45   105, cf. 158
25:46   105
Cf. 26: 69-74   117
Cf. 27:48   61, cf. 145

Mark
3:29   111
5:9   81
Cf. 9:44   cf. 147
Cf. 9:45   105
Cf. 9:46   cf. 147
12:25   75, 115, 115
Cf. 12:42-44   121, cf. 162
Cf. 15:36   61, cf. 145

Luke
Cf. 1:14   99, cf. 156
Cf. 1:19   43
Cf. 1:26-27   43
4:34   73
10:18   63
10:20   109
Cf. 12:5   cf. 147
Cf. 13:28   cf. 157
15:8-10   22
Cf. 16:9   cf. 157
Cf. 16:11   cf. 157
16:24   107
23:43   65, 113

24:12   99

John
3:5   103
3:18   103
Cf. 8:44   63, cf. 145
Cf. 13:23-25   cf. 161
Cf. 13:25   21, 103, cf. 158
Cf. 19:29   61, cf. 145
Cf. 21:11   87, cf. 152

Acts
Cf. 20:9   cf. 162

Ep. Romans
2:14   cf. 156
5:12   93, cf. 154
Cf. 8:10-11   cf. 154
8:21   57
8:22   55, cf. 144

Ep. I Corinthians
Cf. 2:4-16   37
2:9   115
3:11-12   113
3:14-15   113
6:9-10   103
13:9   11, 119
13:9-10   85
Cf. 13:10   117
Cf. 13:12   85, 119
Cf. 13:12   117
Cf. 15:42   99
Cf. 15:44   99
Cf. 15:45   91
15:53   99

Ep. II Corinthians
Cf. 11:33   cf. 162
12:7   73

Ep. Ephesians
1:21   39
6:12   65

Ep. Colossians
    1:16   39

Ep. I Timothy
    5:24   103

Ep. James
    2:10-11   105
    2:19   73

Ep. I John
    3:2   117
    Cf. 3:8   63, *cf. 145*
    5:16   103

Apocalypse
    Cf. 2:23   113
    Cf. 5:2-3   107, *cf. 159*
    Cf. 7:15   41, *cf. 139-140*
    Cf. 12:7   43
    Cf. 21:1-4   99

Index of Patristic & Medieval Works and Councils

Aeneas, bishop of Paris
    Liber adversus Graecos 26, *cf.* 138

Aethicus Ister
    Cosmographia 22, *cf.* 148

Aldhelm
    De Virginitate (prose) *cf.* 139, *cf.* 154
    De Virginitate (verse) *cf.* 139

Ambrose
    In Hexamaeron *cf.* 142

Anonymous
    Altus Prosator 20, *cf.* 149
    Apparebit repentina *cf.* 159
    B Glosses to Bede's *De temporum ratione* 27
    Belfour Homily XI 25
    Canones Hibernenses *cf.* 160
    Catechesis Celtica 23
    Commemoratorium 22
    Commentarius in Iohannem *cf.* 152
    Commentarius in Lucam 22
    Commentary on the Pentateuch *cf.* 157
    Crith gablach *cf.* 163
    De assumptione Sanctae Mariae *cf.* 159-160
    De XII abusiuis saeculi 23, 128, 130, 133, *cf.* 159
    De ecclesiasticis dogmatibus liber 35, 115, *cf.* 137
    Epinal-Erfurt Glossary *cf.* 153
    Excerpta in Evangeliae *cf.* 138
    Expositio IV evangeliorum 21, *cf.* 155
    First Commentary on the Pentateuch (Canterbury school) *cf.* 155
    Florilegium frisingense *cf.* 161
    Glossa ordinaria 27, 28, *cf.* 143
    Gospel of Máel Brigte 24
    Hisperica Famina *cf.* 145, *cf.* 148, *cf.* 149, *cf.* 150
    Irish Penitentials 20
    Liber de numeris 22, *cf.* 155, *cf.* 161
    Liber questionum in evangeliis 20(2)
    Lorica 24
    Old English Martyrology 25
    Pauca de Genesi *cf.* 156
    Pauca problemata de enigmatibus ex tomis canonicis *cf.* 152
    Quicunque vult 26, 35, *cf.* 137
    Reference Bible cf. 147, *cf.* 152
    Saltair na rann 22, 25, 26
    Senchas Már 26
    St. Gall Commentary on Genesis 26, *cf.* 152, *cf.* 153(3), *cf.* 155
    Stavelot Commentary 26
    Visio sancti Pauli *cf.* 159
    Würzburg Glosses to Matthew 21

Augustine of Hippo
    Ad Orosium contra Priscillianistas et Origenistas *cf.* 142
    De civitate Dei 35, 107, *cf.* 137, *cf.* 142, *cf.* 159
    De Genesi ad litteram 47, 51(3), 53, 55, 57, 61(2), 63(2), 67, 69, 73, 75(2), 85, 91, 93(2), 93, 95, 95, 95, 99, 107, 119, 121, *cf.* 140,

184 INDEX OF PATRISTIC & MEDIEVAL WORKS AND COUNCILS

cf. 141(2), cf. 142(5), cf. 143(2),
cf. 144(2), cf. 146(3), cf. 147,
cf. 154(3), cf. 155, cf. 159, cf. 161,
cf. 163
De Genesi ad litteram imperfectum
75
De Genesi contra Manichaeos 61,
cf. 144
De natura boni 35, cf. 137
De ordine 7
De sermone domini in monte 23,
cf. 157
De Trinitate 35, cf. 137
Enarrationes in psalmos 63, 113,
cf. 143
Enchiridion 35, 63, cf. 137, cf. 142
In Iohannis euangelium tractatus 97,
cf. 155
In Psalmo X cf. 143

Augustinus Hibernicus (= the Irish
Augustine) cf. 148, cf. 149(2),
cf. 150(2), cf. 151
De mirabilibus sacrae Scripturae 7,
9-15, 18, 47(2), 49(2), 63, 67(2),
69(3), 75(3), 83(2), 85(5), 130,
cf. 140(3), cf. 141, cf. 142(3),
cf. 144, cf. 145(2), cf. 147(4),
cf. 148(2), cf. 149(3), cf. 150,
cf. 151, cf. 152(3), cf. 153, cf. 160

Bede 18, 25, cf. 149, cf 150
De natura rerum 15-18, 25, cf. 142
De temporum ratione 27, cf. 149
Hexaemeron cf. 162
Historia Ecclesiastica Gentis Anglorum
cf. 161
In cantica canticorum cf. 139
In Lucam 22
In Marcum 22, cf 150
In proverbia Salomonis cf. 154

Caesarius of Arles
Sermones 113, cf. 139, cf. 160

Cogitosus
Vita Brigitae cf. 162

Columbanus
Instructio 35, cf. 137
Regula monachorum cf. 145

Council of Orange cf. 157

IV Council of Toledo cf. 138

XI Council of Toledo 7, 24, 25, cf. 138

Council of Whitby cf. 161

Defensor of Ligugé
Liber scintillarum 7, 15

Gregory the Great
Dialogues cf. 160
Homilia 34 in euangelia 22, 39(3),
41(7), 43(8), 45(4), cf. 138,
cf. 140(3)
Moralia in Iob 23, 30, 77, 79(2),
107, cf. 142, cf. 148, cf. 158(2),
cf. 159, cf. 160
Homilia 4 in Hiezechielem prophetam
cf. 138

Haimo of Auxerre
Commentary on Isaiah 26, 27

Isidore 7, 9, 25, 27, cf. 143
De ecclesiasticis officiis 111, cf. 160
De natura rerum cf. 140
Etymologiae cf. 156
Liber differentiarum (II) 9, 65, 73,
75, 79, 101, 115, 117, 119(3),
cf. 147(3), cf. 148, cf. 157, cf. 160
Quaestiones in Vetus Testamentum
30, cf. 138
Sententiae 22, 23, cf. 147(2), cf. 154

Jerome
- *Commentariorum in Danielem libri III*   cf. 139, cf. 140
- *Commentarius in Ecclesiasten*   cf. 143
- *Commentariorum in Hiezechielem libri XIV*   87, 121, cf. 145, cf. 152, cf. 162(2)
- *Commentariorum in Esaiam libri XVIII*   59, cf. 143, cf. 159
- *Commentariorum in Matthaeum libri IV*   21, cf. 147
- *Epistula 51*   91
- *Epistula 53*   91, 121, cf. 138, cf. 162
- *Epistulae*   65, 122, 130   cf. 139
- Introduction to the Book of Esther   15, 121, cf. 163
- *Liber interpretationis hebraicorum nominum*   41(2), cf. 139(2)

Lathcen mac Baith
- *Egloga quam scripsit Lathcen filius Baith de Moralibus Iob quas Gregorius fecit*   30, cf. 142

Martin of León
- *Sermo secundus in adventu Domini*   28
- *Sermo vicesimus quintus de resurrectione Domini*   28

Pelagius   8, cf. 156-157
- Commentary on St Paul's Epistle to the Romans   cf. 156
- To Demetrias   cf. 156

Peter Lombard
- *Sententiae*   28, cf. 143

Philippus Presbyter
- Commentary on Job   11, 85, 105, cf. 149, cf. 159

Pseudo-Bede
- *Collectanea*   22, cf. 161
- *De sex dierum creatione liber sententiarum ex patribus collectarum*   cf. 145

Pseudo-Cyprian
- *De duodecim abusiuis saeculi*   23, 128, 130, 133, cf. 159

Pseudo-Gennadius
- *Libri ecclesiasticorum dogmatum*   35, 115, cf. 137

Pseudo-Jerome
- *Expositio quattuor euangeliorum*   cf. 155

Pseudo-Rufinus
- *Liber de fide*   35, cf. 137

Quodvultdeus
- *Liber promissionum et praedictorum Dei*   cf. 146
- *De accedentibus ad gratiam sermones*   cf. 146

Rufinus
- *Expositio Symboli*   35, cf. 137

Victorius of Aquitaine
- *Cursus Paschalis*   7, cf. 156

Index of Modern Authors

Arévalo, F.   128, 142, 148, 166(2)
Baluze, E.   128, 166, 174
Bayless, M.   22, 166, 169, 170
Becker, G.   135(5), 170
Bieler, L.   20, 167, 170
Biggs, F.   23, 158, 159, 160, 170, 171, 172
Bisagni, J.   149, 150, 151(2), 170
Bischoff, B.   19, 21(2), 124, 125(2), 126(3), 127(2), 128, 133, 135, 138, 152(2), 155, 170, 174, 177
Blume, Cl.   20, 166, 170
Bracken, D.   23, 147(2), 154, 157, 170
Breen, A.   24, 159, 171
Brown, Sh. A.   8, 156, 157, 158, 173
Burn, A.E.   26, 167, 171
Carey, J.   22(2), 25(2), 26, 141, 158(2), 167, 171
Cartwright, D.E.   11, 150, 152(2), 171
Christ, K.   123, 135, 171
Clayton, M.   160, 171
Colgrave, B.   19, 168, 171
Connolly, S.   162, 168, 171
Contreni, J.J.   27(2), 171
Cross, J.E.   19, 25(3), 26, 27, 171
d'Achery, Dom Luc   128, 134(3), 165, 171
Davidson, G.   138, 171
de Bruyn, Th.   156, 169, 171
Delumeau, J.   145, 172
Díaz y Díaz, M.C.   4, 7(4), 9(2), 11, 15(3), 19, 20, 21, 26(4), 27, 28, 29(5), 123(2), 124, 129, 130, 134, 138, 140, 141(4), 142, 143, 144(2), 145(6), 146, 147(2), 148, 149, 150(2), 154(2), 155(2), 156, 157, 160, 161, 163, 166, 172
diPaolo Healey, A.   159, 172
Dolan, B.   159, 172
Duhem, P.   9(2), 11(2), 149, 152, 172
Dumville, D   125
Esposito, M.   9, 172
Fernández Catón, J.M.   130, 172
Fontaine, J.   140, 169, 172
Ganz, D.   7
Garrett, C.J.R.   150, 172
Glauche, G.   126, 172
Gorman, M.M.   27, 28, 157, 163, 172
Grimm, R.R.   145, 154, 172
Grosjean, P.   30, 172
Gryson, R.   140, 143, 166, 172
Guiley, R.E.   138, 173
Hall, Th.   7
Hamman, A.   165, 167, 170, 173
Hamp, E.P.   156, 173
Herbert, M.   158, 160, 173
Herren, M.W.   7(2), 8, 9, 19(2), 20, 22, 24(2), 139, 145, 148(3), 153, 154, 156-157, 163, 166(2), 167, 173(2)
Holder, A.   139, 168, 173
Hotchkiss, V.   35, 137, 157, 167, 174
Howlett, D.   20, 21, 173
Illich, I.   139, 173
Iogna-Prat, D.   26, 173
Jenkinson   148, 167
Jones, C.W.   19, 27, 168(2), 173
Kattenbusch, F.   138, 173
Kavanagh, A. K.   21, 173
Kelly, F.   163, 173
Kelly, J.F.   156, 166(2), 173

INDEX OF MODERN AUTHORS 187

Kessler, E. 126, 133
Klein, E. 138, 174
Krämer, S. 135, 174
Lapidge, M. 7, 22, 27, 124(2), 125, 138, 139(2), 155, 165, 166(3), 169, 170(2), 174
Lehner, A. 26, 133, 167
Lowe, E.A. 19, 124(3), 125 (3), 126, 127, 133, 174
Löfstedt, B. 20(3), 174
MacGinty, F.P. (= MacGinty, G.) 9, 19, 167, 168, 174
Madoz, J. 24, 174
Mai, A. 146
Manitius, M. 135, 174
Mansi, J.D. 138, 174
Martin, H. 130, 174
McNally, R.E. 155, 161, 167(2), 174
McNamara, M. 158, 160(2), 170, 173, 174
Martène, Ed. 128, 166, 174
Meyer, H. 30, 174
Müller, H. 7
Munk, W.H. 150, 172
Mynors, R.A.B. 19, 168, 171
Ó Carragáin, T. 162, 174
Ó Cróinín, D. 9, 19(2), 156, 167, 174
O'Loughlin, Th. 7, 16, 154, 173, 174
O'Neill, B. 162, 174
Orchard, A.P. McD. 21, 173, 174
O'Sullivan, A. 162(2), 174
Pelikan, J. 35, 137, 157, 167, 174
Peyrafort-Huin, M. 135, 175
Picard, J.-M. 15, 162, 168, 171, 175

Rees, B.R. 156(2), 169, 175
Reilly, E. 162, 174
Rittmueller, J. 20, 24(2), 167, 175
Rosier, J.L. 139, 166, 174
Savigni, R. 26, 175
Sheerin, D. 7
Shimahara, S. 26, 175
Siecienski, E.A. 138, 175
Sims-Williams, P. 22, 157, 175
Smyth, M. 8(3), 9, 11, 12, 15(4), 16, 21, 24(3), 25, 26, 137, 138(2), 140(2), 141(5), 142(4), 143(3), 144(3), 145(4), 146(3), 147, 148(2), 149(6), 150(3), 151(5), 152(3), 153, 154(4), 155, 156, 158(2), 159(4), 160(3), 161(2), 162(2), 163(3), 175
Stegmüller, F. 26, 176
Stevenson, J. 20, 149, 176
Stotz, P. 20, 21, 176
Stuiber, A. 145, 176
Suntrup, R. 30, 174
Thurneysen, R. 19, 176
Vnoucek, J. 163(3), 176
Wallis, F. 144, 149, 152, 168, 176
Warntjes, I. 7, 143, 176
Wawrykow, J.P. 157, 176
Weber, R. et al. 163, 168
Wenger, A. 160, 176
Wieland, G. 26, 176
Wilmart. A. 19, 128, 166, 176
Winterbottom, M. 21, 177
Wright, Ch.D. 9, 19, 22(2), 23(2), 26, 177

Index of Topics

Achab   77, 148
Adam   21, 65, 91, 93, 95, 97, 115, 119, 154, 155
Air   8, 12, 13, 16, 17, 18, 30, 49, 51, 53, 61, 63, 65, 67, 69, 73, 79, 83, 87, 91, 93, 97, 119, 141, 144, 148
Anatholia   97
Angels   8, 14, 16, 22, 30, 39, 43, 45, 63, 69, 73, 75, 77, 79, 93, 101, 105, 107, 115, 117, 119, 138, 140, 142, 146-148, 160
Animation of the stars   59, 142-144
Archangels   39, 43, 140
Arctus   97
Ashes   13, 18, 69, 83, 99, 148
Bad will of the devil   77, 79
Baptism   8, 30, 101, 103, 111, 157, 158, 161
Birds   26, 61, 67, 85, 87, 93, 121, 141, 152-153
Birth   97
Call at Last Judgement   23, 24, 95, 109, 111, 155, 160
Cardinal directions   21, 97, 155, 156
Catholic   8, 37, 55, 59, 63, 65, 121, 156
Celestial Paradise   8, 23, 61, 63, 65, 113, 115, 145
Chapters in DOC   29-31
Charity   8, 23-24, 101, 105, 109
Cherubim   39, 41, 43, 93, 138, 139
Church (the)   8, 37, 91, 117, 138, 143, 147, 160
Clothes   23, 101, 105, 109,
Clouds   12, 13, 18, 49, 61, 63, 67, 69, 71, 73, 83, 87, 141

Cold   67, 69
Common year   10, 85, 152
Computus   59, 143, 149, 151, 152
Constillatio   86-87, 153
Cosmic egg   25, 26, 52, 141
Creation   8, 13, 25, 55, 75, 87, 89, 101, 117, 119, 137, 140, 142, 153, 156, 161
Damnation   8, 73, 77, 103, 105, 107
Daniel   45
Dating of DOC   7-8, 15-18, 24-25
Dealing with contradictory opinions   8, 53, 59, 65, 119, 142, 144
Death   8, 14, 21, 23-25, 30, 37, 57, 65, 75, 77, 93, 95, 97, 101, 103, 107, 113, 117, 145, 154, 155, 159, 160
Devil, demons   13, 22, 31, 63, 65, 73, 75, 77, 79, 81, 101, 105, 107, 145, 147, 158, 159
Disc (re. Firmament)   51, 141
Disc (re. Moon)   57, 143
Disis   97
Dominations   39, 41
Drink   83, 105, 109
Earth   8, 12, 13, 16, 17, 18, 24, 26, 30, 31, 47, 49, 51, 61, 63, 65, 67, 69, 71, 73, 75, 83, 89, 91, 93, 95, 97, 99, 101, 105, 107, 109, 117, 119, 140, 141, 144, 148, 153-155
Easter   21, 143, 156
Ebb   10, 11, 83, 85, 150, 151
Eggshell   25, 26, 51, 141
Elements   15, 17, 51, 53, 69, 83, 89, 97, 119, 141, 142, 145
Elias   115, 117, 148, 160

INDEX OF TOPICS

Embolismic year   10, 85, 152
End of mutability   57, 99, 115, 117, 160
Enumerative style   22-23, 35, 39, 93, 101, 113, 117, 160, 161
Equinox   10, 11, 85, 152, 156
Eschatology   8, 23-24, 30-31
Eternal   22, 30, 31, 35, 37, 65, 73, 101, 103, 105, 107, 109, 145, 155
Eternal fire   73, 75, 103, 105, 107, 111, 158
Evil   8, 35, 41, 65, 79, 95, 101, 105, 109, 115, 137, 154
Ezechiel   39, 162
Fall of angels   8, 13-14, 30, 31, 63, 65, 75, 93, 115, 147
Fall of man   8, 13-14, 22-23, 55, 75, 89, 93, 101, 147, 154, 156
Fenestra   118-119, 161-162
Fig tree   93, 95, 155
Filioque controversy   138
Fire   16, 17, 23, 49, 51, 53, 67, 69, 71, 73, 75, 91, 103, 105, 107, 109, 111, 113, 119, 141, 148, 158-161
Fire of judgement/of Gehenna   23, 24, 103, 109, 111, 113, 160
Firmament   8, 16, 25, 26, 29, 47, 51, 53, 55, 61, 63, 91, 97, 141, 142
Fish   21, 67, 85, 87, 93, 152
Flood (the)   11, 30, 47, 140, 142, 161
Flow   10, 83, 85, 151, 152
Food   14, 75, 101, 105, 109, 113, 148
Fourfold division of mankind   23, 103, 158
Fourfold earth   97
Free will   8, 115, 119, 157, 158
Fugitive slave   22, 77, 147
Gabriel   43, 45
Gift from God   41, 101, 109, 115, 147, 157, 158, 160
Goat skin   121, 162-163
Good   8, 23, 24, 30, 35, 41, 73, 77, 79, 89, 95, 101, 105, 107, 111, 113, 115, 121, 145, 148, 154, 156-160

Grace   8, 37, 103, 119, 157, 158
Guilt   24, 95, 103, 111
Habakkuk   57, 143
Hail   61, 67, 69
Heaven   11, 14, 22, 24, 47, 63, 73, 75, 93, 95, 105, 107, 109, 115, 117, 159
Heavens   16, 47, 49, 55, 61, 63, 65, 67, 73, 97, 99, 117, 141, 143, 156
Hell   8, 23, 24, 27, 105, 107, 159, 160
Hemispheres   49, 61, 67, 69, 71, 140, 144
Higher space of air   8, 17, 61, 63, 65, 97
Holy Spirit   37, 57, 101, 103, 111
Ice   67
Influence of DOC   15-18, 25-29
In metallis   104-105, 158-159
Irish origin of DOC   7, 9-25
Isaiah   39, 97, 105, 117, 138
James (St)   21, 103
Jerusalem   99
Job   69, 77, 79
John (St)   21, 41, 103, 117, 139, 158, 160
John the Baptist   111
Justice   41, 58, 73, 99, 109, 115, 117
King of Babylon   105
Kingdom of Heaven/of God   11, 24, 95, 99, 103, 105, 109, 115, 157
Last Judgement   17, 23, 24, 30, 37, 63, 73, 79, 95, 99, 103, 105, 109, 111, 155, 160
Law of nature   101, 158
ledo   9, 10, 82-83, 84-85, 149-151
Life to come   30, 95, 101, 111, 115, 117
Like angels   14, 22, 75, 95, 107, 115, 117
Like demons   107
Light   22, 27, 47, 55, 57, 59, 79, 117, 119, 140, 162
Lightning   17, 63, 69, 71, 146
Locus amoenus   145
Lower space of air   8, 17, 30, 49, 61, 63, 67, 69, 71, 79, 141, 144
Luminaries   49, 55, 57, 61, 91, 141-145

INDEX OF TOPICS

Lunar month   149, 151, 152
malina   9-11, 82-83, 84-85, 149-151
Man (nature of)   101, 156-158
Mary   37, 43, 160
Meadows of the Holy Books   39, 139
Merit   14, 73, 75, 103, 138, 147, 154, 158
Messages   43, 45, 73, 145
Michael   43, 159
Misimbria   97
Moon   8, 10, 11, 27, 47, 55, 57, 59, 83, 85, 89, 99, 117, 142-144, 149-151, 153
Moses   12, 55, 115, 117, 153, 158, 160
Mount Olympus   61, 144
Mutability   18, 35, 57, 97, 99, 115, 119, 148, 160
Nature   11-13, 16-18, 35, 37, 43, 51, 53, 55, 67, 69, 73, 75, 77, 83, 85, 87, 95, 97, 99, 101, 107, 115, 117, 119, 137, 147, 148, 152, 154, 156-159
Natural good   73, 77, 101, 156-158, 160
Neap tides   149, 150
New earth   55, 97, 99
New Heaven   55, 97, 99, 143, 156
Noah   30, 47, 91
Obedience/disobedience   41, 55, 77, 89, 93, 95, 101, 121
Observation   11, 83, 85, 146, 149-151
Ocean   10, 13, 83
Old age   22, 23, 93, 95, 101, 117, 155
Orb   46-47, 57, 89, 97, 101
Order of the elements   15, 51, 53, 69, 89, 141, 142
Orders of angels   22, 39, 41, 43, 47, 117, 140
Origin of DOC   7, 9-15, 18-24
Original sin   23, 95, 101, 155, 157
Orphic tradition   141
Pain/suffering, old age and death   22, 23, 93, 101, 117, 155, 157
Paradise   8, 14, 23, 24, 55, 61, 63, 65, 75, 89, 91, 93, 95, 113, 115, 145, 154, 155

Paschal Lamb   119, 161
Paul (St)   39, 55, 63, 65, 85, 97, 103, 111, 113, 117, 159, 161
Pelagian ideas   8, 138, 147, 156-158, 161
Peter (St)   21, 99, 117
Places of punishment   63, 73, 103, 105, 107, 158, 160
Poverty   105, 109, 121
Powers   17, 39, 41, 45, 47, 63, 79
Precepts of nature   101
Primacy   89, 91, 154
Principalities   39, 41, 63
Psalmist   41, 47, 51, 67, 69, 97, 103, 105
Punishment   37, 63, 73, 75, 79, 89, 101, 103, 105, 107, 155, 158, 160
Purgatorial/cleansing fire   23, 24, 103, 109, 111, 113, 160
Purgatory   160
Rain   12, 13, 47, 49, 61, 69, 71, 83, 144
Raphael   43
Redemption   8, 14, 37, 55, 65, 73, 75, 99, 101
Repentance   75, 103, 105, 113, 147, 159
Restoration to higher status   14, 55, 57, 75, 97, 99, 143, 147
Resurrection   8, 14, 23, 30, 37, 57, 65, 75, 95, 99, 105, 107, 115, 117
Salt water   12, 13, 18, 69, 83, 87, 148, 149, 151
Salvation   7, 37, 111, 147, 157-159
Satan   22, 30, 63, 73, 107
Sea   10-13, 18, 55, 67, 69, 83, 85, 91, 93, 117, 148-151
Seasons   10, 11, 85, 97
Senses (five)   101
Seraphim   39, 41, 139
Shelter   105, 109
Sion   99
Sin   8, 14, 22-24, 55, 57, 63, 65, 73, 75, 77, 79, 89, 93, 95, 101, 103, 105, 109, 111, 113, 115, 117, 143, 147, 154-157, 160

Sinners   23, 24, 77, 103, 105, 107, 142, 160
Sleep   101, 113, 150
Snow   61, 67, 69, 87
Solstice   11, 85, 152
Slaves   159
Soul   8, 23, 25, 37, 39, 65, 79, 101, 107, 117, 119, 140, 142, 161
Sponge   61, 145, 148
Sphere   8, 25, 57, 140, 143, 144
Spring tides   11, 149, 150, 152
Suffering   23, 55, 93, 95, 97, 101, 105, 109, 113, 115, 144, 148, 153, 155, 157, 159
Sun   8, 27, 47, 55, 57, 59, 89, 99, 115, 117, 142-144, 153
Supercelestial waters   8, 16, 47, 49, 51, 53, 97
Teachings of Scripture   101
Tenth order   22
Terrestrial orb   89, 97
Theodore of Tarsus   8, 25
Tidal mills   151
Tobias   43
Thrones   39, 41, 43
Thunder   17, 61, 69, 71, 146
Tides   9-11, 83, 85, 149-152
Time   10, 22-24, 26, 30, 31, 35, 37, 43, 47, 49, 55, 59, 71, 73, 75, 93, 101, 113, 138, 140, 143, 147, 149-151
Transfiguration   115, 160
Three meanings of Scripture   91, 154
Three ways to sin   101, 157
Three wounds from original sin   23, 93, 95, 101, 155, 157
Trees in Paradise   65, 89, 91, 93, 95, 145
Trinity   8, 35, 37, 133
Unformed matter   117, 161
Utility of the sea   18, 83, 149
Visit the sick/the prisoners   105, 109
Visits to Hell   107, 159-160
Water   8, 11-13, 16-18, 30, 31, 47, 49, 51, 53, 67, 69, 71, 83, 85, 87, 89, 91, 97, 101, 103, 105, 111, 117, 119, 121, 141, 142, 144, 145, 148, 149, 152-154
Wind   49, 61, 67, 69, 144, 146, 151, 153
Works of faith/of mercy   23, 24, 101, 105, 109, 113, 159
Wounds   23, 57, 93, 101, 155
Zachariah   43